W9-AFN-073

American Communication Research—
The Remembered History

LEA's COMMUNICATION SERIES
Jennings Bryant/Dolf Zillmann, General Editors

Select titles in General Theory and Methodology
(Jennings Bryant, Advisory Editor) include:

Potter • An Analysis of Thinking and Research About Qualitative Methods

Perry • Theory and Research in Mass Communication

Casmir • Building Communication Theories: A Socio/Cultural Approach

Harris • Health and the New Media: Technologies Transforming Personal and Public Health

Gonzenbach • The Media, The President, and Public Opinion: A Longitudinal Analysis of the Drug Issue, 1984–1991

For a complete list of other titles in LEA's Communication Series, please contact Lawrence Erlbaum Associates, Publishers.

American Communication Research—
The Remembered History

Edited by

Everette E. Dennis
The Freedom Forum Media Studies Center
New York

Ellen Wartella
University of Texas at Austin

 LAWRENCE ERLBAUM ASSOCIATES, PUBLISHERS
1996   Mahwah, New Jersey

Lawrence Erlbaum Associates, Inc., Publishers
10 Industrial Avenue
Mahwah, New Jersey 07430

Library of Congress Cataloging-in-Publication Data

American communication research—the remembered history
/ edited by
    Everette E. Dennis, Ellen Wartella.
        p.   cm. — (LEA's communication series)
    Includes bibliographical references and indexes.
    ISBN 0-8058-1743-3 (cloth). — ISBN 0-8058-1744-1
(paper)
    1. Communication—Research—United States—His-
tory.
    I. Dennis, Everette E. II. Wartella, Ellen. III. Series.
    P91.5.U5A49 1996
    302.2'072073—dc20   95-40454
                                                     CIP

Books published by Lawrence Erlbaum Associates are printed
on acid-free paper, and their bindings are chosen for strength
and durability.

Printed in the United States of America
10 9 8 7 6 5 4 3 2 1

Contents

Preface
Everette E. Dennis   vii

PART I: THE SCHOOLS OF THOUGHT

1 The European Roots
   Kurt Lang   1

2 The Chicago School and Mass Communication
   Research
   James W. Carey   21

3 The Yale Communication and Attitude-Change
   Program in the 1950s
   William J. McGuire   39

4 Diffusion Research at Columbia
   Elihu Katz   61

5 Children and Television
   Hilde Himmelweit   71

6 The Press as a Social Institution
   Theodore Peterson   85

PART II: EYEWITNESS ACCOUNTS

7   Fashioning Audience Ratings—From Radio to Cable
    Hugh Malcolm Beville   **95**

8   Stanton, Lazarsfeld, and Merton—Pioneers in
    Communication Research
    David L. Sills   **105**

9   A Conversation with Frank Stanton
    Rena Bartos   **117**

10 The Master Teachers
    Wilbur Schramm   **123**

11 Research as an Instrument of Power
    Leo Bogart   **135**

12 Addressing Public Policy
    Douglass Cater   **147**

PART III: REASSESSMENT

13 Constructing a Historiography for North American
    Communication Studies
    Gertrude J. Robinson   **157**

14 The History Reconsidered
    Ellen Wartella   **169**

    Appendix: Biographic Sketches of 65 Contributors to the   **181**
    Field of Communication Research

    About the Contributors and Editors   **193**

    Author Index   **199**

    Subject Index   **203**

Preface

Everette E. Dennis

The importance of the media, both as instruments of communication and as a social force, is well established. Commentators and critics speak of the "centrality" of the media as influential players in society that have an impact on individuals, institutions, and the public at large. Although the precise nature of the media's impact and influence is rarely agreed on, it is clear that most knowledgeable observers in the 1990s readily recognize "media power" in politics, consumer behavior, and other arenas. In fact, to the present generation of scholars, critics, and consumers, the idea that media and media messages have something to do with people's perceptions, attitudes, and opinions seems almost axiomatic.

This was not always so. Although the concept of a "powerful" press stretches back decades, even centuries, this was by no means universally accepted or acknowledged. Media power and influence was not a settled issue; in fact, it was the subject of considerable debate. Of course, this debate began and ensued over many decades during a time when mass communication was actually inventing itself. From the first stirrings of mass magazines with circulations of more than 1 million in the 19th century, through the invention of radio and television, to the modern emergence of computers and satellites, communication has changed utterly, and so has its relationship with the larger society.

From the late 19th century on, scholars—especially historians—acknowledged the role and presence of the press and, later, other media; but they almost always saw them as a peripheral influence—a sentinel sometimes, but rarely a central player in society's drama. Indeed, when in rare instances the press or media were isolated as a variable for study, they were found wanting and not nearly as powerful as was commonly believed.

The whole idea of media research, as it is now called, emerged slowly, and was typically aimed at serving the needs and purposes of vested interests. As media scholar Leo Bogart has written, the term *media* was the invention of advertisers and advertising agencies who looked upon the communication system then and now as so many vehicles for display of their products. In such a context it is easy to understand why some curmudgeonly editorialists still decry the use of the term *media*. It was, however, a desire to know and understand more about the reach and effectiveness of radio in the 1930s and beyond that began to stimulate media research. Later, other policy matters well outside the profit making of business played a role. An interest in the systematic propaganda efforts of the Nazi regime in Germany and the role of public information in time of war led both to formal programs of communication and to a desire to measure their effectiveness.

In the United States, where the explosion of media and media industries happened first, it was natural that efforts at systematic research, disciplined intelligence, and feedback would evolve. Just which media research came first is neither clear nor agreed on, but there were certainly concurrent efforts and activities that sometimes fed on one another and became the raw material for what people would later call communication research.

There were early propaganda studies sponsored by government agencies and private organizations, with universities often contracted to carry out the actual research. The emergence of specific media, such as radio and motion pictures, spawned other research efforts, sometimes to "prove" the efficacy of a given medium as a vehicle for advertising or to show that media content, especially that in movies, was or was not harmful to young people. From the beginning of this century, legal scholars and historians had at least a passing interest in media institutions and media content. Social psychologists, sociologists, psychologists, political scientists, and other scholars and critics similarly traced and tracked media matters when they were of sufficient interest to warrant study. At universities like Chicago and Columbia, the study of communication in the context of urban sociology or market studies was a seemingly natural development. Indeed, institutions like Columbia's Bureau of Applied Social Research, active from the 1930s through the 1970s, pioneered studies of the radio audience. The bureau also probed the media's impact on electoral campaigns. Like so many subsequent efforts, the Columbia program was a nexus of industry and the academy, having developed first as a project supported by radio networks and later attracting the attention of leading scholars looking for projects worth pursuing and financial support.

Social scientists became particularly active in media studies, not as an end in themselves, but as part of a larger project on human behavior or individual cognitions. Usually in the realm of applied research, these efforts abutted similar (and sometimes related) work in journalism schools that had strong reasons for wanting to know more about media and their influences. Although projects at first were simply conducted for their own sake, to ferret out information helpful to business, agriculture, government, or the media, on occasion scholars, as they are wont to do, decided to take stock.

In annual reviews, journal articles, and other venues, scholars would synthesize, trying to capture the state of communication research and its relative importance and impact. They were duly cautious about making exaggerated or outrageous claims and thus applied rigorous standards of proof. When asked whether the media in and of themselves really told people what to think, swayed the masses, or controlled human behavior, the thoughtful answer came back in the negative. The idea of an omnipotent media, which had been championed by propaganda theorists in earlier days, was discounted, and carefully the scholars would talk only of documented, short-term effects on elections, of public health campaigns, and of marketing. Here the media's influence was quickly underplayed and even diminished. The evidence was simply not there, and, in fact, there was every reason to believe that media were only part of a larger chorus of social forces having an impact on human activity.

For at least two generations, not only were media scholars cautious but they lent support to a generalized attitude in American universities that suggested a minimal impact of media in a variety of arenas. Economists, political scientists, and sociologists, for example, rarely discussed media at all, and when they did, in texts and lectures, it was almost in passing. A review of texts from the 1940s through the 1980s, whether in sociology, history, or political science, reveals a backwater perception of the role of the media.

But outside the ivory tower, in the "real world," advertisers were playing up the impact and influence of the media. They argued that without proper advertising and visibility, public support for products or politicians could not be generated. Advertising bureaus associated with various media, such as newspapers, magazines, and television, had teams of researchers out to "prove" that their medium had the greatest reach and the greatest influence on readers or viewers. To these people there was no question that media were powerful and important. At least, that is what they said.

Media in the United States have been mainly, although not exclusively, creatures of commercialism. Public broadcasting is an exception. On occasion, as with broadcasting and advertising, there was modest government intervention and regulation, but for the most part media were left alone to develop and expand their operations. But media owners and executives realized that a powerful and mainly unregulated communication system might be seen as troublesome to government and other institutions, so they had strong incentive to minimize their power and influence.

More than any other occurrence, it was the dawn of the information revolution that underscored the growing influence of media. From electronic direct-marketing efforts for products, candidates, and causes as well as the growing economic power of communication empires, people began to get the idea that, in a world where money talks, these media enterprises were not only highly profitable but they were also influential in many ways. An obvious fact of life for most of the lay public, media were achieving increasing status as an important and vital part of the social landscape. Were they important and influential? Yes, of course, almost everyone agreed—except the scholars.

Slow to come to this view, media scholars continued to use old methods of measurement and to focus on short-term influences rather than more pervasive and longer term impacts for most of the 1960s and 1970s. As greater interest developed in cognitive effects of media as well as the emergence of a critical and cultural studies movement, a body of literature in support of a more powerful media emerged. Strange bedfellows contributed to this now-prevalent idea, ranging from money-oriented marketeers to ideologically bound critics.

In such an atmosphere, and as new studies were published almost daily, media scholars and critics became more introspective about their field, its present state, and its roots. It was common in media studies programs and annual conventions to reflect on the past, to critique it, to illuminate its shortcomings, and for some, to celebrate its achievements.

The people who engaged in this chorus of discussion had different motives, but they collaborated (even when they did not know it) to foster interest in the genealogy of communication research and media studies. Names once only known as items in a graduate student's bibliography became worthy of serious biography.

These were some of the factors that gave impetus to the development of this book, which is linked to a series of lectures and seminars held at The Freedom Forum Media Studies Center (at the time called The Gannett Center for Media Studies) at Columbia between 1985 and 1994. The series on the "History of Mass Communication Research" was organized with the idea that some then-living pioneers of the field would be paired with contemporary critics to inquire into the purpose, meaning, and impact of various research ventures now deemed as important to the building of the field.

So it was that some of the most illustrious people in the field came to Columbia to tell their stories, to debate others, and sometimes to defend or justify their efforts. In other instances, the presenters were highly critical, looking back on the studies of their early days as primitive by contemporary standards.

Those of us associated with this series, while enthusiastic, were skeptical about the practical logistics of bringing together many of the luminaries of the field and whether we would find an appreciative audience. On both counts we were pleased. Every person we asked to speak in the series accepted, some traveling thousands of miles to participate. And every session played to standing-room-only audiences, with scholars, industry researchers, and media professionals petitioning to attend. But we were especially pleased with the yield from the sessions—thoughtful, eyewitness accounts from the pioneers and equally thoughtful, long-view presentations from historians of communication research and researchers themselves. The series accomplished its ultimate goal—to paint a cumulative portrait of media research—and went even further by creating an elegant statement of meaning.

When the series ended, tapes were transcribed, papers were written and rewritten, often benefiting from the lively discussions that were part of the seminar series. Sometimes disturbing and, at the moment, unanswerable questions were raised that stimulated further elaboration or new research. The editors of this volume worked closely with the contributing authors in setting up the original seminar, helping to structure the presentation and discussion, and critiquing early drafts.

In identifying, dissecting, and reassessing the nature and dimensions of the history of communication research, we focused mainly on American research, with some links to Europe and other countries. While trying to catch the drift of what scholars and critics were saying, we made no effort to be comprehensive or all-inclusive, although we, in fact, captured most of the main currents of the American media research experience. The chapters presented in this volume are based both on papers and oral presentations delivered during the series.

We begin with schools of thought: those loci of intellectual activity centered in institutional settings like Columbia or the University of Chicago or in a research tradition tied to substantive areas of study or particular methods, such as the press as a social institution or media and children. These social constructions have proved helpful in charting research directions and purposes. Here we have the benefit of elegant commentaries and insights from some of the field's leading thinkers and analysts: Kurt Lang of the University of Washington, James W. Carey of Columbia University, Theodore Peterson of the University of Illinois, William McGuire of Yale University, Elihu Katz of Hebrew University and the University of Pennsylvania, and Hilde Himmelweit of the University of London. Represented here are the views of sociologists, social psychologists, communication economists, and critics.

Moving from this broad, thematic approach, with chapters by leading researchers, historians, and critics of communication studies, we next meet witnesses to the history of the field, some of them scholars, others practitioners and industry executives who participated in, directed, funded, or otherwise influenced research developments. Here we get insights from people who lived through the developments others can only write and speculate about. Industry leaders and researchers like Hugh Beville of NBC and Leo Bogart of the Newspaper Advertising Bureau give us the tone and texture—the "blood and guts"—of research and reasons industry was motivated to support and sponsor it. We asked David Sills, executive emeritus of the Social Science Research Council in New York, who was associated with Columbia's Bureau of Applied Social Research, to write a special essay for this volume that would tie together the contributions made by Paul F. Lazarsfeld, Frank Stanton, and Robert K. Merton to the industry-research nexus. We have also included an interview with Stanton that was conducted by Rena Bartos for the Advertising Research Foundation. Both Stanton and Merton made remarks at the seminar series but characteristically declined to have them published herein, arguing in their near-perfectionist mode that informal remarks did not effectively represent their earlier published work. With regret we acceded to their wishes and thus included other commentary to portray their vital roles. These voices are augmented by scholar Wilbur Schramm of Iowa, Illinois, and Stanford, himself a pioneer and creative leader. The connection to policy makers is made by Douglass Cater, a leading thinker, government official, and university administrator.

The final section of the book takes stock of the earlier two and offers them up for analysis. Here the historiography of the field is examined by Gertrude Robinson, an internationalist from McGill University, while coeditor and media scholar Ellen Wartella reconsiders the writing of histories of the field and offers an extensive list of brief biographies from which the genealogy of the field can be considered. This work also augments and interprets individuals and schools of research cited throughout the text.

During the editing of this volume, four of the principals whose work is presented here died, including most recently Douglass Cater. This affirmed, sadly, our belief that these reports, essays, and speeches urgently needed to be captured. In the cases of Hilde Himmelweit, Hugh Beville, and Wilbur Schramm, these presentations were among their last formal statements on media research.

For readers intimately acquainted with the history of communication research, this volume will have a familiar ring because it covers some familiar ground, but it also introduces much new material, even some heretofore unpublished accounts and revelations. This new material is sufficiently strong, in our opinion, to warrant publication for the benefit of specialists and other experts. In large part, however, this book is meant for students who do not know the institutional history of the field of media research, have not met its builders, and have only second-hand sources about its original purposes and interpretations.

What is presented here is intended to stimulate thought and inspire appreciation for the origins of the field as well as encourage further research. A comprehensive history of communication research is yet to be written, and institutional portraits and biographies of founding institutions and their leaders are sorely needed. In an era when communication research is recognized as increasingly important to understanding the contours of modern media and modern life, it is appropriate both to elucidate and to foster understanding of early work in the field. To that end this volume is dedicated.

PART **I**

THE SCHOOLS OF THOUGHT

Chapter 1

The European Roots

Kurt Lang
University of Washington

Most U.S. scholars, dependent as they are on what appears in English-language publications, know little about foreign research in mass communication. The *International Encyclopedia of the Social Sciences* (Sills, 1968), to take one example, has seven articles on the mass media. Only the one by Wilbur Schramm, in which he compares "control and public policy" in the United States with that in other countries, draws on a significant amount of foreign language literature (Vol. 3, pp. 55–63). The bibliographies of the other six contain only one foreign entry—and this in a compendium that presents itself as "international." It appears in the article on political communication by Ithiel de Sola Pool (Vol. 3, pp. 90–96), who mentions a German book on the Allied propaganda in World War I—*Weltkrieg ohne Waffen [World War Without Weapons]* by Hans Thimme. Published in 1932, it presented data in support of the political myth that the old imperial German army had not been defeated in the field; the stab in the back it received in 1918 was attributed to foreign propaganda.

In a 1977 report to the British Broadcasting Corp., Elihu Katz flatly asserted that "communication research . . . is surely an American science. It flourished for perhaps two decades under the founding fathers, Paul Lazarsfeld, Harold Lasswell and Carl Hovland" (Katz, 1977, p. 22). I do not dispute that it had indeed flourished under the leadership of these men. But let us also look at what one of these founding fathers wrote, in reference not just to his own role: "Many of the techniques which are now considered American in origin were developed in Europe 50 or a hundred years ago and then exported from the United States after they had been refined and made manageable for use on a mass scale" (Lazarsfeld, 1965, p. v).

This statement comes, quite obviously, from Lazarsfeld, coauthor with Katz of *Personal Influence* (Katz & Lazarsfeld, 1955), a book that helped as much as any other to put to rest by the late 1950s inquiries into the effects of mass communication.

An earlier paper of mine (Lang, 1979) made a similar point but in a different context. That paper argues that much of what was being defined by Europeans as characteristically U.S. communication research (more or less as defined by Katz) had been introduced to the United States from the Old World, mostly by Germans (which in this case included Austrians), or by Americans who had studied in Germany or had been influenced by work in Central Europe during the first third of the 20th century. Siegfried Kracauer, Leo Lowenthal, Ernst Kris, Hans Speier, Herta Herzog, Kurt Lewin, and Karl Deutsch should be recognizable to students of mass communication. They had much influence on the generation educated right after World War II, the generation of which I, too, am a member.

But the European and more specifically the German influence goes back farther still. It is very much in evidence among the social scientists linked to the Chicago School of sociology. Both Robert E. Park and Lasswell had spent time in Germany early in their careers—the former taking a PhD at Heidelberg. Among other Chicagoans, I should also mention Helen M. Hughes, a student of Park, and her much neglected book *News and the Human-Interest Story* (1940). And, of course, there is also the 1947 presidential address to the American Sociological Society by Louis Wirth on consensus and mass communication (1948), which in my judgment is still well worth reading, even though Wirth himself (unlike his two colleagues Herbert Blumer and Philip Hauser) never engaged in anything resembling what we have come to call mass communication research. These three certainly had some familiarity with the German literature on the subject.

I was moved to do the previously mentioned article at the urging of my wife, Gladys Engel Lang. Everything we do is at least in some remote way a joint product. It was written while we were in England, working on an entirely different project. Jeremy Tunstall had asked me to speak to his study group on recent communication research in Germany, which got me into a running controversy with some young academics there, against whom I remonstrated for their limited view of the history of their subject. They perceived a sharp opposition between U.S. media research as personified by Lazarsfeld and German media research, which they equated with the postwar Critical School at Frankfurt. Their view did not encompass the full scope of Lazarsfeld's work, and a number of them, as it turned out in later discussion, acknowledged that they had never even heard of some of the other emigré scholars. My article was intended to correct this rather one-sided and restricted view of the history of communication research.

The subject on which Gladys and I have been working, the building and survival of artistic reputations,[1] has sharpened my consciousness of the selective processes that shape and, to a degree, distort the collective memory of even our own field. Obviously, no one—not even historians—can look at the past with anything but the eyes of their own time. But art historians Rudolph and Margot Wittkower conceded even more when they declared flatly that in art "misinterpretation is one of the great stimuli for keeping the past alive. Only that which strikes a congenial note will be taken up from an immensely rich tradition and revitalized" (Wittkower & Wittkower, 1963, p. 283). Others have pointed to a similar process of reinterpretation. Robert Escarpit (1958) referred to the tendency of writers to fall into oblivion some 10, 20, or 30 years after their death until they become defined as members of some literary collective or movement to make them appear more relevant to a contemporary public.

Something like this has happened in sociology and in the sociology of mass communication. Not only do we forget the past but we manage to see a past that fits our preconceptions. The current interest in the forerunners of our discipline, which I heartily welcome, strikes me as an effort to legitimate a discipline in danger of becoming overly concerned with de-contextualized minutia and of producing increasingly repetitive findings. Linking it to a rich intellectual tradition helps to support our claim. Significantly enough, Lazarsfeld, during the last two decades of his life, had also turned his attention to the precursors of modern empirical and statistical research methods; he also wrote on the theorists of public opinion.

It seems to me that the appeal of the critical approach to some of our colleagues is a symptom of the same concern. Its more radical adherents have been prone to overlook such historical facts as the involvement of one of its main apostles, Theodor Adorno, in empirical research. Not only had he been, while in the United States, the senior author of the monumental, though somewhat misguided, study of the authoritarian personality (Adorno, Frenkel-Brunswik, Levinson, & Sanford, 1950), but upon his return to Germany he worked to introduce the empirical methods he had once, and others have since, denigrated as "administrative" research into sociology in order to prevent it from remaining simply a humanistic discipline (*Geisteswissenschaft*). The dissemination given Adorno's dispute with Lazarsfeld over administrative research and, of course, to his more esoteric writings has been at the expense of other aspects of his past.

Having so far focused on the United States, let me turn to Europe. The same commercial and business interests that are known to have affected the direction of U.S. communication research also influenced the direction

---

[1]This was January 1986. The results of this study have since been published in Lang and Lang (1990) and in several articles.

it took in Europe. But there was, it appears to me, at least one important difference between the two continents: A number of European scholars who wrote on the press did so after extensive experience in journalism. This holds for Albert Schaeffle, Karl Buecher, Emil Loebl, Siegfried Kracauer, and also, let us not forget, for Max Weber. The only one among the early Americans with this kind of dual career that readily comes to mind is Park. In France, Germany, and England, leading academics have generally had easier access to journalistic outlets. The association may account for the fact that as early as 1916, and partly under the impetus of World War I, plans for a university-based institute to study the press (Institut fuer Zeitung-swissenschaft) at Leipzig were drawn up, soon to be followed, after the war, by the *Zeitschrift fuer Zeitungskunde [Journal Newspaper Studies]*, a journal devoted to studies of the subject. Buecher, a respected economist, was the guiding spirit behind both.

Remember also that these projects preceded the advent of the two broadcast media—radio and television. The first did not become an important social force until around 1930, and no one at the time thought seriously about television. The press—the penny press, the yellow press, the tabloids, the community newspaper, and the more serious journals of opinion—was just about all there was to fit the label of "mass" communication. There was some interest as well in general reading habits. As movies made their appearance on the scene, these also became the subject of sociological study. One early study of the cinema was based on a questionnaire, albeit not a very sophisticated one, that asked people directly about what had moved them to go to a movie, whether they stayed to the end, and about any "artistic impressions" conveyed to them (Altenloh, 1914). It was a start, even though the approach may have been somewhat naïve by contemporary standards.

The interest of scholars in mass communication goes back much earlier of course. The question is where to begin. One likely candidate would be Karl Marx, who followed the European career path by writing for several newspapers, including the *New York Tribune*, but never focused on the press as an object of analysis. There is, however, Alexis de Tocqueville, whose writing on the role of the newspaper in the United States in the formation of public opinion predates Marx. It needs to be pointed out that the highly politicized French press and the part it had played in the Revolution had left a strong impression on French writers throughout the 19th century. They were highly conscious of the influence newspapers and periodicals could exercise. Indicative of this interest is the monumental eight-volume work by Eugène Hatin on the literary and political history of the press in France (1859–1864), which was followed 2 years later by his *Bibliographie historique et critique de la presse périodique française . . . précédé d'un essai historique et statistique sur la naissance et les progrès de la presse périodique dans les deux mondes* (1866) [*Historical and Critical Bibliography of the Periodical Press in France...preceded by an Historical and Statistical Essay on the birth and the Progress of the Periodical Press in the Two Worlds*]. This extensive bibliography was preceded by a historical and statistical essay on the birth and progress of the periodical press in the Old and New Worlds. It provided the kind of statistical information on which later analysts could build.

Turning to the Germans, it seems to me that their studies had greater influence on the United States. In 1857, the economist Karl Knies published a book on the telegraph, in which he dealt extensively with the economics of information flow. I personally have never held a copy of that book in my hand, but the number of references to it allow one to conclude that it had some influence. The relationship between news reporting and the telegraph, first recognized well over 100 years ago, is once again being investigated by several scholars, including Richard Kielbowicz, a colleague of mine at the University of Washington.

The interest of Knies extended beyond the influence of a single invention, even one as important as the telegraph. Approaching his subject from an economic perspective, he contended that news communication between localities was complementary to exchange relationships, if not directly mandated by them. This line of thought was further developed by Buecher as well as by members of the Chicago School of sociologists in their ecological studies of newspaper circulation. More generally, what Knies implied, namely that functional relationships precede participation in a common normative order, has become a generally accepted postulate within the social science community.

But more than anyone else, it was Karl Buecher who took the lead in the development of the new field he called *Zeitungskunde*—a rough equivalent of mass communication research. Buecher, as mentioned, was among those who had begun their careers as working journalists. After becoming an academic, in his writings he addressed the many aspects of the press—its nature and function as an institution, journalistic practice, and the education of journalists—contained in the volume of his collected essays on the subject (Buecher, 1926). He also developed the kind of economic statistics on newspapers and the newspaper industry that have become common in the industrialized nations. Buecher must be judged as a major figure in every sense of the word. Available in English in a collection titled *Industrial Evolution* (1901) is his essay on the genesis of journalism, which treats the newspaper as:

> primarily a commercial contrivance, forming one of the most important pillars of contemporary economic activity. . . . In fact, the newspaper forms a link in the chain of modern commercial machinery; it is one of those contrivances by which in society the exchange of intellectual and material goods is facilitated.

It futher bemoans the fact that "those departments of knowledge that cannot form the basis of an academic career are inadequately investigated. This is the fate of journalism" (pp. 215–216).

Other important work to come out of Germany were Ludwig Salomon's three-volume history on the German press (1900–1906), which dealt in a remarkably thorough fashion with developments up to 1850, and a book by H. Wuttke (1875) dealing with the press and the emergence of public opinion. The latter topic takes us back to the phenomenon that had so intrigued Tocqueville. In the chapter of his *Democracy in America* on the relation between associations and newspapers, he raised the question of how to obtain cooperation in some common enterprise "when men are no longer united among themselves by firm and lasting ties." Men cannot combine, he wrote, until a "newspaper takes up the notion or the feeling which had occurred simultaneously, but singly to each of them. . . . The newspaper brought them together and keeps them united." From this he concluded that "newspapers make associations, and associations make newspapers" (Tocqueville, 1900, p. 119).

Notice that the argument in these extracts is not that the newspaper functions as a creator of opinions but rather that it articulates opinions that have no other vehicle of expression. There is nothing of the supposedly "all powerful" media in this passage nor in any of the other work I shall be citing. I cannot refrain from repeated reminders that this frequently cited theory never really had any followers among persons we would consider social scientists. But it was congruent with the popular fears about the effectiveness of the propaganda of totalitarian regimes and was used as a straw man that helped dramatize conclusions drawn from empirical findings in a U.S. context and make them appear more novel than they actually were. The theory has been buried rhetorically a countless number of times.

The relation between press and party (or association), so important throughout the 19th century, was also addressed by Emil Loebl, deputy editor in chief of the *Wiener Zeitung*, in a book titled *Kultur und Presse* [*Culture and Press*] (Loebl, 1903). This book was quite influential and helped establish *Zeitungskunde* as an academic discipline. It was mentioned favorably by Weber in his 1910 address to the first meeting of the German sociological association but is little known today and available in only a few U.S. libraries. Loebl's treatment is not so much historical as systematic and critical, with each chapter proceeding from definitions and concepts to analyze the organization of newspapers, the content of newspapers, and journalistic practices. Subjects examined include professional journalism and its relation to society, the anonymity of authorship and journalistic education, the function of the press and the resources at its disposal, its relation to politics and governmental authority, and the value of press freedom and the theory that supports it.

Loebl also had something to say about public opinion, which he saw as the product of two factors: an "original and living idea" and a "multiplier." (The last term is his.) Usually but not invariably this multiplier function is performed by the press. He was careful to note that public opinion also exists outside the press and sometimes develops, even attains power, in opposition to it. Thus, "the propagator of an idea disposes over other means for the dissemination and the reinforcement of his idea: books, a parliamentary platform, associations, assemblies, public lectures, informal get-togethers, and direct muted agitation from person to person" (1903, p. 255). The quote underlines that he, and others, were aware of the importance of personal influence, particularly in those instances where public opinion developed "without or even against the press."

Nevertheless, Ferdinand Toennies, in his lament nearly 20 years later, in his *Kritik der oeffentlichen Meinung* [*Critique of Public Opinion*] (1922), that the power of public opinion had often been equated with the power of the press, could still take Loebl to task for not recognizing the full import of his observation about the press as only one influence on public opinion among others. The power of the press was simply the more obvious; it was further magnified by the fact that "behind a newspaper, especially a big newspaper, stood the power of a political party, which frequently is also a part of economic and intellectual life or at least is closely connected with these" (p. 254).

In his *Kritik*, Toennies drew extensively on the existing literature and case material. He was very much aware also of the significant sociological reflection on the press in *L'opinion et la foule* [*Opinion and the Crowd*] by Gabriel Tarde (1901), who had been a strong influence on Park. Although Toennies differed with Tarde, he goes out of his way to pay his respect to the work of a man whose views have all too often been lumped with the far more extravagant formulations of Gustave Le Bon, his contemporary, about the irrationality and emotionality one encountered at times in the public sphere. In contrast to Le Bon, who saw evidence of the influence of the crowd wherever he happened to look, Tarde believed that publics were taking over from crowds, a development he attributed to the printing press and newspapers. This expanded communication enabled large numbers of persons, even if geographically dispersed, to know about the same news at the same time and to arrive at a unity of belief and, possibly, of action. Reading gave people an opportunity for reflection, which made publics jointly created by personal conversation and the printed word more rational than crowds.

Although Tarde here was following a line of thought previously developed by Tocqueville, he was also very aware that newspapers, when playing on emotions, could make people more "crowd-like." The previous essay (1901) was first published in 1899 when France was polarized over the Dreyfus affair, and few would have questioned that the French press, with its highly partisan reporting, had done its best to play on emotions. This context is a clue to why Tarde should have gone out of his way to discuss the affinities and differences between opinion and the mentality of crowds.

Questions about the effects of propaganda and of the sensationalism exhibited by the yellow press are also closely related to public opinion. I do no more than illustrate the thinking of some British scholars at the time. For instance, Graham Wallas asserted that group cooperation had rested to a great degree on personal knowledge and contact, but the coming of the Great Society had changed all this. "The largest visible crowd," he wrote, "is . . . only a tiny fraction of a modern nation. A modern civilized man can, therefore, never see or hear the nation of which he is a member" (Wallas, 1921, p. 78) even though some tangible image of its character and objectives is a prerequisite for common action but obviously lacking in the average man. Such images, Wallas believed, came mostly from newspapers that "often color the news." Wallas was a major influence on Walter Lippmann, who soon after published his own classic work on public opinion with its critique of journalism (1922). The concerns of these two men were real, but although recognizing that newspapers are powerful, neither even suggests that the press (or the media) were "all powerful."

Another very interesting book of this era on the influence of the press is by the economist Francis W. Hirst (1913). From vivid accounts of the events and press coverage during six war scares and financial panics, he drew this conclusion:

> A nation is not a crowd. To evoke a national panic in a modern state is a very difficult operation. . . . But . . . the semblance of a panic may be created even in an educated country like ours—enough, let us say, to increase the sale of newspapers, guns and stores, battleships or flying machines. What the newspapers can do, and what they cannot do, is worth ascertaining and describing. . . . The fuss and fury of our yellow press, though it thrills smart society in London, though it may sway the minds and policy of Ministers, produces no proportionate effect on the individual citizen. . . . [The typical Englishman] did not believe all that he was told. This is worth remembering; for we are always overapt to confuse the minds and opinions of our people with the nonsense they read. (pp. 1–4)

That the press exerts its power largely through its effect on members of the elite is one of the main points we made in our book on Watergate (Lang & Lang, 1983). It also fits very well with what Toennies said about the press being the "battle ground" for political conflict and the most important means for making public opinion "known" to those who claim to be responding to such opinion. Furthermore, the notion of misrepresentation of reality became most obvious during World War I and gave rise to studies of these misrepresentations as propaganda. The American most closely identified with this interest is Harold Lasswell.

One can easily distinguish between two types of research on the effects of propaganda. The first focuses on the questionable accuracy of reports that people were prone to accept as truth and the circumstances likely to produce gross distortions. Studies of this type have obvious relevance for the training of journalists even though one no longer encounters many references to these early studies by Europeans—only to Lippmann. One famous but by now nearly forgotten study by van Gennep, the ethnographer and folklorist, involved arranging to have someone dressed as a clown burst into his class on psychology pursued by a Black person with a revolver in his hand. As the clown fell, the Black person leapt upon him, fired, and then both rushed out. Written accounts by students who had been observers to this deliberately contrived event that lasted some 40 seconds turned out to be rather inaccurate. Had these eye-witness reports been passed on to others, they would have fit the model of rumor Gordon W. Allport and Leo Postman (1947) extracted from serial reproduction experiments they conducted three decades later.

The link between cognitive error, propaganda, and press coverage is brought out more clearly in a case study by Fernand van Langenhove (1916), a Belgian, of stories of *francs-tireurs* (snipers) operating in civilian clothes behind German lines. He traced these stories to fear and confusion experienced by soldiers, whose informal accounts were then picked up by newspapers and incorporated into the official German view.

The second type of propaganda research has to do with the actual performance of the press and the detection and analysis of propaganda. An early U.S. study by Wilcox (1900) that classified space devoted to different categories of news seems to have been the first systematic and quantitative content analysis. Henry de Noussance (1902) undertook a similar count of the lines in 20 Parisian and 7 provincial newspapers on a single day. About a dozen years later, a German study of 13 Berlin and 17 German provincial newspapers for an entire week used the same categories as in the French study to extend the comparisons to the press in the capitals of the two nations and to their provincial press (Stoklossa, 1910). These studies looked at the extent to which the press was neglecting its moral obligations.

The previously mentioned study by van Langenhove used essentially ethnographic methods to trace the "natural history" of a news story. There were others. One we cited in *Collective Dynamics* was by Arthur Ponsonby, an Englishman. In his *Falsehood in Wartime*, published in 1930, he documented how a news story evolved as each paper picked it up from another as in the serial transmission of the classic rumor experiment (cited by Lang & Lang, 1961, p. 62).

Having dealt with content, I should also say a few words about the earlier audience research, much of it conducted within a political or moralistic context. Glancing through some of the British social surveys, like those by Charles Booth and by Benjamin Seebohm Rowntree, which are in the University of Washington library, I could not find any probes into what ordinary poor people were reading at the time. There were a few references to what newspaper vendors sold but nothing about what newspaper readers actually read. About the same time, two German pastors used a questionnaire to conduct a study for the Allgemeine Konferenz des Deutschen Sittlichkeitsverein (Conference of the German Association on Morality), in which they looked into the "influence of a bad press and cheap literature." Returns were obtained from some 14,000 Protestant ministers from all over Germany. What I know of this study comes only from Anthony Oberschall's review of the empirical German literature (1965, pp. 32f). I do not know about any effects they may have found, but it is noteworthy as an early attempt to obtain systematic data from informants.

Meanwhile, librarians were beginning to examine the circulation of library books. One such study, also cited by Oberschall (1965, pp. 83f), distinguished between "proletarian and bourgeois" readers according to their occupations. It includes a list of the most-read books in the various categories. There were more than 50 tables in this study published in 1910.

Another interesting questionnaire study explored the work situation and living conditions of workers as well as their feelings and thoughts about these aspects of their lives. It had a question on books respondents had read (Levenstein, 1912). Its observation was perhaps a little tendentious, as were others of this sort, in noting that most workers were heavily into the socialist and trade-union literature. A study of movies, published around the same time, has already been mentioned (Altenloh, 1914).

All in all, there were few studies directly aimed at assessing effects. Without detailed investigation of communication behavior, conclusions rested heavily on inferences from content, especially if this could be correlated to behavioral indicators. One monograph, based on a PhD thesis at the University of Halle (Wittwer, 1914), managed to introduce a time dimension into its investigation of the relationship between the trend in the social democratic vote and the circulation of the social democratic press in Germany between 1908 and 1913. Both had increased in the interval—the former from 27% to 35% and the latter from 1.5% to 2.2%. The finding is open to several interpretations. One could say that socialist gains occurred despite rather low penetration of party newspapers, or one could point out that the two slopes rose in roughly parallel fashion. Insofar as the proportionate increase in social democratic readership was actually larger than the increase in the vote, the second argument, though plausible, is less than fully convincing.

This way of gauging media effects is obviously flawed, but it does not suggest the simple-minded "hypodermic" or "bullet" theory, against which contemporary scholars continue to rail. Not only Toennies but others as well expressed doubts about being able to ascertain the drift in public opinion from the press. James Bryce (1921), for one, declared that "the press . . . is not a safe guide, since the circulation of a journal does not necessarily measure the prevalence of the views it advocates" (Vol. 1, p. 155). To recognize public opinion, one has also to pay attention to what one hears everywhere and what one sees in the form of marches, demonstrations, and other forms of protest.

On the effect the press had on public opinion, even the earliest scholars pointed to the importance of contextual influences. Thus, Tocqueville asserted that the singular power of the press was "much greater in France than in the United States." One reason he gives for this has to do with the large amounts of space in U.S. newspapers given to advertisements, whereas commercial space is very limited in France, and the most essential part of every issue is taken up by discussion of the politics of the day, commercial space being very limited. He continued with the following:

It has been demonstrated by observation [but obviously not the kind of observation that we would accept as "hard" data]. . . that the influence of a power is increased in proportion as its direction is rendered more central. In France the press combines a two-fold centralization; almost all its power is centered in the same spot, and vested in the same hands, for its organs are far from numerous. . . . Neither of these kinds of centralization exists in America. The United States have no metropolis; the intelligence as well as the power of the country are dispersed abroad, and . . . cross each other in every direction. . . . The number of periodical and occasional publications which appear in the United States actually surpasses belief. . . . There is scarcely a hamlet without its own newspaper. (Toqueville, 1947, p. 107)

But Tocqueville also acknowledged that the influence of the press in the United States was immense:

When a great number of organs of the press adopt the same line of conduct, their influence becomes irresistible; and public opinion, when it is perpetually assailed from the same side, eventually yields to the attack. In the United States each separate journal exercises but little authority, but the power of the periodical press is only second to that of the people. (1947, p. 107)

This is the proposition that the effects of mass communication are greatest in the presence of a media monopoly or, more accurately, on there being a significant degree of uniformity across media outlets. Tocqueville was aware of the pluralism of U.S. society and its capability to produce the cross pressures, whose importance in politics had long ago been recognized by Montesquieu. A lot of what a later generation discovered was anticipated.

Buecher had already observed that editors set what nowadays we would call the public agenda, but with the qualification that this power was attenuated by their economic interest, which made them responsive to the interests of their readers. He probably would have agreed with Toennies that the historical importance of the press had to do with the way it enabled the liberal parties to advance against the hegemony of conservative thought (Toennies, 1922, p. 255). But even here the press was only a means. Said Toennies, "Now, if and insofar as public opinion is subject to the same influences and developmental causations as the press, public opinion will be reflected in the press, so that the power of the press expresses the power of public opinion" (p. 256). But this coincidence, he said a page later, is limited except insofar as there exists a latent but unrecognized unanimity, anticipating in this respect more recent views on hegemony and other thoughts associated with the Critical School.

What about the effects of advertising? Buecher made use of a rather extensive German literature on the subject going back before World War I. In addition to the written literature, Buecher drew on information provided by German consulates about advertising in other countries, particularly in the United States and Great Britain. For him advertising included all means of self-promotion, even the most subtle ones, such as the ways in which academics might seek to gain students for the courses they teach or otherwise enhance their reputations. The extension of promotional techniques beyond the narrowly economic realm, he observed, had gone farthest in the United States. To a German, the term *Reklame* still connoted a certain deception, which kept them from accepting it as an important fact of economic life (Buecher, 1925b).

That the book, the first form of mass communication and the first commodity to be mass produced, should also be the first to be promoted by advertising was no coincidence for Buecher. But the marketing analysts were hardly naïve. The German Buecherverein (Association of German Book Publishers), in a study it undertook in 1926, knew already that most book buying was a response, not to printed advertisements, but to word-of-mouth (Schuecking, 1939). No sweeping conclusions about mass media influence versus personal influence were drawn. Buecher coupled his eloquent exposition on the importance of advertising with the same considered skepticism that marks all his writing. "Precisely because it is so difficult to discover the suitable message in each special case," he wrote in an essay first published in 1916, "advertising in general becomes a refuge for people who claim to be experts, who promise far more than they are able to deliver" (Buecher, 1925b, p. 315). This sounds very much like a theme more recently pursued by Michael Schudson (1984) in his book on advertising.

Buecher saw the effectiveness of advertising campaigns as limited by the difficulty one inevitably faced in promoting a poor product. Advertising, he maintained, afforded consumers an opportunity for critical selection they would not have if dependent on what was on the shelves. It was best suited for the introduction of new products, but even here campaigns were subject to the law of diminishing returns, now called a ceiling effect. Once something had been publicized and people are buying it, additional effort will bring no more than occasional gleanings from those potential buyers who had been previously overlooked. Campaigns lose effectiveness as they "use themselves up" (Buecher, 1925b, p. 319). Many campaign studies have gone into the field, not when a new product was launched but only after a commercial or political brand name had already established itself.

Lastly, let me turn to the proposal Weber (1924) presented to the first meeting of the German Sociological Society for a monumental, all-encompassing, empirical study of the press. Weber took its significance in modern society for granted. All one had to do, he said, was try to imagine what life would be like without it. Here are the main questions he wanted this research to illuminate.

First, what gets in the papers and what does not? He referred to the principle of parliamentary privilege (especially in England), which conflicted with the dependence of the representatives on the good will of the press.

Second, what are the views, current and past, on the question of publicity and with what social and ideological positions are they correlated? The research was to ascertain what was there but should not be contaminated by any sign of advocacy because it could not be completed successfully without the cooperation from the press itself.

A third set of problems related to how policies and practices about what was privileged and what was legitimately in the public domain, such as the Pentagon Papers or other "confidential" government material, affected the distribution of power. Weber acknowledged that publicity would have less effect on science than on performances dependent on good reviews. The investigation of the relation of the press to the political parties, to the world of business and industry, and to all interests that are influenced by and exert an influence on public life loomed as a real challenge to sociology.

Fourth, what are the causes and consequences of the tension between the press as a source of political and other information and the press as an advertising medium? He referred to differences between France and Germany on this score.

Fifth, what are the effects of size? Are large newspapers with higher capital investment more or less careful not to alienate their readerships, particularly if they depend on newsstand sales? The issue remains highly relevant for current policy.

Sixth, what are the implications of chain ownership and monopoly for public opinion?

Seventh, Weber raised a series of questions about journalistic practices. Were differences in journalistic practices affected by the relationship of a paper to its sources and by its dependence on newsstand sales (as opposed to subscriptions and deliveries)? Were journalistic practices affected by a tradition in which institutional authority weighed more heavily than the intellectual acuity or celebrity status of the writer? How important were free-lance contributions? Was there a general trend toward more "factual" reporting as opposed to commentary? And, more generally, what were the main sources of information for newspapers: their own sources, press associations, handouts, and so forth?

Eighth, Weber argued for studies of the journalistic profession and the career prospects of journalists and how they varied in different countries. For example, is journalism a natural stepping stone into politics? What are the social origins of journalists and their educational backgrounds?

The ninth set of questions relates to the effect of the readership. To what kind of reading matter have people become accustomed? Do newspapers displace books? What are the effects of constant stimulation by news with rapidly shifting foci of attention? What is the effect on culture in general?

Having raised these questions, Weber ended with a rhetorical one about where the material for such study was to be found. His answer:

> In the papers themselves, and we will, to put it frankly, proceed in the most pedestrian manner, by measuring with calipers and compass, how the content of the press has shifted quantitatively in the course of the last generation and not ignore the advertising sections, the feature section, the balance between features and editorials, between editorials and news, and between what comes in and what is actually utilized. . . . We have the beginnings of such investigations . . . but only the very beginning. And on the basis of these quantitative findings we will then turn to the qualitative ones. (Weber, 1924, p. 441)

To what extent were these formulations by Europeans assimilated into the U.S. mainstream of mass communication research? On the negative side, I note that this particular address by Weber, who is so widely celebrated in this country, was not even listed in either of two very comprehensive bibliographies by Lasswell and his associates (Lasswell, Smith, & Casey, 1935; Smith, Lasswell, & Casey, 1946) and has rarely, at least not until recently, been acknowledged.

There is, however, another side to the story. The examination of the newspaper and its relation to the community, as in Park's studies of the immigrant press, was to become a part of the Chicago tradition. In his later years, Park also wrote some seminal papers on the sociological nature of news. Even before this, he had been the obvious catalyst for at least two dissertations on the subject—one by Carroll Dewitt Clark in 1931; the second by Helen M. Hughes, which became the basis for her book (1940).

The content analysis studies of propaganda by Lasswell and the survey of Washington correspondents by Leo Rosten are also very much in line with Weber's call for empirical investigations. Both Lasswell and Rosten came out of the Chicago School.

A second element of continuity resides in the underlying reformist and meliorist motivation underlying later U.S. studies. It found perhaps the clearest expression in the Payne Fund Studies of movies from 1929 to 1932, which focused on whether movie-going promoted delinquent or violent behavior among adolescents (for summary, see Charters, 1933). It is equally present in the studies of propaganda (during the 1930s) and in much of the early work of the Bureau of Applied Social Research, with its thinly veiled concern about whether the potential of radio as a medium for education and the dissemination of culture was being fully realized. Although some critics may not be willing to concede as much, I am convinced that many, but by no means all, of the issues addressed during the years of the Office of Radio Research at Princeton University arose from the same concerns that had moved their European precursors. Both sides of the Atlantic have moved ahead, and they are not as far apart as some would have us believe.

Why should the European tradition and the U.S. tradition have so often been thought of as antithetical to one another? It seems to me that this exaggeration of differences has something to do with the "minimal effects" theorem and its effect on Americans, many of whom, especially at Columbia, advertised their work as a long overdue corrective against the theory of the "all powerful" media. That theory, however, rests on a popular myth; it has never been formulated as a scientific proposition. I, for one, have as yet to find a footnote to a scholarly book or article that espouses it. There has come into being, nevertheless, an intellectual or scholarly myth with remarkably wide currency, namely, that it was left to the scholars of the 1940s and 1950s to have been the first ever to put the power of the media into perspective. Americans, convinced of this myth, have also exported it along with their refinements in methodology, which do indeed represent real contributions. A sequel to the original myth is the presumption that only in the past two decades have we gradually been "rediscovering" that the media may in fact be just a little more powerful than scholars were able to conclude from research during and after World War II.

I am not simply making things up. Oberschall, on whom I have drawn and whose scholarly work I greatly respect, characterized the notions of Buecher on the influence of the press on public opinion as simplistic and essentially "conspiratorial." Buecher believed, according to Oberschall, whom I quote, that "everything is thought out in advance (for the reader). In every corner, in every little notice of the paper, the news-reports are mixed in with value judgments, opinions and feelings. In the end this foreign conception weighs down on one's own powers of judgment as lead" (Oberschall, 1965, p. 110).

Oberschall (1965) further attributed to Buecher an exaggerated notion about the "suggestivity of printed matter" and the belief that the morality of the press will become the "morality of the masses" and asserted that his concept of public opinion, being of the cultural critical variety, was not geared to empirical testing (p. 110). To document that Buecher conceived of public opinion as undifferentiated and irrational, subject to wide and irregular fluctuations, Oberschall ended with a quote from a volume unfortunately not available in my library:

> "Public opinion is the judgment of society, strongly saturated with affectual and will components, a mass psychological reaction which turns affirmatively or negatively against certain events, measures or established facts." In this conceptualization, comments Oberschall, the question whether certain individuals and groups are more susceptible than others of being influenced by various modes of communication was never raised. (Buecher, 1926, cited in Oberschall, p. 110).

"Never" is a strong word and can be refuted by a single instance. The following passages, which I managed to find in what was available at the University of Washington libraries, are enough to refute so sweeping a generalization. All of them come from an article on the anonymity of the press contained in the collection titled *Die Entstehung der Wirtschaft* [*Industrial Evolution*](Buecher, 1925a).

Here he began with a brief historical account together with some explanations of how editorials came to be unsigned and articles and sources kept anonymous. He continued noting two developments: Readers were turning away from the party press to the nonpartisan newspapers and the reliance on news services. This meant that the "press in the entire educated part of the world carried the same news about the same matters" (Buecher, 1925a, p. 263), and the content of the papers had actually become so similar during the recent war that it no longer mattered which ones a person read (p. 264). From there he proceeded to argue for the elimination of anonymity on the assumption that this would raise the status of journalists and make them less dependent on the whims of publishers. The content of the newspaper would be elevated as a result. He did indeed impute a certain "power of suggestion" to the printed word and traced this to the way "all news presents itself with the same claim for reliability and credibility [to]

be uncritically accepted" by many uneducated people but also the educated. But "if the reader has a critical disposition, then he will meet
everything with the same deep-rooted mistrust. If he is by nature trusting,
then everything the paper brings will be gospel for him, to be passed on
just as he received it" (pp. 284, 286). He argued against anonymity on the
ground that readers who are given sources will have the means to exercise
their critical faculty.

The reference to the suggestibility of readers contains no imputation of
blind trust. Actually Buecher developed this notion in much the same way
as did Tarde. Both worked from the postulate that the newspaper readers
have in their mind some image of others reading the same thing as they
are. These others function like a reference group. Inasmuch as papers treat
what they write about as self-evident and the "facts" they convey as beyond
challenge or question, Buecher reasoned, people may feel isolated when
they dissent. But he never implied that such a reaction was automatic.

Having reviewed some of these early writings, I ask once again: Why do
so many of us harbor the idea that the analyses by early social scientists of
the undeniably great power of the press (and the media generally) paid no
attention to the mediating conditions that sometimes enhanced and at other
times limited its control over the masses? I can think of three reasons. One
is, of course, historical. The flow of information between the European
forerunners and social science as it was developing in the United States was
disrupted by the rise of fascism and the war that followed. To be sure, many
Europeans, especially Germans, came to the United States, but they became
involved in social science as it was developing here.

Second, a lot of the early material simply is not available except in a few
major libraries. I alluded to difficulties I, myself, had in finding material.
Many communication researchers, even students of international communication, do not read foreign languages, and much of the material I discussed has never been translated.

The third reason touches on a more important sociological principle. It
has something to do with how social scientists work and the way even they,
like physicists, are prone to make priority claims. I refer you to articles by
Robert K. Merton (1957) in which he noted the keen competition among
scientists to be first. A similar kind of competition exists among social
scientists, though perhaps in a muted form, because many interesting
findings are at least somewhat serendipitous, belonging in the category of
unanticipated discoveries. In these instances, whoever chances on a previously unobserved phenomenon often does not know what to make of it.
Much rests on the interpretation. The discovery process involves a certain
rhetoric—the rhetoric of discovery.

Because of the relatively undeveloped theoretical infrastructure in most
social sciences, the competition for priority is heavy on rhetoric. Taken by

themselves, one's findings may not seem at all significant, but linking them to some important current of thought in the literature can make them so. The compulsion to show that one is working in a grand tradition, or on a major problem, increases to the degree that the findings fail to speak for themselves. But in making the case that one's findings seriously modify or, better yet, contradict a widely accepted theoretical position, one does indeed enhance their significance. Here social scientists operate very much like artists, where every group, at least since modernism came to the fore in the 19th century, has tried to define itself as secessionist, emphasizing its differences with an establishment dominated by an older generation. Artistic styles have come to change ever more frequently, and artistic generations are being compressed. We are encountering something similar within sociology, where one stands to gain especially by defining oneself as different from the established tradition. In this way, one can claim having made a theoretical breakthrough.

Some of the priority claims established by the rhetoric of the ascending Columbia University school of communication research clearly rest on a deficient historical memory. In saying this, I do not mean to take away from its real contributions. I have read their studies with profit, and I do not intend to substitute a new myth of the glorious past. My concern is over the redefinition made possible in part by the organized power of an academic group, which by deluding itself also deluded others into believing that none of the ideas they labored to produce had ever been anticipated.

Lazarsfeld, for one, must have known this because toward the end of his career he became increasingly concerned with the work of his precursors. Many others are only just beginning to learn, partly through some of the things Lazarsfeld wrote in his later years, about the intellectual debt we owe to forgotten scholarship.

REFERENCES

Adorno, T. W., Frenkel-Brunswik, E., Levinson, D. J., & Sanford, R. N. (1950). *The authoritarian personality*. New York: Harper.
Allport, G. W., & Postman, L. (1947). *The psychology of rumor*. New York: Holt.
Altenloh, E. (1914). *Zur Soziologie des Kino* [*On the sociology of the cinema*]. Jena: Diederichs.
Bryce, J. (1921). *Modern democracies* (Vols. 1–2.). New York: Macmillan.
Buecher, K. (1901). The genesis of journalism (S. M. Wickett, Trans.). In *Industrial evolution* [Translated from third edition, *Die Entstehung der Wirtschaft*, published 1900] (pp. 215–243). New York: Holt.
Buecher, K. (1925a). Die Anonymitaet in den Zeitungen [*Anonymity in newspapers*]. *Die Entstehung der Volkswirtschaft* [*The origin of the political economy*] (Vol. 2, pp. 245–292). Munich: H. Laupp.
Buecher, K. (1925b). *Die wirtschaftliche Reklame* [*Economic advertising*]. *Die Entstehung der Volkswirtschaft* [*The origin of the political economy*] (Vol. 1, pp. 293–322). Munich: Laupp.

Buecher, K. (1926). *Gesammelte Aufsaetze zur Zeitungskunde [Collected essays on mass communications]*. Tuebingen: Laupp.

Charters, W. W. (1933). *Motion pictures and youth, a summary*. New York: Macmillan.

Clark, C. D. (1931). *News: A sociological study*. Unpublished doctoral dissertation, University of Chicago.

Escarpit, R. (1958). *Sociologie de la littérature [Sociology of literature]*. Paris: Presses Universitaires de France.

Hatin, E. (1859–1864). *Histoire politique et littéraire de la presse en France [Political and literary history of the press in France]* (Vols. 1–8). Paris: Pulet-Malassis & de Broise.

Hatin, E. (1866). *Bibliographie historique et critique de la presse périodique francaise . . . précédé d'un essai historique et statistique sur la naissance et le progrès de la presse périodique dans les deux mondes [Historical and critical bibliography of the periodical press in France . . .proceded by an historical and statistical essay on the birth and the progress of the periodical press in the two worlds]*. Paris: Firmon-Didot.

Hirst, F. W. (1913). *Six panics and other essays*. London: Methuen.

Hughes, H. M. (1940). *News and the human-interest story.*Chicago: University of Chicago Press.

Katz, E. (1977). *Social research on broadcasting: Proposals for further development* [Report to the British Broadcasting Corp.]. London: BBC.

Katz, E., & Lazarsfeld, P. F. (1955). *Personal influence: The part played by people in the flow of mass communications*. Glencoe, IL: The Free Press.

Knies, K. (1857). *Der Telegraph als Verkehrsmittel: Mit Eroerterungen ueber den Nachrichtenverkehr ueberhaupt [The Telegraph as means of communication: With examinations of news service in general]*. Tuebingen: Laupp.

Lang, G. E., & Lang, K. (1983). *The battle for public opinion: The president, the press, and the polls during Watergate*. New York: Columbia University Press.

Lang, G. E., & Lang, K. (1990). *Etched in memory: The building and survival of artistic reputation*. Chapel Hill: University of North Carolina Press.

Lang, K. (1979). The critical functions of communication research: Observations on German-American influences. *Media, Culture and Society, 1*, 83–96.

Lang, K., & Lang G. E. (1961). *Collective dynamics*. New York: Crowell.

Langenhove, F. van (1916). *The growth of a legend*. New York: Putnam.

Lasswell, H. D., Smith, B. L., & Casey, R. D. (1935). *Propaganda and promotional activities*. Minneapolis: University of Minnesota Press.

Lazarsfeld, P. F. (1965). Preface. In A. Oberschall (Ed.), *Empirical social research in Germany 1848–1914*, (pp. v–viii). Paris: Mouton.

Levenstein, A. (1912). *Die Arbeiterfrage [The labor question]*. Munich: Reinhardt.

Lippmann, W. (1922). *Public opinion*. New York: Macmillan.

Loebl, E. (1903). *Kultur und Presse [Culture and press]*. Leipzig: Duncker & Humblot.

Merton, R. K. (1957). Priorities in scientific discoveries. *American Sociological Review, 22*, 286–324.

Noussance, H. de. (1902, June). Que vaut la presse quotidienne française. *Revue hebdomadaire [Weekly Review]*, 1–26.

Oberschall, A. (1965). *Empirical social research in Germany, 1848–1914*. Paris: Mouton.

Salomon, L. (1900–1906). *Geschichte des deutschen Zeitungswesens [History of the German press]* (Vols. 1–3.). Oldenburg/Leipzig: Schartz.

Schudson, M. (1984). *Advertising, the uneasy persuasion: Its dubious impact on society*. New York: Basic Books.

Schuecking, L. L. (1939). *The sociology of literary taste* (E. W. Dicks, Trans.). London: Oxford University Press. (Original work published 1931)

Sills, D. L. (Ed.). (1968). *International encyclopedia of the social sciences* (Vols. 1–17). New York: Macmillan & The Free Press.

Smith, B. L., Lasswell, H. D., & Casey R. D. (1946). *Propaganda, communication and public opinion.* Princeton, NJ: Princeton University Press.

Stoklossa, P. (1910). Der Inhalt der Zeitungen. *Zeitschrift der gesamten Staatswissenschaft [Journal of general political science], 66*, 555–565.

Tarde, G. (1901). *L'opinion et la foule [Opinion and the crowd].* Paris: Alcan.

Thimme, H. (1932). *Weltkrieg ohne Waffen: Die Propaganda der Westmaechte gegen Deutschland [World war without weapons: The propaganda of the western powers against Germany].* Stuttgart: Cotta.

Tocqueville, A. de (1900). *Democracy in America* (H. Reeves, Trans.). London/New York: Colonial Press.

Tocqueville, A. de (1947). *Democracy in America.* New York: Galaxy.

Toennies, F. (1922). *Kritik der oeffentlichen Meinung [Critique of Public Opinion].* Berlin: Springer.

Wallas, G. (1921). *Our social heritage.* New Haven, CT: Yale University Press.

Weber, M. (1924). Rede auf dem ersten Deutschen Soziologentage in Frankfurt 1910 [Address at the first German conference of sociology]. In *Gesammelte Aufsaetze zur Soziologie und Sozialpolitik [Collected essays on sociology and social policy]* (pp. 431-449). Tuebingen: J. B. C. Mohr.

Wilcox, D. F. (1900). The American newspaper. *Annals of the American Academy of Political and Social Science, 16,* 56–92.

Wirth, L. (1948). Consensus and mass communications. *American Sociological Review, 30,* 1–15.

Wittkower, R., & Wittkower, M. (1963). *Born under Saturn: The character and conduct of artists.* New York: Random House.

Wittwer, M. (1914). *Das deutsche Zeitungswesen in seiner neueren Entwicklung [The German press in its latest developments].* Unpublished doctoral dissertation, University of Halle, Halle a. d. Saale.

Wuttke, H. (1875). *Die deutschen Zeitschriften und die Entstehung der oeffentlichen Meinung [The German journals and the origins of public opinion.]* Leipzig: Kruger.

Chapter 2

The Chicago School and Mass Communication Research

James W. Carey
Columbia University

Strictly speaking, there is no history of mass communication research. From the 17th century forward, one finds scholars, scientists, lawyers, clerics, men of letters, journalists, politicians, and free-lance intellectuals writing about the printing press, broadsides, penny dreadfuls, censorship, the Star Chamber, the urban public, freedom of speech and press, and a host of related topics and issues. Similarly, as the 19th century progressed, an increasing number of essays appeared on the telegraph, the rise of advertising, the economic power of newspapers, the growth of the national magazine, and the emergence of the "press baron." However, this motley collection of books, essays, speeches, memoirs, autobiographies, political interventions, and ideological tracts hardly constituted a history of the mass media or even the materials necessary to an understanding of such institutions.

Rather, the history of mass communication research is a recent literary genre, albeit a minor one: It is a self-conscious creation (and now an endless recreation) that sifts, sorts, and rearranges the accumulated literary debris into a coherent narrative. The narrative that emerges serves ultimately a variety of purposes: principally to focus, justify, and legitimate a 20th-century invention, the mass media, and to give direction and intellectual status to professional teaching and research concerning these same institutions. But it is hardly an innocent history, for it was invented for political reasons: to cast loyalties, resolve disputes, guide public policy, confuse opposition, and legitimate institutions; in short, the history that emerged was a minor episode in the social-political and ideological struggles of the 20th century.

By the 1950s, the history of mass communication research had achieved textual status (it was a recognizable species of writing) and certain "studies," essays, books, and intellectual figures (e.g., Paul Lazarsfeld and Wilbur Schramm) had become part of a minor canon that were required reading on university syllabi. Once formulated, the history almost instantly achieved boilerplate status and was endlessly retailed in textbooks, essays, research reports, and on any given academic day was providing an easy and unearned introduction to a subject matter in classrooms across the country.

The history, reduced to a sketch and a caricature, went—actually, it still goes—something like this. Mass communication research began in the years surrounding World War I as a response to a widespread fear of propaganda: wartime propaganda by the major military powers, peacetime propaganda by organized interests, particularly the modern corporation and the business class. The fear of propaganda was fueled by the spread and increasing sophistication of advertising and public relations, but the indictment of these practices moved from the arena of news and public affairs across the landscape of mass-produced culture and entertainment. If the cognitive and attitudinal life of the citizen was under assault by propaganda, the moral, appreciative, and affective life of children (and the child in us all) was similarly assailed by a banal and pernicious system of cultural production emanating from massive, concentrated institutions. As the "jazz age" turned into the Great Depression, the fears of propaganda and the media were confirmed by the mass movements in politics and culture typical of that period and by a series of specific and startling events of which Orson Welles' radio broadcast "The War of the Worlds" stood as an archetype. In the standard history, this random assortment of fears, alarms, jeremiads, political pronouncements, and a few pieces of empirical research were collapsed into the "hypodermic-needle model" or "bullet theory" or "model of unlimited effects" of the mass media, for they converged on a common conclusion: The media collectively, but in particular the newer, illiterate media of radio and film, possessed extraordinary power to shape the beliefs and conduct of ordinary men and women.

However, the standard history continues, this conclusion was supported by nothing more than speculation, conjecture, anecdotal evidence, and ideological axe grinding. None of the conclusions was theoretically or empirically grounded; none was supported by systematic research. Inferential and unjustified leaps were made from patterns of ownership and control (by business elites and reactionary entrepreneurs) to the quality and import of "messages" and from the content of messages (Father Coughlin's radio addresses, for example) to effects on conduct and attitudes. In short, unjustified connections were made between the presence of a cause and the stipulation of an effect, the appearance of a stimulus and the automatic production of a response, without evidence concerning the intervening and mediating linkages between medium, message, and effect.

However, the standard history continues, beginning in the late 1930s and progressively throughout the 1940s, a body of empirically sophisticated and theoretically grounded research began to appear, largely at Columbia University's Bureau of Applied Social Research and the Division of Information and Education at the War Department, that decisively cut against the hypodermic-needle model of media effects. What was discovered, almost fortuitously it seems, was a bizarre situation in which there were causes without effects, stimuli without responses. That is, hardly anyone denied the charges that the media contained propaganda and degenerate culture, but most investigators produced evidence that the content or intentions were rarely tied to effects or consequences. What was also discovered, in the standard rendition, was that individuals, the members of the audience, were protected from the deleterious possibilities inherent in the mass media by a group of predispositional or mediating factors. Some of these factors were psychological—people interpreted messages and retained meanings in the light of their own needs and desires—and some of these factors were social—people interpreted messages and assigned meanings as part of an interactive network of stable social groups to which they belonged. Both sets of factors conspired to protect individuals from everything but the most marginal effects of the mass media. Some individuals (a few) under some circumstances (rare) were directly affected by the mass media. Otherwise, media propaganda and mass culture were held at bay by an invisible shield erected by a universally resistant psyche and a universally present network of social groups. This conclusion was presented in summary form as early as 1948 in an *American Scholar* essay by Joseph Klapper, "The Mass Media and the Engineering of Consent" (1948) and fully articulated 12 years later, with all the empirical evidence assembled, as his summary judgment of *The Effects of Mass Communication* (1960).

Klapper concluded that the fears of propaganda, of manipulative elites, of media-induced extremist behavior, were misplaced and hysterical. Empirical research, he believed, had carefully documented the factors that made individuals resistant to mass persuasion. He concluded that the mass media could have an effect on their audiences only when the media moved in concert with the natural predispositions of an audience, when they were impelling the audience in directions ordained by the general culture rather than working against it. Given the conservative bias of the media and of social life generally, Klapper concluded that the preponderant effect was the reinforcement of the status quo. There was, therefore, little to fear from extremist behavior or anti-democratic social movements. The media were at one, if not by design and intent, at least by results and consequences, with the democratic, individualist, decentralist traditions of the country. All in all, this was a pretty rosy picture, particularly given the sharp national conflicts and deep ideological divisions present in the postwar world.

With the conclusion firmly established that the media had but limited effects, the research agenda was largely a mopping-up operation: the closer and more detailed specification of the specific operation of mediating and intervening factors. Consequently, Klapper (1963) tried to turn research in another direction, toward what he called a "phenomenistic approach" and what others called the study of "uses and gratifications" (Katz & Foulkes, 1962). In a well-known line, interest shifted from what it was that the media did to people toward what it was people did with the media. This was then a shift in interest and attention from the source to the receiver and a relocation of the point of power in the process: The audience controlled the producers. Except for some special problems (violence and pornography are the best-known examples) and some special groups (principally children), interest in direct effects and propaganda withered away. The settled and established consensus and conclusion to the history was that the media might have special and limited effects on some topics and some groups, that they might direct attention to some problems and away from others, thereby setting a social and political agenda of sorts, but the media did not constitute a social problem, did not debase the culture or promote extremism; the media were, in short, in concert with rather than in opposition to the fundamentally democratic and egalitarian forces in the culture.

There is, inevitably, some truth in this standard history, but it is powerfully misleading and of late there have been attempts to recast it and recover the pertinence and sophistication of the research and speculation on propaganda that was a hallmark of the 1920s (see Sproule, 1989). But what must be emphasized here is that the standard history had, or at least was subsequently endowed, with a practical political purpose. It attempted to negate or at least deflect the characteristic critiques of modern, liberal, capitalist democracies. Those critiques, whether of the left or right, identified dominative forces and totalitarian tendencies within all the Western democracies and tied these tendencies to certain features inherent in the structure, content, and ownership patterns of the mass media. These critiques are frequently lumped together as "the theory of mass society," a pastiche containing distinctively radical and distinctively conservative analyses of modern society. Daniel Bell (1961) gave the theory one kind of summary:

> The conception of "mass society" can be summarized as follows: The revolutions in transport and communications have brought men into closer contact with each other and bound them in new ways; the division of labor has made

them more interdependent; tremors in one part of the society affect all others. Despite this greater interdependence, however, individuals have grown more estranged from one another. The old primary group ties of family and local community have been shattered; ancient parochial faiths are questioned; few unifying values have taken their place. Most important, the critical standards of an educated elite no longer shape opinion or taste. As a result, mores and morals are in constant flux, relations between individuals are tangential or compartmentalized rather than organic. At the same time greater mobility, spatial and social, intensifies concern over status. Instead of a fixed or known status symbolized by dress or title, each person assumes a multiplicity of roles and constantly has to prove himself in a succession of new situations. Because of all this, the individual loses a coherent sense of self. His anxieties increase. There ensues a search for new faiths. The stage is thus set for the charismatic leader, the secular messiah, who, by bestowing upon each person the semblance of necessary grace and fullness of personality, supplies a substitute for the older unifying belief that the mass society has destroyed. (pp. 21–22)

The key event in the evolution of mass society was the development of the mass media. As Raymond and Alice Bauer (1960) put it, the population, as conceived by the theory of mass society, was "atomized" by industrialism and developed, as a result, "an insatiable appetite for narcotizing diversion, a circumstance which makes them susceptible to the machinations of the few who control the media of communications. One result of this process . . . is that the groundwork is laid for totalitarianism" (p. 5).

As I said, the theory of mass society was actually a synthesis of two rather different critiques of modern life, one conservative and one radical. Both critiques shared, however, the belief that all the forces of modernity—technology, economic development, literacy, mass democracy—conspired to erode the protective standards and covering that ensured social stability and a reasonable politics and culture. They differed rather considerably, however, concerning whose standards were being eroded and who was being disabled from exercising political leadership. The conservative critique focused on the erosion of the position and standards of traditional elites in the arts, academy, and civil service as mass participation in culture and politics was mobilized through, among other things, the mass media. The radical critique, predictably, focused on just the opposite, on the demobilization of the masses, on their exposure to manipulative control, and on the intent of domineering elites to contain any movement aimed at radical change.

Synthesized into a more or less coherent position, the theory of mass society contended that the media of communication were simultaneously an agent for destroying intellectual and artistic standards and the elites who bore them and a means for exercising dominion over and control of ordinary men and women. Both elites and masses, set free from, liberated from, tradition and traditional ways of life, were promptly reabsorbed into the market and consumerism, into mass politics and mass consumption. The only winners in this game were commercial elites and their technocratic servants in the professions, including the personnel of the mass media.

The history of mass communication created, then, as its necessary double, the theory of mass society and, naturally, constituted that theory in its most vulnerable form: as a straw man that would topple before the thinnest empirical evidence. The theory was patched together out of lines drawn from unlikely allies: T. S. Eliot and Karl Marx, Max Weber and Emile Durkheim, Alexis de Tocqueville and Dwight MacDonald, and a spurious coherence imputed to the whole. Such a jerry-built structure was easy enough to topple, but the actual demolition often concealed the real intent behind the creation of both the history of mass communication research and the theory of mass society, namely, the attempt to contain and neutralize those intellectuals pursuing a critical theory of modern society among whom the Frankfurt School, exiled in the United States, was merely the most prominent group.

My aim here, however, is not so much to assess the political intent and efficacy of the standard history of mass communication as it is to insist that even on its own terms that history is radically truncated and incomplete. This is not the place to rewrite that history *in toto* but to begin the work of correction and completion. Let me briefly stitch into the narrative two other traditions that are critical to understanding how thought in this field developed.

It is proper to suggest, I believe, that for most of the 19th century there was nothing in form or content that could be considered a precursor literature to the mass communication research of this century. There were, of course, intelligent and scholarly reflections on the newspaper, telegraph, and magazine, but these media individually or the mass media—a more recent coinage—were not taken to be a social or intellectual problem. The agenda of intellectual life in 19th-century United States was largely set by a species of utilitarianism that came into the culture by a particularly narrow reading of John Locke. The central problem in utilitarianism is the question of freedom and, therefore, the mass media (better, the press) were thought of almost exclusively within the terms laid down by utilitarianism. The central terms were freedom and the public; the central problem was the stipulation of the conditions of a free public life. What we might call more generally liberal theory emphasized that "society is grounded in a solidary public that is conceived as virtuous" (Mayhew, 1984, p. 1279). Public opinion—the opinions uttered in public—was taken to be a constituent component of the liberal social order, a force in the creation and expression of a civic consciousness. When the entire public was conceived as a rational body engaged in discussion through printed media, the press was directly involved in the formation, maintenance, and expression of liberal society.

The term *public* is the key to understanding utilitarian thought. The public is a group bound by reason and united in conversation that seeks to place a limit on state power. Faith in the public is clearest not when liberals discuss the social contract but when they identify the social foundations of the public in the process of free communication. "The utilitarian argument asserts that in any free exchange of ideas among rational thinkers, truth will emerge victorious" (Mayhew, 1984, p. 1283). This idea provides utilitarianism with a concrete policy: freedom of debate, preaching, speaking, writing, and most important, freedom of publication were the means of founding order in society on reason in the individual. "Let each person be free to argue as reason guides. If all have reason and if reason is capable of discerning truth, all will ultimately come to truth" (Mayhew, 1984, p. 1283). In the liberal tradition, the conditions of freedom guaranteed the solidarity of society. "There can hardly be—or so the utilitarian thinkers suppose—a better foundation for social life than universal acceptance of truth" (Mayhew, 1984, p. 1283).

There is a second way, a more economistic way, of characterizing the liberal-utilitarian tradition, a way that places less emphasis on the public and solidarity and more on the individual and individual desire. Utilitarianism assumes that, strictly speaking, the ends of human action are random or exogenous. Rational knowledge could not be gained of human values or purposes. The best we can do is rationally judge the fitting together of ends and means. One can attain rational knowledge of the primal allocation of resources among means and toward given ends, but one can gain no rational knowledge of the selection of ends. Apples are as good as oranges; baseball as good as poetry. All that can be determined is the rational means to satisfy subjective and irrational desire. Truth in this tradition is a property of the rational determination of means. In turn, the rationality of means depended on freedom and the availability of information. More precisely, it was freedom that guaranteed the availability of perfect information and perfect information that guaranteed the rationality of means. In summary then: If men are free, they will have perfect information; if perfect information, they can be rational in choosing the most effective means to their individual ends, and if so, in a manner never quite explained, social solidarity will result. So the problem that concerned writers about the press in the Anglo-American tradition was how to secure the conditions of freedom against the forces that would undermine it. These forces were considered to be political and institutional, not psychological. Once freedom was secured against these forces, truth and social progress were guaranteed.

There is, then, a coherent literature concerning mass communication, broadly conceived, that stretches back to the 19th century, one that was nourished by the English Enlightenment, by such venerated works as John Milton's *Areopagitica* and John Stuart Mill's *On Liberty*, and by the theory of markets and individuals contained in classical economic theory. As these texts were absorbed into U.S. culture, a literature was produced on the Constitution and the Bill of Rights, on landmark legal cases, and on the philosophy of freedom that was and, in many ways, remains the fundamental U.S. outlook on the mass media (see Siebert, Peterson, & Schramm, 1956). It is discontinuous with the modern work on communication effects, for it was organized, paradigmatically, around a radically different problem. One of the linkages between the utilitarian texts and the modern ones, between the problem of freedom and the problem of effects, is found in the person of Walter Lippmann. Lippmann's *Public Opinion* (1922) is the originating book in the modern history of communication research. Its title may be *Public Opinion*, but its subject and central actor is the mass media, particularly the news media (Lippmann, 1914). The book founded a tradition of research as it changed the central problem in the study of the mass media.

Although I have told this story before, it bears repeating if only to clarify the role Lippmann played in this history. In 1914, Lippmann published *Drift and Mastery*, a book whose very title tells us of the mood of the year. The country, the entire Western world, was at drift: Things were out of control, the Great War was about to commence. How were we to avoid drift and regain mastery; how was the course of human events to be brought back under human control? During the war, Lippmann went to work for President Woodrow Wilson, provided the first draft of the Fourteen Points on which the peace settlement was to be based, and later attended the negotiations at Versailles. Like so many others, he was disappointed by the outcome of the negotiations and the subsequent failure of the League of Nations. He wrote as follows of the chaotic scene at Versailles:

> The pathetically limited education of officials at the conference, trained to inert and pleasant ways of life, prevented them from seeing or understanding the strange world before them. All they knew, all they cared for, all that life meant to them, seemed to be slipping away to red ruin. And so in panic they ceased to be reporters and began bombarding the Chancellories at home with gossip and frantic explanation. The clamor converged on Paris and all the winds of doctrine were sent whirling about. Every dinner table, every lobby, almost every special interview, every subordinate delegate, every expert adviser was a focus of intrigue, bluster, manufactured rumor. The hotels were choked with delegations representing, pretending to represent, hoping to represent every group of people in the world. The newspaper correspondents struggling with this illusive and all-pervading chaos were squeezed between

the appetites of their readers for news and the desire of the men with whom the decisions rested not to throw the negotiations into a cyclone of distortion. (Cited by Steel, 1980, p. 152)

Lippmann's *Public Opinion* was an extended reflection of his experience at Paris and Versailles. His conclusion was a dour one. One will not get out of drift and achieve mastery by relying on the public or the newspapers. There is no such thing as informed public opinion, and therefore, that opinion cannot master events. Voters are inherently incompetent to direct public affairs. "They arrive in the middle of the third act and leave before the last curtain, staying just long enough to decide who is the hero and who is the villain" (cited by Rossiter & Lare, 1963, p. 108). Lippmann concluded: "The common interest in life largely eludes public opinion entirely and can be managed only by a specialized class. I set no great store on what can be done by public opinion or the action of the masses" (Lippmann, 1922, p. 310). The road away from drift and toward mastery was not through the public, not through public opinion, not really through the newspaper. The only hope lay in taking the weight off the public's shoulders, recognizing that the average citizen did not have the capacity, the interest, or the competence to direct society. Mastery would come only through a class of experts, a new order of samurai, who would mold the public mind and character: men and women dedicated to making democracy work for the masses whether the masses wanted it or not.

Lippmann, in effect, took the public out of politics and politics out of public life. In a phrase of the moment, he depoliticized the public sphere. Lippmann turned the political world over to private and specialized interests, albeit interests regulated by his new samurai class. Lippmann wrote, of course, in the heyday of science, when science was taken to be the exemplar of a culture as a whole. He assumed that scientists were a transcendent class, without interests and objectives: philosopher-kings of the new world.

> The burden of carrying on the work of the world, of inventing, creating, executing, of attempting justice, formulating laws and moral codes, of dealing with the technique and the substance, lies not upon public opinion and not upon government but on those who are responsibly concerned as agents in the affair. Where problems arise, the ideal is a settlement by the particular interests involved. They alone know what the trouble really is. (Lippmann, 1925, p. 73)

Note the structure of Lippmann's argument: A free system of communication will not guarantee perfect information and, therefore, there are no guarantees of truth even when the conditions of freedom are secure. Moreover, the enemies of freedom are no longer the state and the imperfections of the market, but they are in the nature of the news and news gathering, in the psychological dispositions of the audience, and in the scale and organization of modern life. Lippmann, in fact, redefined the problem of the media from one of morals, politics, and freedom to one of psychology and epistemology. He established the tradition of propaganda analysis and simultaneously, by framing the problem not as one of normative political theory but as one of human psychology, opened up the tradition of effects analysis that was to dominate the literature less than two decades after the publication of *Public Opinion*.

The trick Lippmann pulled off was this: He legitimated a democratic politics of publicity and experts while confirming the psychological incompetence of people to participate in it. He tried to show how there could be, as in the title of Robert Entman's book, *Democracy Without Citizens* (1989), while preserving a valuable role for the mass media. This was the same conclusion arrived at in the history of effects research: People could immerse themselves in a media system saturated by propaganda and mass culture, defend themselves against this onslaught by arational psychological and social mechanisms, and yet neither the "stimulus" nor the "response" would threaten the underlying conditions of democracy.

But Lippmann did more than anticipate and clear the ground for effects research. He also rejected, sometimes quite explicitly, the work of John Dewey and other members of the Chicago School of Social Thought. It was Dewey, along with George Herbert Mead, Robert E. Park, and Charles Cooley, who reacted against the form in which utilitarianism was incarnated in the late 19th century, namely Social Darwinism, and in that reaction formed the most distinctive and, I believe, the most useful view of communication and the mass media in the U.S. tradition. The work of Dewey and his colleagues is also omitted from the standard history of mass communication research, but it, along with Lippmann and liberal theory, provides the necessary linkage between the theory of the public and freedom typical of the 19th century and the theory of media effects typical of the 20th.

One way of catching the distinctiveness of the views of Dewey and other members of the Chicago School is through the commonplace observation that the liberal and utilitarian tradition never effectively crossed the Rhine, and, as a result, a counterutilitarian tradition developed throughout the 19th century in German scholarship. Hanno Hardt's useful *Social Theories of the Press: Early German and American Perspectives* (1975) details the work of a group of thinkers—Karl Knies, Albert Schaffle, Karl Buecher, Ferdnand Toennies, and Max Weber—whose work was in significant ways a critique of utilitarianism and utilitarian views of freedom and communication. They in turn shifted the central problem of communication from one of freedom within the context of publics and markets to that of social integration and domination. They turned from the liberal question—What are the conditions of freedom?—to the inverse question—How is it that the social order is integrated through communication? Here a new set of concerns emerges: function, integration, legitimacy, power, and control. They invert, in short, the relation between freedom and solidarity.

The members of the group that gathered around Dewey, originally at the University of Michigan, were all deeply influenced by and affiliated with the German scholarly traditions that descended from Hegel or later took their advanced academic work in Germany. When this German tradition settled in Ann Arbor, Michigan, and later resettled in Chicago and New York, it was reconstituted as a distinctively U.S. outlook and was addressed to distinctively U.S. concerns (Carey, 1989).

At Ann Arbor, in the period between 1882 and 1887, Dewey was a professor of philosophy and Park was his student. Cooley was another student in the department at the same time. Mead was a faculty colleague, and this quartet was joined by a strange, itinerant New York journalist, Franklin Ford, about whom little is known other than what Dewey wrote. Ford wandered into Ann Arbor with a plan to publish a newspaper, *Thought News*, that was to be the first truly scientific newspaper. Park went on to a career in journalism beginning in Minneapolis, Minnesota, then in Detroit. While he was in Detroit in the late 1880s and early 1890s, he reconnected with Dewey and Mead, and the group set about publishing *Thought News*, the first newspaper based on a scientific method of reporting.

Ford had worked for a forerunner of Dun & Bradstreet, the commercial credit house. This company was one of the first to make extensive use of the telegraph in gathering credit information and intelligence. He wanted a newspaper that was as fair, accurate, objective, and honest as the credit information gathered by the company. Ford developed a plan for a national newspaper with separate editions for various regions, professions, and functions. His plan was a technologically primitive version of an integrated computer communications facility. *Thought News* was to be a newspaper, a professional journal, a library, and a reference service—all integrated into one flexible organization.

They planned the first issue, they printed it, and, as Dewey said later, "We pied the type." They ran out of money. But the experience had a profound effect on Dewey, and he later wrote William James to the effect that it was Ford who changed his interest in philosophy and directed his attention away from metaphysics and epistemology and onto problems of politics, morals, education, and the news.

In 1894, Dewey joined the faculty at the newly opened University of Chicago. Park went off to graduate school in Germany, spent 10 years as the secretary and publicist for Booker T. Washington, and finally came back to Chicago in the years just before World War I. But from the 1890s forward, when Dewey and Mead came to Chicago, there was an attempt by this group to develop a different tradition of analysis of communication and the mass media.

I want to offer one interpretation of that tradition, albeit a contestable one, that starts from a remark by Carl Hovland, namely, that in the United States, communication is a substitute for tradition. In the absence of a shared and inherited culture, communication has to accomplish the tasks of social integration that were elsewhere the product of tradition. This interpretation emphasized that there was not a shared traditional culture available to people who were forming new communities and institutions, particularly on the frontier or in the Western regions. In the absence of a shared sentiment, the only means by which these communities could be organized and held together was through discussion, debate, negotiation, and communication. Social order was neither inherited nor unconsciously achieved but actually hammered out as diverse people assembled to create a common culture and to embody that culture in actual social institutions. This attitude looked toward the future, not the past, as the source of social cohesion: The meaning of things, the character of social relations, and the structure of institutions had to be actively created rather than merely drawn out of existing stocks of knowledge and culture. Communication, at least in 19th-century United States, was an active process of community creation and maintenance. It was not a place for lonely individuals. Freedom was not a mere negative product of removing restraints or leaving people alone. Freedom required, first of all, the institutions—government, courts, schools, churches, public houses—of civic and civil life. It required, as well, more subtle cultural creations: modes of conduct, styles of speaking, modes of address, instruments of social control, and ostracism.

It is this unromantic view of the sheer necessities of social life that led to Dewey's oft-quoted line that "society exists not only by transmission, by communication, but it may be fairly said to exist in transmission, in communication" (1916, p. 5).

The first site of this process of community creation was on the frontier where strangers came together and had to negotiate a world out of diverse and conflicting cultural resources. This was a task of creating actual physical communities: town building and building the institutions of local life. This occupied a full century as the nation expanded west and south. It was carried out by groups of strangers who did not necessarily share a common background, experience, or tradition. What tradition is to the rest, communication is to us: the process and resource through which we constitute ourselves and the little worlds we inhabit. By making a revolutionary break, we oriented to the future, not the past, to posterity, not tradition, and this made us unusually reliant on explicit processes and procedures of debate, discussion, negotiation: mutual sense making in radically undefined situations. It is this sense of communication, the sense of community building, of communion, that gives the word one kind of weight in our culture. This creative aspect of culture has an antinomian counterpart. We ceaselessly create communities out of need, desire, and necessity but then continually try to escape from the authority of what we have created. We are forever building a city on the hill and then promptly planning to get out of town to avoid the authority and constraint of our creation. Both the creation and the escape, the organization and disorganization, involve intense episodes in sense making, in the formation and reformation of human identity, in communication in its most fundamental sense.

One recognizes here the genesis of an expressive and interpretive theory of culture. To use a contemporary phrase, Stanley Cavell states that culture and communication is a process of "wording the world together." This was a particular task: Common words had to be found to create and express a common world. But, the stronger claim is that in the absence of a common means of communication there cannot be a common world. Theory and action are indisolvably linked in community creation.

The network of communities painfully created in the 19th century was progressively dismantled during the turn of the 20th as the frontier closed and the cities that now dominated the culture swelled through immigration from abroad and domestic movement from farm to city and South to North. This was a second phase of community creation now carried out along the ecological frontier of urban life. New forms of racial, ethnic, religious, and class communities were created in the cities simultaneous with attempts to give institutional and cultural shape to these new urban containers. The creation of ethnic communities was the crucial event of this phase, and Thomas and Znaniecki's *The Polish Peasant in Europe and America* (1918) was the single most important study. Ethnic communities were not merely transplants of intact cultures from the Old World to the New World. In fact, ethnic groups were formed in the diaspora. The Irish, Italians, Jews, and Poles were in significant ways creatures of the New World. Distinct people, identified with different regions, speaking different dialects or languages were formed, partly by self-identification, partly by social imposition, into self-conscious groups, aware of or made to accept a common heritage and fate. Again, these groups created new institutions of neighborhood life—newspapers, entertainment centers, churches, hospitals, orphanages, poor houses, and friendly and burial societies—along with distinctive patterns of social interaction, ethnic and social types, new forms of language, and particular types and styles of popular art.

This second wave of community creation, which involved the simultaneous destruction and transformation of older patterns of living and settlement, was also a radical and creative cultural achievement. Recognition of this continuous and ceaseless process of community creation and re-creation gave rise to a peculiarly U.S. version of the theory of mass society. Its European counterpart charted a transit from *Gemeinschaft* to *Gesellschaft*, organic to mechanical solidarity, feudalism to capitalism or, in C. Wright Mills' later phrase, from a community of publics to a society of masses. U.S. history and experience lacked one pole of this contrast. The product of revolutionary circumstances on a "virgin continent," we were never a *Gemeinschaft* society, never one of status or organic solidarity, without a feudal tradition; never, strictly speaking, a community of publics. Without a point of origin in traditional society, we could hardly have a place of destination in a mass society. Instead, the Chicago School suggested that we go through recurring, even ceaseless cycles of social organization, disorganization, and then social reorganization—cycles when existing patterns of social interaction and relations, social institutions and forms of life, even forms of individual identity are broken down and dispersed. What follows is a moment of mass society, when social disorganization reigns, when identities and relations are in flux and change. However, this phase itself is never permanent, for the social system is reorganized and restructured: New identities emerge; new patterns of social relations, usually quite surprising and unpredictable, are forged.

The period that was formative in the intellectual life of these scholars, from the 1890s to World War I, provoked a crisis in social representation, as the national system of end points in communication was extended into the small towns and hamlets that had been bypassed in the earlier extension of the railroad and telegraph. The maturing of the wire services, the growth of national magazines, the development of national retail organizations and catalog sales, free rural delivery, national advertising and marketing, and national political parties all had the effect of eclipsing the local, of terminating the existence of self-contained, island communities. Urbanization, industrialization, the maturing of industrial capitalism (with increasingly international connections), the closing of the frontier, the eclipse of agriculture as a predominant way of life and with it the country town as a cultural force were the events that set the agenda for these intellectuals. It was in this milieu of a national, urban society, a society that both invaded and transcended the local, that the nature of communication and community had to be re-thought. But problems of scale and identity were the same, though larger, as had bedeviled U.S. life from the outset: democracy versus scale, capitalism versus republican politics, Puritanism versus antinomianism, a continental political economy versus local life.

Surrounding those structural changes were a variety of cultural and social movements that were both "responses" and assertions: progressivism, populism, the creation of ethnic groups, nativism, the know-nothings, women's suffrage, temperance, the Grange. These movements expressed a restless search for new identities and new forms of cultural and political life. Taken together, these movements offered new ways of being for a new type of society. The 1890s appears to be a moment when people actively shed their past, shed old ways of being and belonging, and created a society in motion that lacked a clear sense of where it was going or what it would be when it got there.

The social psychology of this process was best laid out by Cooley. The transformations created by the turn of the century from an agricultural to an industrial society, from the rural and small to the urban and large would not lead to a permanent change of a mass society of atomized individuals. Cooley's social psychology was a continuing argument against the frontier individualism that dominated liberal thought and the urban atomization that haunted the European imagination. He recognized that even in the modern world, the human personality would be formed within the context of local life, within a network of social interaction. However, a question needed to be answered: If the old small-scale, local communities of 19th-century United States were eclipsed by the formation of large-scale cities and a national society, what would replace the local community as the agency of character formation, the site where a looking glass self-developed, where the significant other and the generalized other came together to form an I and a me? Cooley invented the notion of the "primary group" to carry this indispensable burden. The primary group is, of course, a gross abstraction. Cooley was thinking of the nuclear family, the tiny circle of friends and relatives who surrounded it, and the urban neighborhood. Now that the primary group in this sense has been pretty much destroyed, destroyed at the moment Elihu Katz and Lazarsfeld (1955) were rediscovering it as the anchor point in their analysis of media effects, Cooley might seem a little quaint. But the question he leaves behind is still on the agenda. What kind of people are we to become in the postmodern world where courts, counselors, schools, child-care centers, self-help groups, and a variety of family types (single parent, blended, hinged, seriatim) assume the social role of the primary group?

To understand the problems that Dewey, Cooley, and Park were attacking and the "structure of feeling," to use Raymond Williams' phrase, of the era in which they worked, we might raise parallel questions about our own time, about what is happening to us now that the fruits of the progressive era have yielded a more global or at least transnational structure of politics, commerce, and culture. What is the relation between the social disorganization of our time and the new forms of communication that have emerged since World War II? How does one represent the social totality and the period through which we are living?—The global village? spaceship earth? the postindustrial, postmodern, posteverything society? Who are we in this new age?—world citizens? feminists? postmarxists? neoconservatives? religious fundamentalists? What are we going to do about the new plutocrats,

Donald Trump, T. Boone Pickens, Ivan Boesky? To which identity and culture are we socializing our children?

The point is this: Although the process of social and cultural change is ceaseless, particularly in the United States where little is solid and most things continuously melt into air, there are critical junctures where the social capsule breaks open, and the fundamental coordinates of individual identity and group life are broken up. The work of Dewey and the sociologists who followed him, the symbolic interactionists, is particularly apt and useful in these moments of rupture and less so in moments of relative stasis. The moments of rupture are times when ceaseless, impersonal competition among inchoate formations are translated into structured conflict. At these moments new forms of social drama are created, new social antagonisms defined and sharpened, new social types created, and new cultural forms of address, interaction, and relationship developed.

This attempt to develop a structural ecology of urban life in relation to communication was also a means of writing a phenomenology of modern consciousness. Cooley's injunction that the solid facts of society are the imaginations people have of one another artlessly mirrors Park's romantic reminder that we have to get behind people's eyes to get to the thrill of it all. These are merely naïve but expressive injunctions to create an empirical sociology of street life, of gang life, of community life, of group life on which to construct a phenomenology of the actual process of symbolic construction and reconstruction, action and interaction, in which community life was forged.

The media of communication entered this social process at two critical points. First, it was the hope of Dewey, and to a lesser degree Cooley, Park, and others, that the media of communication might re-create public life, might bring a great community of rational public discourse into existence. In this view, the public of democratic theory, eclipsed by the enormous technical expansion of social life, might be reborn in the modern mass media. Although Dewey recognized the importance of the network of small-scale groups to the formation of a social fabric, he took this recognition as a prelude to transcendence. For Dewey, communication was an ethical principle. Whatever inhibited communication, whatever inhibited the sharing, widening, and expansion of experience was an obstacle to be overcome. We learn from one another, from our difference as well as our similarity. The new media offered an unparalleled opportunity to widen the arena of learning, the capacity to accept but transcend the particular, to join a wider community of citizens without sacrificing our private identity as members of particular, limited social formations. It was this hope, the optimism that fueled it, and the reformist energies that it unleashed that was much opposed by Marxism and led to the split between Marxism and pragmatism, a split that opened a theoretical space through which marched the positivist, expert-oriented social science that defined the effects tradition. The split was one of the minor tragedies of modern politics. The Chicago School certainly failed in its attempt to reconstitute a democratic public life and was absurdly utopian in its hopes for the democratic potential of the mass media. Nonetheless, it kept alive a minor but enduring tradition that today has been reworked and reinvigorated (see Barber, 1984).

The second reference point for the mass media was in the more conflict-oriented sociology of Park. In this scheme the media of communication became sites of competition and conflict, sites where latent antagonisms were fashioned into explicit drama. This occurred as groups struggled to control the means of cultural production at every level of social life. In local communities groups attempted to seize newspapers and other journals to lay down definitions of group life, identity, and purpose. Within the Black community, there were struggles to control the forms of expressive life in the Black press, to control the definitions of Black culture (Kreiling, 1973). These struggles were duplicated in the national media in attempts to define the history, culture, purpose, and constituent groups which made up U.S. life. To this end, virtually all the books that came forward from Chicago sociology—books on the gang, the Gold Coast, the Negro community in Chicago, the Polish peasant—devoted part of the analysis to the ways in which the media, as active sites of conflict and struggle, both defined and expressed these communities.

What gave the Chicago view a certain distinctiveness is that it veered away from the question of communication effects and toward that of cultural struggle. At the same time, it viewed struggle not merely in class and economic terms but extended it to a full array of interests: aesthetic, moral, political, and spiritual. Such struggles were, of course, conducted on class lines but also along other fronts: racial, religious, ethnic, status, regional, and, we would have to add today, gender.

This expansive view of an actual social process, an intense interest in its phenomenology, and a historical understanding of how the media of communication enter a ceaseless temporal process of change (rather than a static snapshot of having or not having an effect) is the important but forgotten episode in the standard history of mass communication research.

REFERENCES

Barber, B. (1984). *Strong democracy*. Berkeley: University of California Press.
Bauer, R., & Bauer, A. (1960). America, mass society and mass media. *Journal of Social Issues*, 16(3), 3–66.
Bell, D. (1961). *The end of ideology*. New York: Collier.

Carey, J. W. (1989). Communications and the progressives. *Critical Studies in Mass Communication, 6*(3), 264–282.

Dewey, J. (1916). *Democracy and education.* New York: Macmillan.

Entman, R. (1989). *Democracy without citizens.* New York: Oxford University Press.

Hardt, H. (1975). *Social theories of the press: Early German and American perspectives.* Beverly Hills, CA: Sage.

Katz, E., & Foulkes, D. (1962). On the use of the mass media as "escape": Clarification of a concept. *Public Opinion Quarterly, 26*(3), 377–388.

Katz, E., & Lazarsfeld, P. (1955). *Personal influence.* Glencoe, IL: The Free Press.

Klapper, J. (1948). Mass media and the engineering of consent. *American Scholar, 17*(4), 419–429.

Klapper, J. (1960). *The effects of mass communication.* Glencoe, IL: The Free Press.

Klapper, J. (1963). Mass communication research: An old road resurveyed. *Public Opinion Quarterly. 27*(4), 515–527.

Kreiling, A. L. (1973). *The making of racial identities in the black press: A cultural analysis of race journalism in Chicago, 1878–1929.* Unpublished doctoral dissertation, University of Illinois.

Lippmann, W. (1914). *Drift and mastery.* New York: Mitchell-Kennerly.

Lippmann, W. (1922). *Public opinion.* New York: Macmillan.

Lippmann, W. (1925). *The phantom public.* New York: Macmillan.

Mayhew, L. (1984). In defense of modernity: Talcott Parsons and the utilitarian tradition. *American Journal of Sociology, 89*(6), 1273–1305. The entire paragraph is largely a paraphrase of arguments in Mayhew's splendid essay.

Rossiter, C., & Lare, J. (1963). *The Essential Lippmann.* New York: Random House.

Siebert, F. S., Peterson, T. B., & Schramm, W. (1956). *Four theories of the press.* Urbana: University of Illinois Press.

Sproule, M. J. (1989). Progressive propaganda critics and the magic bullet myth. *Critical Studies in Mass Communication, 6*(3), 225–246.

Steel, R. (1980). *Walter Lippman and the American century.* Boston: Little Brown.

Thomas, W. I., & Znaniecki, F. (1918). *The Polish peasant in Europe and America.* Chicago: University of Chicago Press.

Chapter **3**

The Yale Communication and Attitude-Change Program in the 1950s

William J. McGuire
Yale University

Carl Hovland's attitude-change project at Yale in the 1950s was one of many diverse independent groups out of which the present communication research movement has grown. The Hovland group, like many of the others, was centered on a charismatic leader who recruited a talented team to investigate selected aspects of a broad spectrum of communication issues. In retrospect, the contemporaneous appearance of so many contributory groups at mid-20th century suggests that communication studies was an idea whose time had come.

These founding groups arose in diverse disciplines. The Hovland–Yale attitude-change group came from psychology; Paul Lazarsfeld's radio-research group at Columbia was composed predominantly of sociologists; Harold Lasswell and his colleagues tended to come from political science and law; Wilbur Schramm's group at Illinois initially included humanists and journalists; and Claude Shannon's Bell Labs group came from electrical engineering. Linguistics seems to have been inappropriately underrepresented, unless we include marginally related scholars like Thomas Sebeok or Edward Sapir, or if we include Charles E. Osgood's psycholinguistics group at Illinois (who were more "psycho" than "linguistics"). These streams from multidisciplinary sources have now melded fairly comfortably into the communication field as we know it, but to understand the work of each seminal group and its ultimate contribution to the unified field, it is important to understand the disciplinary context in which the group developed.

In carrying out my assignment here to describe the Hovland–Yale communication and attitude-change group during its heyday in the middle of the 20th century, I first describe the psychological context out of which it arose and within whose constraints it evolved. The middle section of this chapter describes the 1950s Hovland–Yale group itself, how it worked and what it achieved. The third part of the chapter describes how we got here from there, the later evolution of the 1950s Hovland–Yale research, and its transformed manifestations in today's communication field.

PSYCHOLOGICAL ORIGINS OF THE YALE COMMUNICATION AND PERSUASION PROJECT

If it is a wise child who knows its own father, then psychology has always laid claim to this wisdom: Received history is that the "big bang" that gave birth to the field occurred precisely with Wilhelm Wundt's establishing the Psychologisches Institut at Leipzig in 1879. Social psychology, the subdiscipline in which the Hovland–Yale group was situated, arrived a generation later. The two earliest textbooks called *Social Psychology* both appeared in 1908, one by the psychologist William McDougall, published in London, and the other by the sociologist E. A. Ross, published in New York. Hovland himself and some other members of the Yale communication project (including this writer) came from general experimental rather than social psychology, but the movement can best be understood within the social psychological tradition that quickly absorbed it.

The European Prehistory

As H. Ebbinghaus (1908) aptly phrased it, psychology has a long past but only a short history. History began as psychology became empirical, thus gaining academic respectability and even being trusted to move out of the philosophy parental nest and become a new department. Through the first quarter of the 20th century North American psychology showed a cultural lag, running up a vast trade imbalance, living off imports mainly from Europe, especially Germany. The received history of the discipline (Boring, 1929/1950) emphasizes the European origins of North American psychology, stressing especially the role of Wundt and other German psychologists. As regards the role of Wundt specifically, there is a current controversy within the parochial ranks of historians of social psychology

(Farr, 1983) as to whether Boring emphasized the wrong Wundt, stressing his 19th-century work on individual psychology to the neglect of his more social-psychological culminating work, *Völkerpsychologie* [*Folk Psychology*], published in the 20th century in 10 volumes (Wundt, 1900–1920). An obscure but useful prehistory of social psychology is provided by F. B. Karpf (1932), the first half of which describes the European origins and the second half, the early social psychological work in North America. The broad conceptual issues and the historical debates that emerged early were of little interest to Hovland, whose style was to start with ad hoc theorizing about some interesting relation among variables and then get on with an ambitious program of empirical work. He approached some observed relation, not from a general theoretical perspective, but rather by using multiple theories eclectically to identify the bases and limits of the independent-to-dependent variable relations. However, we mention these ancient happenings because in recent times they have been raised within the social representation movement to question the nature and limitations of the contribution made by the Hovland communication and attitude-change project at Yale in the 1950s.

The Five Eras of U.S. Empirical Social Psychology

The Successive Hegemonies. Empirical work in social psychology advanced slowly during the first quarter of the 20th century in North America and Europe, but by the 1920s it achieved a level that gave it visibility and a respectable status within U.S. psychology that it has subsequently maintained. The advance of psychology from the 1920s through the 1990s has involved a series of five successive overlapping hegemonies. The first is the 1920s and 1930s era, which focused on attitude measurements and, to a lesser extent, on attitudes' relation to behavior. There followed a 1935–1955 interlude when the exciting topic in social psychology was group dynamics. The third era, the 1950s and 1960s, focused on attitude-change research. The first half of this third era was dominated by the Hovland–Yale group and its convergent style of research on attitude change; the second half, the 1960s, was dominated by the Festinger–Stanford group, using a divergent research style to study dissonance theory implications regarding the relation between attitudes and behavior. The fourth ascendancy, dominating the 1965–1985 era, focused on social cognition, the cognitive transformation of social information. We are currently experiencing a fifth hegemony, an attitude-system era preoccupied with the structure and functioning of systems of attitudes. A more detailed description of these five eras can be found in W. J. McGuire (1986).

Five Overlapping Hegemonies That Constitute the Progress
of Social Psychology in the 20th Century

1. Attitude-measurement era (1920s and 1930s)
2. Group-dynamics era (1935 to 1955)
3. Attitude-change era (1950s and 1960s)
   a. The 1950s convergent style (Hovland–Yale)
   b. The 1960s divergent style (Festinger–Stanford)
4. Social-cognition era (1965–1985)
5. Attitude structure era (1980s and 1990s)

The Centrality of Attitudes in Social Psychology. The Hovland–Yale group's particular contribution to communication research focused on attitude change. Indeed, the Communication Research program at Yale was known locally as "the attitude-change project." This focus is quite appropriate for a social psychology movement because attitudes have been the central topic of social psychology in three of the five successive eras that have constituted its progress since the 1920s. Indeed, attitudes were early identified as the central concern of social psychology by commentators as disparate and early as the sociologists W. I. Thomas and F. Znaniecki (1918) and the behavioral psychologist J. B. Watson (1925).

Although attitudes have been an abiding concern of social psychology, a closer examination of the five eras of social psychology shows that the recurring interest in attitudes escalated in sophistication from era to era. The 1920s and 1930s attitude-measurement era focused on individual attitudes in their static state, measuring them at a given moment in time. By the 1950s and 1960s attitude-change era, in which the Hovland–Yale group played a major part, the interest continued to focus on individual attitudes, but in their dynamic, changing aspect; the Hovland–Yale group and other researchers in that era were interested in how various components of persuasive communications contributed to attitude change. More recently, the attitude-systems era that is flourishing in the 1980s and 1990s goes beyond individual attitudes to the structure of systems of attitudes. The Hovland–Yale communication and persuasion research in the 1950s grew out of the earlier static-attitude measurement work in the 1920s and 1930s; correspondingly, that Hovland 1950s research has blossomed into the current attitude systems work, as I describe in the final section of this chapter.

THE HOVLAND–YALE 1950s COMMUNICATION AND PERSUASION PROJECT

The third era of social psychology, the 1950s and 1960s decades when the work focused on attitude change, was the major single psychological input into founding the field of communication research as we now know it. There were additional psychological contributions of very high quality at that time and later, such as the work by Charles E. Osgood and his associates on the dimensions of meaning (Osgood, Suci, & Tannenbaum, 1957) or the work of George Miller (1951) and Roger Brown (1958) on psycholinguistics. Although these contributions were of exquisite quality in themselves, they were done on a relatively narrow scale. The Hovland–Yale Communication and Persuasion group was the biggest single force within psychology's communication-relevant attitude-change movement, particularly in the 1950s.

To describe this Hovland–Yale group and its contribution I consider first the Yale setting in which the work was done and then deal successively with the relevant biography of the founding father, Carl Hovland, the product produced by the group, and the group's working methods and organization. The Hovland–Yale group dominated only the first of the two decades of attitude-change ascendancy, especially in the 1950s; by the 1960s the Festinger cognitive dissonance group at Stanford outpaced the Hovland group. Therefore, to do justice to the influence of the whole of the 1950s and 1960s attitude-change era, I shall add a brief comment on the Festinger–Stanford work in the 1960s and then discuss the convergent versus divergent styles that differentiated the working methods of the Yale versus Stanford groups.

I should reveal my personal involvements in the several psychological centers that made contributions to establishing the field of communication during the 1950s, because my account here draws on this personal experience as well as on second-hand knowledge of the group and the published research. My personal involvement in the Hovland–Yale group is somewhat peripheral in the sense that I was a secondary member of the group and that this attitude-change work was a secondary interest in the spectrum of research in which I was engaged.

From 1951 to 1954 I was a graduate student at Yale University working in the area of human learning. Although Hovland was formally the main adviser on my doctoral dissertation on memory, my research had nothing to do with attitude change, and I scarcely knew of the existence of the communication and persuasion group while I was a graduate student. In 1954-55, I went to the University of Minnesota as a postdoctoral fellow and worked with Leon Festinger on dissonance theory just before he moved to Stanford University. I returned to Yale as a junior faculty member for the 1955–1958 period, and then some of my research work was included in Hovland's communication and persuasion project. From Yale I went to the University of Illinois from 1958 to 1961, where my joint appointment included the Communication Research Institute, after Wilbur Schramm had left it for Stanford but when it was still under the active and productive directorship of Charles E. Osgood.

Yale and the Institute of Human Relations Before Mid-Century

Three distinctive features characterized the Yale Psychology Department during the 1950s. First was its recognized excellence derived not from the attitude-change research but from the Hullian (1943) learning-theory work. Yale psychology dominated the discipline during the 1940s and 1950s to an extent rare in academic history, comparable to Columbia University's dominance of anthropology during the Boas era, the University of California at Berkeley's brief hegemony over physics, or the University of Chicago's over sociology. When I applied for graduate school in 1950 I was an out-of-touch philosophy student at the University of Louvain with my nonmainstream undergraduate education obtained at a Jesuit university. When I decided to return to the United States to enter a doctoral program in psychology and was admitted to Harvard, Princeton, and Yale, I hesitated not at all in choosing Yale. In 1950 Yale was the place to be, reputationally and actually.

A second characteristic of Yale psychology was its tradition and its aspiration, even if largely unrealized, to be interdisciplinary. The physical manifestation of this aspiration was the Institute of Human Relations (IHR), both as an organizational unit and as a building founded in the early 1930s and financed by Rockefeller funds at a level generous for those days. The IHR's goal was to integrate the work of 10 or 15 talented academics from a half-dozen different disciplines (psychology, anthropology, law, medicine, political science, etc.).

The IHR faded gradually out of existence in the 1960s (Morawski, 1986). Even though the effort to lower between-disciplinary walls became less successful as the years went by, the thought hovered like an *éminence gris* sustained by architecture, organization, and funding. The interdisciplinary efforts had occasional substantial successes. Groups of talented people from within and outside psychology gathered around Clark Hull to use behavioristic theory to investigate theory-relevant and societal-relevant problems. As regards basic research, the volume on rote learning by Hull and his colleagues (1940) brought together psychologists, mathematicians, and symbolic logicians. On the applied side, the *Frustration and Aggression* volume (Dollard, Miller, Doob, Mowrer, & Sears, 1939) became a classic. Evening meetings in the IHR Blue Room continued into the 1950s to bring together people from different fields for intellectual exchange and left a legend of a once-and-future Camelot embracing disciplines without walls.

The third distinctive feature of Yale in the 1950s was the openness of its administration, which functioned in a decentralized and egalitarian style. There were some grand old men (and an occasional grand old woman) on the scene—Charles Yerkes, Walter Miles, Catherine Cox Miles, Clark Hull—but the power lay with the middle-aged people like Hovland, Neal Miller, Irvin Child, Irving Janis, Leonard Doob, and Frank Beach, among others. Other young birds of passage also left their intellectual marks, such as Charles E. Osgood, O. Hobart Mowrer, and Kenneth Spence. These leaders were generally open to new ideas and were sufficiently entertained by cultivating their own research gardens to leave their junior colleagues to cultivate different blooms in different gardens, if they preferred.

Illustrative of this openness and youth orientation was the recruitment of junior faculty relevant to the Hovland–Yale communication and persuasion group. Academic institutions in the United States typically diversify hiring of junior faculty across many universities. However, Hovland sought talent without worrying about diversity of institutional background. When he returned to Yale as chair in 1945, Hovland brought into the department a set of talented people (Janis, Fred Sheffield, Arthur Lumsdaine, etc.), all coming from the Army Information and Education Branch. Again, in 1955, the year of my appointment to the Yale faculty, Hovland simultaneously brought into the department Arthur R. Cohen, Milton Rosenberg, and Irving Sarnoff, all of whom had just obtained their PhD's in social psychology at the University of Michigan (and also Jack Brehm, almost a Michigander). Hovland had recognized that the psychology-sociology PhD program at Michigan was attracting (and therefore turning out) superb young people. The psychology department at Yale, although modest in size, was open to bringing in five new junior members in the same year, in the same area, most from the same institutions. Such willingness to "go for the gold," even at the sacrifice of other criteria, is rare in academia.

The Founding Father, Carl I. Hovland

Carl I. Hovland (1912–1961) grew up in Chicago, land of broad shoulders and distant horizons, and was marked by the "dust bowl empiricism" often found in Midwesterners whose research style is characterized by low-order theorizing and systematic experimentation. He obtained his undergraduate and MA degrees in psychology at Northwestern University and then moved to Yale for good, completing his doctoral studies between 1933 and 1936, and then immediately appointed to the Yale faculty, staying until his death in 1961, except for a 1942–1945 leave of absence when he worked in the War Department's Information and Education Branch where he began his communication and persuasion research. His precociousness partly compensates for his premature death.

Hovland's Prewar Research. Before his wartime leave of absence from Yale, Hovland was an experimental psychologist (he would now be called a "cognitive" psychologist) rather than a social psychologist. He was a graduate student assistant to Clark Hull and worked with him and other members of the IHR, but he did not share Hull's (1943) penchant for high-level theoretical formulations. Rather, from his student days Hovland focused on specific relations such as stimulus generalization, the reminiscence phenomenon, or the serial-position effect. His most elegant research used the hypothetico-deductive method favored by Hull and his mathematician and logician colleagues to account for a variety of rote memorization relations (Hull et al., 1940). This mathematico-deductive volume has received little recognition but it is as elegant a volume as ever published in psychology. Defenders of erotica assert that no one ever lost her or his virginity to a book, but my stumbling upon that volume in my undergraduate browsing days seduced me into psychology. Another quite different gem that he published the same year, as part of the IHR interdisciplinary group working on frustration and aggression, is the Hovland and Sears (1940) study showing the relation, over a century of U.S. history, between the number of lynchings and economic indices such as the price of cotton.

Hovland's prewar research gave little indication that he would switch his research topic from human learning to communication and persuasion. His youthful work was well received, making the precocious Hovland already recognized at age 30 as one of the leaders in psychology. His prewar and wartime work were similar in style, but his subject matter switch was quite abrupt and discontinuous. One possible link is that Hovland's mentor, Hull, before he became a stimulus–response (S–R) reinforcement behavioral theorist working with rats and memory machines, had conducted during the 1920s an elegant experimental analysis of hypnosis and suggestibility (Hull, 1933), but Hull had discontinued his suggestibility research before Hovland arrived at Yale.

Dr. Win-the-War. When the United States entered World War II at the end of 1941 many psychologists, including Hovland, left academia to do war research, usually in the Army or the Army Air Corps, on topics such as pilot selection and soldier morale and training. These psychologists could apply their special skills to national needs and at the same time avoid less interesting and less safe military assignments. Some entered as officers, such as John Flanagan and Stuart Cook, whereas others, like M. Brewster Smith, were enlisted men, rank usually reflecting seniority. Hovland, however, remained in civilian status during his 1942–1945 War Department stint in the research branch of the Information and Education Division. Director of the professional staff was Samuel A. Stouffer, under whom there was a survey section headed by Leonard S. Cottrell, Jr., and an experimental section headed by Hovland.

Hovland's main War Department research was on the motivational and morale effects of the army's information and education programs, especially of the *Why We Fight* films. Hovland's group not only assessed the general effectiveness of the films in enhancing soldiers' motivation but also obtained information of theoretical interest by including in the designs and analyses independent variables (e.g., viewer intelligence, immediate versus delayed effects, effects of one-sided versus more balanced presentations, the importance of active participation, etc.) whose main and interaction effects tested theoretical implications. The summary of the group's work appeared as Volume III in the "American Soldier" series (Hovland, Lumsdaine, & Sheffield, 1949), which can be considered the first major contribution of social psychology's third, attitude change, era. With elegant symmetry, Volume IV of the "American Soldier" series (Stouffer, 1950) can be considered the last major contribution of the first attitude-measurement era.

Moving the Attitude-Change Research to Yale. At the end of the war Hovland returned to Yale as chair of the Psychology Department and obtained Rockefeller Foundation support to continue his wartime work on persuasion as the Yale Studies on Communication and Attitudes. Rockefeller money had supported social and behavioral science at Yale for the previous two decades through IHR. These funds enabled Hovland to bring with him some of the researchers from the experimental division of the Army Information and Education group, including Janis, Sheffield, and Lumsdaine, soon supplemented by Harold Kelley. From the outset, graduate students, such as Walter Weiss, Herbert Kelman, Harriet Linton, Elaine Graham Bell, Bert King, Gerald Lesser, Wallace Mandel, Enid Hobart Campbell, David Sears, Phil Zimbardo, and Timothy Brock, were heavily involved. By the mid-1950s additional faculty members were added to the group, including Robert P. Abelson, Arthur R. Cohen, Milton J. Rosenberg, Jack W. Brehm, Irving Sarmoff, Norman H. Anderson, and the writer William J. McGuire. Social psychologists at other institutions, such as Muzafer Sherif at Oklahoma and Abraham S. Luchins at Oregon, also carried out research as part of Hovland's communication and attitude-change project.

Individual studies were often published as journal articles, but almost all the Hovland groups' communication and persuasion research is also described in six volumes. The World War II research in 1942–1945 is published as Volume III of the "American Soldier" series (Hovland et al.,

1949). The other five volumes were published in a Yale University Press series. Much of the early postwar work at Yale is summarized in Hovland, Janis, and Kelley (1953), *Communication and Persuasion: Psychological Studies of Opinion Change*. During the remaining years before Hovland's early death in 1961, there appeared four further volumes of a more monographic nature, each focused on a specific topic. They include *The Order of Presentation in Persuasion* (Hovland, 1957); *Personality and Persuasibility* (Hovland & Janis, 1959); *Attitude Organization and Change* (Hovland & Rosenberg, 1960); and *Social Judgment* (Sherif & Hovland, 1961). Already by the mid- or late 1950s the interest of most of the participants, including Hovland, had evolved into areas other than communication and attitude change.

Work Style in the Hovland–Yale Group. The communication and attitude-change group at Yale was a comfortable and productive work setting for researchers who wanted to choose their own topics and study them in their own way. Hovland has been called the world's most nonauthoritarian leader, and his nondirective style tended to attract and retain independent researchers. Hovland's style had four notable characteristics: It was relation focused in problem selection, eclectic in theoretical orientation, decentralized in organization, and synthesizing in contribution. Each of these four characteristics merits some description.

Hovland never met a hypothesis he didn't like. He never worried about recruiting people who were interested in the right thing but seemed rather to regard any topic as potentially interesting. Whenever he discovered that an associate was knowledgeable about a topic, Hovland probed this person's area of expertise extensively and in depth. A colleague once remarked that every time he met with Hovland he came away feeling like a squeezed orange. Hovland did have personal topics of interest (although these changed rapidly), but he did not actively recruit others to work on his ideas. His conversations were almost wholly taken up with the other person's interests rather than his own, as if he enjoyed talking to people about topics they knew more about than he did.

Hovland's eclecticism came out in his selection of people, issues, work styles, and especially theories. From the outset he sought good people regardless of their intellectual backgrounds, the topics they wished to study, their explanatory styles, or their preferred modes of research. His intellectual point of departure was typically some specific relation (e.g., the persistence of induced attitude change, the relative merits of ignoring versus refuting the opposition arguments, how the source of the communication affected the impact of its contents, etc.) rather than some specific theoretical viewpoint. Some members of the Yale 1950s group were ideologues, guided in their problem selection and solution by one or another theory. It never bothered Hovland that members of the group working on the same problem were driven by antagonistic theories that made opposite predictions. For example, at one point several members of the group were interested in the effects of active participation in persuasive communication, particularly in how being forced to defend overtly a position discrepant from one's private position might result in internalizing the overtly defended position. Irving Janis, on the basis of an incentive theory, predicted a positive relation between inducement and internalized attitude change in this situation, whereas Bob Cohen's dissonance-theory position predicted a negative relation. Such theoretical conflict did not seem to bother Hovland at all, and he may not even have appreciated that it bothered the antagonistic theorists.

The Yale communication and attitude-change group was a decentralized organization. Hovland's nonauthoritarian, nondirective leadership style resulted in a minimum of meetings. Members of the group seldom proselytized one another or graduate students to collaborate. At most, an occasional pair might start collaborating and recruit graduate students, as when Cohen and Jack Brehm worked together on dissonance theory's implications for attitude change and were joined by Tim Brock, Phil Zimbardo, and other graduate students. Many of the faculty members worked alone or with a graduate student or two and were often aware of what the other members were doing only in general terms.

What helped keep this decentralized, individualistic organization from becoming undesirably anarchical was Hovland's particular intellectual excellence as a synthesizer. He could attend a symposium of papers that seemed to have little in common and, if called on to summarize them, seemed able on the spot to abstract out their unifying themes and show that the papers converged in interesting and complex ways to produce a coherent picture. Hovland's ability as a listener kept him aware of what a wide variety of people were doing, while his synthesizing predilections allowed him to see connections that other people missed. When he heard that one was about to visit another university, he might suggest several people there whom one should talk with because his or her work was relevant to one's own. One's subsequent conversations with these locals often bore out Hovland's predictions of mutual interests.

That the last four volumes of the Hovland–Yale group's contributions focused on specific themes (e.g., the 1957 volume on order effects within persuasive communications, the 1959 volume on personality correlates of persuasibility, etc.) might suggest that the group was organized to work in some integrated way around designated basic themes. Actually the thematic clustering was largely *a posteriori*. At some point Hovland would have noticed a common theme that cut across the work of a half-dozen members of the group, such as how the ordering of material in the communication affected persuasive impact, a general topic in various aspects of which several of us had gotten interested for idiosyncratic reasons. If there seemed enough interest, we would agree to hold off journal submission and instead publish the studies together in a volume of the Yale University Press series on "Attitude and Communication," typically with introductory and concluding integrations by Hovland.

The group had its share of autocrats and prima donnas, and there were occasionally mild antagonisms between individuals, but on the whole it was a happy ship and a productive one. As I compare it to many other institutional settings in which I have worked, I am led to ascribe its productive and pleasant aspects to the benign intellectual and administrative styles of Hovland. It was an added pleasure that he took responsibility for fund-raising and did it so effectively that we others spent little, if any, time applying for grants.

THE FESTINGER-STANFORD GROUP IN THE 1960s

Hovland's group at Yale in the 1950s was a major influence in establishing the field of communication research as we now know it. Indeed, Schramm (1985) cited Hovland as the largest single contributor to founding the communication field. This superlative might be going a bit far; Schramm himself may be more deserving of it than is Hovland. A more defensible accolade is that Hovland's was the biggest contribution to communication made from within psychology. To put the Hovland–Yale communication and attitude-change project in the proper psychological perspective, it should be remembered that the attitude change-era stretched through the 1950s and 1960s. The Hovland group dominated only the first decade, and by the early 1960s, the center of gravity had shifted west to the Festinger dissonance-theory group at Stanford. This latter group contributed to communication research but less than did the Hovland–Yale group. The Festinger group had more influence on the course of social psychology than did the Hovland group and so deserves some brief description here.

Festinger's work grew out of the group-dynamics movement founded by Kurt Lewin, a leader more charismatic than Hovland and as pre-eminently representative of the Central European intelligentsia as Hovland was *ganz Amerikanisch*. Lewin (1890–1947), a generation older than Hovland, moved to the United States when the National Socialists attained power in Germany in 1933 and worked successively at the University of Iowa and at the Massachusetts Institute of Technology. At both institutions he gathered around him remarkable graduate students and colleagues, even more talented than the Hovland–Yale group, one of the earliest of whom was Festinger. Lewin was signally able to combine theoretical relevance with societal relevance, encouraging his students in the use of abstract approaches like topology and field theory as well as encouraging them to study practical problems and use clever laboratory simulations of the real world.

Festinger shared Lewin's interest in basic research, including quantitative methods (particularly low-parametric statistics) and general theoretical viewpoints, but he was indifferent, at best, to the National Training Laboratories and other applied aspects of Lewin's group-dynamics movement. Festinger and his students did early work on concepts like level of aspiration, social pressure in informal groups, and social comparisons before they focused for much of the 1950s and early 1960s on dissonance theory (Festinger, 1957, 1964), first at Minnesota and then at Stanford. At both places he gathered around him remarkable graduate students, and in the 1960s, Stanford was definitely the place to go in social psychology doctoral programs. By the time Festinger left Stanford in 1968 for the New School for Social Research in New York City, his own interests had shifted away from dissonance theory and from social psychology in general to quite different topics, such as vision, but several generations of his students continued to work on dissonance theory (Wicklund & Brehm, 1976). Some communication researchers used dissonance-theory concepts, but the dissonance theorists themselves had little interest in communication processes or even in Festinger's (1959) own, earlier, communication research.

The Contrasting Convergent and Divergent Research Styles

The Nature of Research Style. Carrying out any specific research project involves a series of steps, including selecting the problem, formulating it as a hypothetical relation among variables, embedding it in appropriate theoretical housings, devising ways to manipulate the independent variable(s) and to measure the dependent variable, identifying variables to be controlled and ways of controlling them, deciding on which variables are to be included in the initial experimental design, developing an appropriate procedure, selecting the sample to be observed, carrying out the data collection ethically and validly, doing the descriptive and inferential statistics, interpreting the relations obtained, writing up the report, and utilizing the findings. Each such step is a decision point at which a choice must be made among alternatives. The alternative chosen at any one step is likely to restrict the alternatives available at later choice points, so only certain patterns of choices through the steps are feasible. A researcher's preferred pattern of choices constitutes his or her research style. At any period most researchers in a subdiscipline congregate in the use of a few Establishment styles. Social psychology's attitude-change decades at mid-century supplied an interesting contrast between two popular styles, the convergent style preferred by the Hovland–Yale group in the 1950s and the divergent style favored by the Festinger–Stanford group in the 1960s.

The Convergent Style.   The fundamental difference between the two styles is established at the very first decision point: the researcher's conceptual point of departure, that is, his or her mode of selecting questions and answers to be investigated. A convergent theorist like Hovland is relation oriented rather than theory oriented. Hovland would develop a tenacious interest in a particular dependent variable, such as attitude change, and then develop a program of research on how the attitude change is affected by some intriguing independent variable, such as order of presentation in the communication, source effects, personality characteristics, or delayed-action time effects. The convergent stylist does not neglect theory altogether but uses low-level theorizing eclectically. For example, in studying conditions under which persuasive communications may have a delayed-action effect on attitude change, Hovland et al. (1949) hypothesized a half-dozen different theoretical reasons for predicting delayed-action effects and then tested several of them via their distinctive mediational or interactional implications. We call this style convergent because these stylists bring a variety of theories convergently to bear on the relation of interest.

The Divergent Style.   Divergent stylists, such as Festinger and his Stanford students in the 1960s, have the opposite priorities as their point of departure. They take a theoretical position (social comparison theory, dissonance theory, attribution theory, etc.) as their conceptual point of departure and bring that theory to bear divergently on any number of relations. Thus, Festinger and his students applied dissonance theory divergently to a variety of problems, such as selective avoidance of discrepant information, internalization resulting from forced overt compliance, and postdecisional re-evaluation of alternatives.

This initial contrast in conceptual point of departure between the convergent and divergent theorists has continuing ramifications at later choice points in the research process. For example, as regards experimental design, convergent theorists include multiple variables and predict interaction effects, whereas divergent theorists include few variables and predict main effects. Convergent stylists use rather weak independent variable manipulations and superficial procedures, whereas the divergent stylists use strong independent variable manipulations and elaborate procedures whose success they check out, eliminating subjects when indicated. As regards dependent variables, convergent theorists tend to use sensitive and reliable multi-item measures that allow use of complex descriptive and inferential statistics, whereas divergent theorists cavalierly use single-item measures of the dependent variable that limit them to relatively insensitive statistics, such as chi-square.

In the third of a century since the attitude-change era, divergent stylists have been in the ascendancy in social psychology, whereas in the communication area the convergent style is more popular. Enthusiasts for one style tend to criticize the other, but each style offers advantages. Researchers should be encouraged to use the style with which they resonate most creatively, but they should also recognize that some topics may intrinsically be better studied by one rather than another style. Often, one style of research tends, by historical accident, to become dominantly used by researchers in an area. Hence, research training in communication and other fields should reduce stereotypy by deliberately acquainting students with alternative styles better to sensitize the student to his or her own proclivities and to the availability of alternative ways of doing research.

The Systems Style. Both the divergent and convergent styles are subspecies of a unilinear style of theorizing and experimenting in that both assume the process under study consists of a series of successive variables (independent, interactional, mediational, and dependent) operating on one another via one main causal path. Attitude-change studies and communication research in general may be passing into an era where these convergent and divergent unilinear approaches will be replaced (or at least supplemented) by systems approaches. The conceptual approach of a systems stylist involves identifying a wide variety of variables complexly related within a system and then hypothesizing multiple causal pathways that interrelate these variables, including feedback loops. The systems stylist collects time-series data on a large set of these variables and uses confirmatory-factor analysis, structural-equation models, or other modes of causal analysis to identify the multiple causal pathways. These matters of research style have been discussed more fully elsewhere (McGuire, 1983).

GETTING HERE FROM THERE

Our assignment, to discuss the Hovland communication and attitude-change project at Yale, required our focusing particularly on its prime decade of the 1950s (and to a lesser extent the 1960s). We put the period in context at the outset of the chapter by describing the psychological (particularly the social-psychological) origins of this Hovland–Yale program. This last section of the chapter describes the subsequent vicissitudes of the Hovland–Yale legacy to explain the product and processes by which it is manifested in current communication research. We discuss in turn

Hovland's later contributions subsequent to his communication and persuasion research, the post-Hovland shift toward conceptualizing attitude change as a more active process than he regarded it, and critiques of the attitude-change movement mounted by the current social-representation movement, active in Western Europe and increasingly active in Latin America.

Hovland's Later Work

After the publication of the second of the six Hovland attitude-change volumes, *Communication and Persuasion* (Hovland et al. 1953), Hovland's personal research interests largely shifted to other topics, although administratively he stayed close to the Yale communication and persuasion group by providing encouragement and obtaining for the participants a level of financial support from private foundations that was substantial by 1950s standards.

In the last 10 years of his life Hovland's interests shifted to the area of concept communication and computer simulation of cognition, topics on which he did pioneering work and that were only distantly related to his attitude-change research of the 1942–1952 period. Hence Hovland's career, which began precociously with his entering doctoral training at Yale in 1933 and ended prematurely with his death in 1961, was divided into three successive phases in which he focused on quite different topics. In his 1933–1942 early work at Yale he gained national recognition for his work on verbal learning; then from 1942 to 1952, first in the U.S. War Department and then at Yale, he engaged in the communication and persuasion research that concerns us here. Finally, from 1953 to 1961 he developed new approaches to the microanalysis of thought processes. This later work on the formation and communication of concepts focused particularly on the informational value of positive versus negative instances in idiot-savant intelligent machines as contrasted with actual human-concept communicating. Both his conceptual and empirical work on this positivity-asymmetry topic were extremely elegant (Hovland, 1952; Hunt & Hovland, 1960). At his death, he was laying the foundation of the field of computer simulation of cognition (Hovland & Hunt, 1960).

Hovland's organizational work during his final years also deserves mention. He was in the forefront of interesting foundations and industries in supporting research in social cognition and played a prominent advisory role in the Rockefeller Foundation, Ford Foundation, Social Science Research Council, and Russell Sage Foundation. In the industrial sector, he was particularly active in the Bell Telephone Laboratories and, to a lesser extent, in the General Electric Co. in getting these leading industrial research centers to include social and cognitive psychology. These psychological units that Hovland established in the leading industrial research centers were productive during their brief lives, but they did not long survive him. Psychologists and other social and behavioral scientists came increasingly to depend on federal government agencies (particularly the National Science Foundation and the National Institutes of Health) rather than the private sector for research support. The governmental agencies distribute research funds more by peer review groups than by the old-boy networks within which Hovland worked so effectively. Interestingly, communication research has continued to depend relatively more on the private foundations such as Markle, Annenberg, and Gannett.

Shortly before he died, Hovland returned to a communication topic that has been of continuing interest, namely, how communication research done in a laboratory and in the field (particularly survey research) yields systematically different results. Hovland's interest in these differences may have begun in his War Department days (1942–1945), when Stouffer's research branch was divided into two analytical sections—the survey section headed by Leonard Cottrell and the experimental section headed by Hovland. When near the end of his life Hovland received the American Psychological Association's highest award, the Distinguished Scientific Contribution Award, he devoted his acceptance address (Hovland, 1959) to discussing the complementary and mutually correcting contributions of survey research and laboratory experimental research, particularly on communication topics.

The Post-Hovland Conceptual Evolution
Toward the Active-Audience Model

The audience of persuasive communication was conceptualized by Hovland as a passive receiver of the information contained in the message. In conjecturing how some variable (e.g., source credibility, level of fear appeal, or time passage) affected the attitude-change impact of the message, Hovland would think in terms of how it affected mediating information-encoding steps such as attention, comprehension, and agreement. That he used this passive-audience concept is not surprising considering Hovland's background in the 1933–1942 period when his interest focused on memorization and rote learning.

Revisionism of this passive-receiver concept of the audience began early. My own research from the outset took issue with the Hovland–Yale passive concept, in that I ascribed more active roles to the person in persuasion situations. Whereas Hovland conceived attitude change as being induced by the target person's absorption of new information contained in a communication from an outside source, my own work stressed internally induced attitude change, that is, persuading the person by increasing the salience of information already within his or her own cognitive system by Socratic questioning or by directed-thinking tasks (McGuire, 1960; McGuire & McGuire, 1991). The active-receiver concept is also used in my research on immunization against persuasion (McGuire, 1964) and on anticipatory belief change following forewarning of persuasive attack (McGuire, 1969).

A whole school of active-receiver researchers grew up at Ohio State University in the cognitive-response movement (Greenwald, Brock, & Ostrom, 1968; Petty, Ostrom, & Brock, 1981). Currently, the most creative uses of the active-receiver concept are found in the work stemming from R. E. Petty and J. T. Cacioppo's (1986) evaluation-likelihood model of persuasion and Chaiken's (1987) heuristic processing conceptualization of alternative paths to persuasion. These active-receiver conceptualizations of attitude change have rich implication for communication research. Although the active-receiver concept has emerged as a corrective to the Hovland–Yale 1950s passive-receiver concept, the passive tradition remains dominant within social psychology, as reflected in the best current review (Eagly & Chaiken, 1993) of psychological research on communication and persuasion. A newly emerging attitude-systems era of research in North American social psychology is described in McGuire (1986).

The Social-Representation Movement

The active-receiver revisionism of the Hovland–Yale 1950s attitude research developed contemporaneously with a more radical revisionism, the social-representation movement started by S. Moscovici (1982). The social representationalists argue that the "Anglo-Saxon" attitude movement typical of Americans emphasizes differences among individuals—how the population is widely distributed on attitudinal dimensions like conservativism or nationalism. The social-representation theorists, in the tradition of Durkheim's (1898) *Représentations individuelles et représentations collectives [Individual Representations and Collective Representations]* and W. Wundt's (1900–1920) *Völkerpsychologie [Folk Psychology]*, study instead social representations shared by members of a community. The argument is made that the U.S. way of studying attitudes as divisive obscures the role of collective representations that forge shared ideologies within a community. R. Farr and Moscovici (1984) discuss further the distinction between attitudes and representations.

My theory of knowledge (McGuire, 1984, 1989), like Saussure's (1916/1959), stresses that mental constructs (variables) develop by mutual distinctions and that judgments consist of relations between variables. Hence, attitudes or representations have meaning insofar as they distinguish among individuals or groups. If the social representationalists are advancing the question it is by pointing out, not within-group commonalities of representations, but between-groups as well as between-individuals differences in modal representations.

The Hovland–Yale Contributions to Communication Research

The communication and persuasion research inaugurated, inspired, and guided by Hovland, at first in the War Department from 1942 to 1945 and then at Yale until his death in 1961, made a major contribution to one area of the communication field as we now know it, namely, the psychology of social influence. Particularly, the Hovland group studied how the various aspects of a communication (source, message, channel, etc.) contribute to its attitude-change impact. The Hovland–Yale contribution to this topic was substantial, but the group contributed nothing to many other topics in the broad spectrum of communication research such as analysis of dialogue, control and organization of the mass media, contents of the media, and nonverbal communication.

Hovland's contribution was not in terms of radical theorizing or broad new insights. Rather, he was guided by low-level, common-sense theorizing that served by identifying independent variables adumbrated in Lasswell's (1948) classical analysis of communication as a matter of who says what to whom in what channel with what effect? Perhaps more influential than Hovland's substantive contributions on the topic were his methods contributions, showing how an integrated program on a communication topic could be developed and how individual studies could be carried out at a very high level of sophistication. As regards method, Hovland left a convergent model of strategy and tactics in programmatic research that can be emulated not only in the subject matter topics on which he worked but in many other areas of communication research.

REFERENCES

Boring, E. G. (1929/1950). *A History of Experimental Psychology* (1st ed., 1929; 2nd ed., 1950). New York: Appleton-Century Crofts.

Brown, R. (1958). *Words and things*. Glencoe, IL: The Free Press.

Chaiken, S. (1987). The heuristic model of persuasion. In M. P. Zanna, J. M. Olson, & C. P. Herman (Eds.), *Social influence: The Ontario symposium* (Vol. 5, pp. 3–39). Hillsdale, NJ: Lawrence Erlbaum Associates.

Dollard, J. H., Miller, N. E., Doob, L. W., Mowrer, O. H., & Sears, R. R. (1939). *Frustration and aggression.* New Haven, CT: Yale University Press.

Durkheim, E. (1898). Représentations individuelles et représentations collectives [Individual representations and collective representations]. *Revue de Metaphysique et de Morale, 6,* 273–302.

Eagly, A. H., & Chaiken, S. (1993). *The psychology of attitudes.* Orlando, FL: Harcourt Brace Jovanovich.

Ebbinghaus, H. (1908). *Abriss der psychologie [Outline of psychology].* Leipzig: Veit.

Farr, R. (1983). Wilhelm Wundt (1832–1920) and the origins of psychology as an experimental social science. *British Journal of Social Psychology, 22,* 289–301.

Farr, R., & Moscovici, S. (Eds.). (1984). *Social representations.* Cambridge: Cambridge University Press.

Festinger, L. (1957). *A theory of cognitive dissonance.* Stanford, CA: Stanford University Press.

Festinger, L. (1959). Informal social communication. *Psychological Review, 57,* 271–282.

Festinger, L. (1964). *Conflict, decision, and dissonance.* Stanford, CA: Stanford University Press.

Greenwald, A. G., Brock, T. S., & Ostrom, T. M. (Eds.). (1968). *Psychological foundations of attitudes.* New York: Academic Press.

Hovland, C. I. (1952). A "communication analysis" of concept learning. *Psychological Review, 59,* 461–472.

Hovland, C. I. (Ed.). (1957). *The order of presentation in persuasion.* New Haven, CT: Yale University Press.

Hovland, C. I. (1959). Reconciling conflicting results derived from experimental and survey studies of attitude change. *American Psychologist, 14,* 8–17.

Hovland, C. I., & Hunt, E. B. (1960). Computer simulation of concept attainment. *Behavioral Science, 5,* 265–267.

Hovland, C. I., & Janis, I. L. (Eds.) (1959). *Personality and persuasibility.* New Haven, CT: Yale University Press.

Hovland, C. I., Janis, I. L., & Kelley, H. H. (1953). *Communication and persuasion.* New Haven, CT: Yale University Press.

Hovland, C. I., Lumsdaine, A. A., & Sheffield, F. D. (1949). *Studies in social psychology in World War II* (Vol. 3 of *Experiments on Mass Communication*). Princeton, NJ: Princeton University Press.

Hovland, C. I., & Rosenberg, M. J. (Eds.). (1960). *Attitude organization and change.* New Haven, CT: Yale University Press.

Hovland, C. I., & Sears, R. R. (1940). Minor studies of aggression: VI. Correlations of lynchings with economic indices. *Journal of Psychology, 9,* 301–310.

Hull, C. L. (1933). *Hypnosis and suggestibility.* New York: Appleton-Century Crofts.

Hull, C. L. (1943). *Principles of behavior.* New York: Appleton-Century Crofts.

Hull, C. L., Hovland, C. I., Ross, R. T., Hall, M., Perkins, D. T., & Fitch, F. B. (1940). *Mathematico-deductive theory of rote learning.* New Haven, CT: Yale University Press.

Hunt, E. B., & Hovland, C. I. (1960). Order of consideration of different types of concepts. *Journal of Experimental Psychology, 59,* 220–225.

Karpf, F. B. (1932). *American social psychology: Its origins, development, and European background.* New York: McGraw Hill.

Lasswell, H. (1948). The structure and function of communication in society. In L. Bryson (Ed.), *The communication of ideas: A series of addresses* (pp. 37–51). New York: Harper.

McDougall, W. (1908). *Social psychology.* New York: Macmillan.

McGuire, W. J. (1960). A syllogistic analysis of cognitive relationships. In C. I. Hovland & M. J. Rosenberg (Eds.), *Attitude organization and change* (pp. 65–111). New Haven, CT: Yale University Press.

McGuire, W. J. (1964). Inducing resistance to persuasion: Some contemporary approaches. In L. Berkowitz (Ed.), *Advances in experimental social psychology* (Vol. 1, pp. 191–229). New York: Academic Press.

McGuire, W. J. (1969). Suspiciousness of experimenter's intent as an artifact in social research. In R. Rosenthal & R. Rosnow (Eds.), *Artifacts in behavioral research* (pp. 13–57). New York: Academic Press.

McGuire, W. J. (1983). A contextualist theory of knowledge: Its implications for innovation and reform in psychological research. In L. Berkowitz (Ed.), *Advances in experimental social psychology* (Vol. 16, pp. 1–47). New York: Academic Press.

McGuire, W. J. (1984). Search for the self: Going beyond self-esteem and the reactive self. In R. A. Zucker, J. Aronoff, & A. I. Rabin (Eds.), *Personality and the prediction of behavior* (pp. 73–120). New York: Academic Press.

McGuire, W. J. (1986). The vicissitudes of attitudes and similar representational constructs in twentieth-century psychology. *European Journal of Social Psychology, 16,* 89–130.

McGuire, W. J. (1989). A perspectivist approach to the strategic planning of programmatic scientific research. In B. Gholson, W. R. Shadish, Jr., R. A. Neimeyer, & A. C. Houts (Eds.), *The psychology of science: Contributions to metascience* (pp. 214–245). New York: Cambridge University Press.

McGuire, W. J., & McGuire, C. V. (1991). The content, structure, and operation of thought systems. In R. S. Wyer, Jr., & T. K. Srull (Eds.), *Advances in social cognition* (Vol. 4, pp. 1–78). Hillsdale, NJ: Lawrence Erlbaum Associates.

Miller, G. A. (1951). *Language and communication.* New York: McGraw-Hill.

Morawski, J. G. (1986). Organizing knowledge and behavior at Yale's Institute of Human Relations. *Isis, 77,* 219–242.

Moscovici, S. (1982). The coming era of representations. In J.-P. Codol & J.-P. Leyens (Eds.), *Cognitive analysis of social behavior* (pp. 115–150). The Hague: Nijhoff.

Osgood, C. E., Suci, G. J., & Tannenbaum, P. H. (1957). *The measurement of meaning.* Urbana: University of Illinois Press.

Petty, R. E., & Cacioppo, J. T. (1986). *Communication and persuasion: Central and peripheral routes to attitude change.* New York: Springer Verlag.

Petty, R. E., Ostrom, T. M., & Brock, T. C. (Eds.). (1981). *Cognitive responses in persuasion.* Hillsdale, NJ: Lawrence Erlbaum Associates.

Ross, E. A. (1908). *Social psychology.* New York: Macmillan.

Saussure, F. de (1959). *Cours de linguistique générale* [Course in general linguistics] (W. Baskin, Trans.). New York: Philosophical Library. (Original work published 1916)

Schramm, W. (1985). The beginnings of communication study in the United States. In E. M. Rogers & F. Balle (Eds.), *The media revolution in America and Western Europe* (pp. 200–211). Norwood, NJ: Ablex.

Sherif, M., & Hovland, C. I. (1961). *Social judgment: Assimilation and contrast effects in communication and attitude change.* New Haven, CT: Yale University Press.

Stouffer, S. A. (Ed.). (1950). *Studies in social psychology in World War II. Vol. 4: Measurement and prediction.* Princeton, NJ: Princeton University Press.

Thomas, W. I., & Znaniecki, F. (1918). *The Polish peasant in Europe and America.* Chicago: University of Chicago Press.

Watson, J. B. (1925). *Behaviorism.* New York: Norton.

Wicklund, R. A., & Brehm, J. W. (1976). *Perspectives on cognitive dissonance.* Hillsdale, NJ: Lawrence Erlbaum Associates.

Wundt, W. (1900–1920). *Völkerpsychologie: Eine Untersuchung der Entwicklungs-gesetze von Sprache, Mythus, und Sitte [Folk psychology: An investigation of the developmental laws of language, myth and morals]* (Vols. 1–10). Leipzig: Engelmann.

Chapter 4

Diffusion Research at Columbia

Elihu Katz
Hebrew University
University of Pennsylvania

Media research begat diffusion research at Columbia's Bureau of Applied Social Research beginning with *The People's Choice*—the 1940 voting study by Paul Lazarsfeld and others.[1] This study focused on how people make up their minds in election campaigns; it was designed as a study of the role of the media in decision making. *The People's Choice* (1944) led to the so-called Rovere Study, Robert Merton's study (1949) of local and cosmopolitan influences in the town of Dover, New Jersey, and the Decatur Study, which Paul Lazarsfeld and I published 9 years later as *Personal Influence* (Lazarsfeld & Katz, 1955). These were followed by *Voting* (1954), the voting study reported by Bernard Berelson, Lazarsfeld, and W. N. McPhee. This tradition of work, which mutes the power of the media, was summarized and packaged neatly by Joseph Klapper in *The Effects of Mass Communication* in 1960, although the proposal for that book had been around for a long time, possibly since 1949.

The focus of this series of studies is on decision making by individuals. The key concepts, beginning with *The People's Choice*, are as follows:

1. The panel method—Lazarsfeld's method of repeated interviews of the same people over time. This was a very important contribution to

---

[1]Of course, diffusionism has a long history that can be traced to debates with evolutionism and independent invention as theories of culture. The entry on diffusionism in Sills (1968) siscusses the evolution of this concept. Also see Katz, Levin, and Hamilton (1963). The "beginning" at Columbia refers only to a particular empirical tradition.

communication research that, unfortunately, has not been very well continued. The panel method measures stability and change of individuals over time, whether or not the aggregate remains stable.

2. The "Index of Political Predispositions," which was based on the acknowledgment that class, religion, and family played a large role in inclining people toward a particular party loyalty. These three constituted a kind of homing device pointing people to where they really belonged in the political system.

3. A conception of the media as having more to do with the activation of predispositions and reinforcement than with conversion, that is, people were strengthened in whatever they brought with them to their media experience.

It is the primary group, though, that emerges as the hero in this list of concepts. The family is found to be a source of social pressure and, together with friends and other associates, the locus of informal advice. "Opinion leader" in this case means brother-in-law or friend, not banker or vice president of the United States. Operationally it was found that the small number of respondents who changed their voting intentions during the election campaign would assign influence to "brother-in-law" much more than they would say "newspaper" or "radio." To locate these opinion leaders, this study asked people, "Are you an opinion leader?" (not in those words) and compared those who said "Yes" with those who said "No," and inferred from that self-designation a classification of opinion leaders and presumed followers. Those who designated themselves as opinion leaders were found to be relatively more exposed to media coverage of the campaign. Thus emerged from *The People's Choice* the idea of a two-step flow of communication—from the mass media to opinion leaders and from opinion leaders to other members of their primary groups.

The two-step flow idea continued as a theme through the succeeding Bureau studies. The Rovere Study by Merton then distinguished between types of leaders by area of influence: cosmopolitan leaders and local leaders. It was a study paid for by *Time* magazine using a reputational method for designating opinion leadership, much like the method that political scientists recognize as characterizing community studies, trying to find out whom people turn to when they are trying to find out what is going on in town.

In *Personal Influence* (Lazarsfeld & Katz, 1955), an actual snowball technique was used, starting with an individual who said, "I have changed the coffee brand I drink, the fashions I wear, the kinds of movies I go to; and I have made changes in my politics." When the decision maker indicated another person as a source of influence, the interviewer went to find his or her opinion leader. Thus, part of the analysis was based on dyads, that is to say, people who named each other. These studies that get both members of the interaction into the research led from the individual as decision maker to social molecules.

I was a very naïve young graduate student at the time the study was published as Lazarsfeld and Katz. There were a lot of negotiations going on between 1945 and 1956, a lot of memo writing and a lot of potential coauthors, all of whom were somehow off-base from Lazarsfeld's point of view. It speaks poorly of me that I do not know the politics of this, but it is a very interesting period. C. Wright Mills is a major figure at this point, but he is very inconsistent as far as I read his memoranda and reports of the interactions between him and Lazarsfeld. Mills is unhappy that the media are not more directly influential and claims that they somehow work through these interpersonal networks. And he is also unhappy about the opinion leader as brother-in-law rather than as vertical cross-class influence; he was looking for rather more vertical interclass influence in the social structure than the horizontal image of opinion leadership suggested. In fact, the area of politics—as distinguished from marketing, fashions, and movie-going—*does* display more cross-class influence than do the other areas. But I do not go into the story of these interactions, partly because I am not an expert, partly because I am probably biased.

My role in this parade of collaborators was to propose to Lazarsfeld that if interpersonal influence is relevant to understanding the flow of mass communication, then small-group research, which was emerging as a new specialty in U.S. sociology in those days, should have something to say to mass communication. This was a nice marriage for a while. It was very unusual, very unexpected, because mass communication research derives from a mass-society model and, like mass production, was symbolic of modernity. The idea that interpersonal influence in small groups should somehow be a part of the flow of mass communication was a nice kind of paradox. So it was my job and then my PhD thesis to write a review of small-group research for its possible interest for the study of mass communication. That work became Part I of *Personal Influence.* I then reanalyzed all of the data having to do with the two-step flow of communication that had emerged from earlier studies. *Voting* (Berelson et al., 1954) also reiterated the two-step flow, but it also began to cope with the dilemma of mass apathy; the earlier studies—*The People's Choice*, Rovere, *Personal Influence*—all had begun to perceive the mass audience as somehow more active, more involved, and more political. *Voting* grappled with the dilemma of how a mass democracy works when most of the people are ignorant and apathetic.

So we are talking about a largely individualistic tradition of work on individual decision making, amended by Lazarsfeld's latent interest in collective behavior. His interest needs to be spelled out and really has not been, but it resulted in the addition of the notion of interpersonal relations to individualistic decision making and ultimately contributed to the major interest, nowadays, in social-network theory. If one looks at survey research as interviews with atomized individuals, situated as far apart as possible, then the addition of sociometry to survey research is like building a molecule around each of those atoms in the survey sample. That was the beginning of something very hopeful, which has not really been continued, because the group of young Turks at Columbia University's Bureau of Applied Social Research decided at the time that this was not real sociology. It was still too individualistic. Building a molecule around the atom in a sample is a nice idea, they agreed, but what really needs doing, if one is interested in change in a social system, is to trace the flow of some innovation through the elaborate networks that constitute a society, taking account not only of time, which the panel method began to do, but also of social structure. One requires some clearer image of community or of society than simply aggregating sociometric molecules around the atoms in a survey.

We tried to invent something more sociological, and we called it diffusion research. Diffusion research traces some innovation—an idea, a fashion, a new technology, and so on—as it makes its way through a social system. As the innovation travels through channels of communication, within a culture, over time, it is adopted by units—individuals, corporations, schools, or any other entity—that are variously connected to each other in some kind of structure. Those were the elements of the diffusion model. We were saying that in order to study change—to track an innovation as it is diffusing through these networks—measures of time and measures of social structure are needed.

There was a knock on the door just then. It was the Pfizer Corp. asking the Bureau of Applied Social Research to study the influence of its ads and publications on doctors' decision making. To which we said, "Well, we are not really interested in that sort of thing anymore. What is really interesting is tracking the flow of new ideas." This was the famous Bureau/client relation, of which the key line was to tell the client, " What *you* are really interested in is the following," which means, "What *we* are really interested in is the following, and it may serve you better as well." So Pfizer was told, "You are really interested in how new drugs make their way through a medical community, taking account of formal influences such as the media, taking account of interpersonal relations and networks of doctors, taking account of individual decision making, and so forth." Pfizer commissioned the study, and it was reported in a book called *Medical Innovation* (Coleman, Katz, & Menzel, 1966).

The drug study, so called, fulfilled all of the criteria that we had defined as prerequisite for diffusion research. We were granted permission in four

Midwestern cities to audit the prescriptions on file in all of the pharmacies in the four towns in order to locate the first prescription written by each doctor for a new antibiotic. It was the first of a new series of several drugs associated with the generic name *tetracycline*. We could then tag each doctor as to the first date on which he or she wrote a prescription for this new drug. So we had a measure of time. We got a measure of social structure by using straight sociometry. Again, to our surprise, the doctors all cooperated very nicely. They told us whom they consulted when they had a particular problem, and so on. So we were able to trace the flow of this drug through the networks described by the sociometric method. In addition, we were interested in identifying which doctors go to medical meetings and which doctors read which journals, and so on. The process of subjective decision making as reconstructed by the doctor-respondents themselves could then be contextualized in time and social space. This was the beginning of the transformation of the opinion leader or decision studies into the diffusion mode. This is where the drug study fits in the line of work that began with *The People's Choice* and continued through the Rovere, Decatur, and Elmira (Berelson et al., 1954) studies as well as others.

The drug study was interesting because it dealt another blow to the idea of a mass-society model for the study of communication. Although this was a professional community that could be said to be exempt from the atomized, isolated, alleged victimization of consumers television and newspapers, it tended to strengthen the conclusion of the earlier studies that the mass-society model needs to be subsumed by some kind of elaborate interaction among networks of individuals and the media of mass communication. In this case, a formal personal influence—drug company salesmen, who were an unashamed source of influence on doctors' decisions—were an addition to the mass media.

The drug study allowed the Bureau researchers to realize that they were in the diffusion business for real and to discover a study that had been done by rural sociologists some 15 years earlier, which had almost exactly the same design that we had invented on our own. This was the study of the diffusion of hybrid corn in Iowa by Ryan and Gross (1945), two rural sociologists (Gross was actually an educational sociologist). They had seed salesmen, we had drug salesmen. They had "neighboring" as a measure of interpersonal interaction, we had the sociometry of shoptalk, and so on.

The findings of the two studies were very much alike: Sociometric ties affect time of adoption. Earlier adopters are more conservative in the *extent* of their adoption: The pioneer adopters are very wary of how much they will adopt, so they adopt only little bits of the innovation and try it out for themselves. There are phases in decision making: No one adopts in response to only one source of influence. There are typically three sources that affect the decisions of both doctors and farmers: The first is a salesman, the second is mass communication, and the third is interpersonal influence. If asked what is the most important source in one's decision, the farmers say other farmers, but the doctors do not say other doctors; they are more likely to say drug company salesmen, but it is a bad question to begin with. There was a two-step flow of communication in both cases. The doctors who went to meetings were more looked up to for influence and so on.

We argued among ourselves about the role of simultaneity in the adoption of innovation. How did we get to the idea of simultaneity? The strongest correlation in the study was between the number of sociometric choices received and the time of adoption of the innovation. The more integrated the doctor in the networks of communication, the earlier he or she adopted this particular innovation. So we asked, "Is it possible that innovativeness explains popularity?" We ruled that out. Then we asked, "What if it is the other way, that integration explains innovativeness?" And we tried several ideas. One is that the doctors who are more integrated are more secure—they have less to lose, more credibility. Secondly, the doctors who are leaders have to act as pioneers in a kind of exchange theory—noblesse oblige—they have to show initiative. The third possibility, the one that we settled on in the end, was that it is likely that the doctors who are more integrated are also more centrally located in the networks of communication, informal and formal, and therefore are better informed about the experiences and opinions of others. In addition, they are the ones who go to meetings, and so on. Then we tested this interpretation against other data we had. We asked, "Do people who are related to each other sociometrically adopt together?" We found that the answer was yes, but only in the early phases, that is, in the more risky phases of the adoption of a new drug. These interpretations continue to invite interest among social-network theorists and researchers, and the data have been reanalyzed at least twice.

We also realized that we were in the same business as the rural sociologists, and that people studying innovation-flow in ostensibly unrelated traditions are not so far apart. Mass communication research is not so different from some of the other social sciences and humanities. It is not just rural sociology and mass communication that are also concerned with diffusion. For example, scholars of the history of religion want to know how Islam or Christianity spread. Did these religions spread by means of the two-step flow of communication? The answer is maybe. What about the epidemiological concern with diffusion of disease? How about archaeology and anthropology, two fields obviously interested in cross-cultural contact? I have not mentioned early diffusionism, but there was a major movement in anthropology that looked to diffusion as the key to understanding social change in the world. It was based on locating centers of innovation—say, the Fertile Crescent. Communication concerns of this kind are endemic in the different traditions in the social sciences. We realized that we had something to say to them and that they had something to say to us. Some of this comes out in a study on the diffusion of fluoridation among U.S. cities (Crain, Katz, & Rosenthal, 1969). There we looked at the cities as units of adoption and at the sociometry of intercity relations. What does one city say to another city? For example, if there is a large fluoridation fight in one city, its sociometric partner will be slower to adopt fluoridation than would have been expected.

Diffusion research had its own crisis, as did the two-step flow decision-making tradition. As the decision tradition gave way to the diffusion tradition, so the diffusion tradition began to collapse in the face of various problems. Somehow the mass media got lost in the transition. It was not clear which kinds of connections existed between the mass media and interpersonal networks. The interpersonal networks became too sovereign in this tradition, or so I think.

Also, diffusionism was heavily criticized for emphasizing the concept of functional compatibility. Things were adopted because they somehow fit a pre-existing frame, which is a sort of cousin to the idea of reinforcement; there is never a change, people are always adopting something that fits the frame of reference they began with. There is a sense that change is just more of the same. Clearly in the case of diffusion, one might want to use the notion of compatibility to explain that Tribe A, with a patrilineal tradition, adopted Christianity because the symbols of Christianity are more compatible with patrilinealism, whereas Tribe B with a matrilineal tradition did not. This seems to work out very nicely, but it clearly ignores the issue of power. How can you talk about the diffusion of Islam or Christianity without talking about power? Here were these very naïve functionalists talking about diffusion research without much reference to power, and that was really a crisis for the diffusion model.

A third problem was that the diffusing item would not stand still. That is to say, as something diffuses it changes its meaning, so that the form might be the same but the meaning might be different. The sewing machine might move from Midwest United States to the front porches of Tanzania, but the meaning of the sewing machine in Tanzania might be quite different. Thus, the idea of decoding functions and the meaning of forms itself became a central concern, and diffusion research did not cope with this very well.

There was a clear shift out of diffusion research into the modernization movement. Led by Everett Rogers (1962), there was a great move to translate diffusionism into the study of third-world modernization. New crises developed, first from the inherent frustration of achieving short-run change, and second from the gradual emergence of a pious feeling that the whole of the technical-assistance movement, however altruistic and well intentioned, was in fact an imposition. The researchers were collaborating in what was, in effect, a hegemonic project. The problem was how to get initiative from the bottom up rather than from the top down.

Then diffusion research had its own crisis, not just in the communication research business but elsewhere. And yet there are constant revivals of an interest in diffusion research. One is the current concern with the movement of television programs in the world that allegedly creates a cultural imperialism of U.S. mass communication. In fact, a large proportion of television time—certainly prime-time television—is taken up in other countries by imported U.S. shows such as *Dallas* and *Dynasty*. This turns out to be of some interest not only in mapping program flow but in getting into the business of decoding. What does *Dallas* mean in Japan, where it failed, or in Germany or Israel, where it was a giant success? Is it understood? What difference do subtitles make? Is it understood the same way in different places? How is it decoded? Does it enter people's lives? If so, how?

I think there is a connection between this diffusion tradition and the idea that the media can themselves create new networks, new connections, and new social structures. From this technological point of view, diffusion research concerns not only pre-existing channels through which ideas flow but it may also look at media as some kind of stimulus or influence on the construction of networks themselves. Look at the newspaper and European nation building, for example, that linked people over the heads of family and region to some national center. People realized that when they saw their local dialect in print, that all Italians more or less had the same language. The beginning of nation building, then, can be partly attributed to the medium of the newspaper in Europe. Other examples include the printing press and its role in the Protestant Reformation. James W. Carey's (1988) study of the telegraph looks at the means by which U.S. business could be operated simultaneously as one national market: Because of the simultaneity of the telegraph, people did not have to lose hours bidding in the New York Stock Exchange if they happened to be elsewhere. These things created new social structures, which again connect diffusionism not only to the notion of the flow of content through pre-existing networks but also to the idea that the media are creatures of these very social networks through which things spread and vice versa.

Diffusion research was a sociological interlude in mass communication research. It somehow reintroduced the idea of social structure into media studies and connected mass communication research with other traditions of social science and humanities that were interested in the study of change. I do think that mass communication was not sociological enough and still is not. We are at a moment when if one thinks of powerful effects, one finds that one can explain them better by macrosociology, including how societies deploy the technology, than by social psychology. One can explain

Renaissance scholarship or the early history of science or the Protestant Reformation on the basis of the development of new communication technologies. Look at Carey on the telegraph and Karl Deutsch on the newspaper and nationalism and look at how the Jewish people survived, and one begins to see effects associated with media of communication that are so much more powerful than the kinds of small effects that we desperately look for in the study of individualistic change of decision or attitudes. And looking at mass media as a decision problem was in itself an anomaly. Why is it, of all the possible effects that could have been chosen in studying mass communication, communication researchers chose to study change of opinion and attitude?

I want to end in noting that Carey, who proposed that there are two main themes in communication research, is right. One deals with flow or transportation, and the other is about meaning. Ostensible rivals, these two themes are linked in the history of mass communication research, sometimes one is on the ascendance, sometimes the other, and obviously we are at a point where the two are strongly interlinked.

REFERENCES

Berelson, B., Lazarsfeld, P. F., & McPhee, W. N. (1954). *Voting: A study of opinion formation in a presidential campaign*. Chicago: University of Chicago Press.

Carey, J. W. (1988). *Communication as culture: Essays on media and society*. London: Unwin Hymen.

Coleman, J. W., Katz, E., & Menzel, H. (1966). *Medical innovation: A diffusion study*. Indianapolis: Bobbs-Merrill Co.

Crain, R. L., Katz, E., & Rosenthal, D. (1969). *The politics of community of conflict: The fluoridation decision*. Indianapolis: Bobbs-Merrill Co.

Katz, E., Levin, M. L., & Hamilton, H. (1963). Traditions of research on the diffusion of innovation. *American Sociology Review, 28*, 237–252.

Klapper, J. (1960). *The effects of mass communication*. New York: The Free Press.

Lazarsfeld, P. F., & Katz, E. (1955). *Personal influence: The part played by people in the flow of mass communication*. Glencoe, IL: The Free Press.

Lazarsfeld, P. F., Berelson, B., & Gaudet, H. (1944). *The people's choice: How the voter makes up his mind in a presidential campaign*. New York: Duell, Sloan and Pearce.

Merton, R. K. (1949). Patterns of influence: A study of interpersonal influence and communications behavior in a local community. In P. F. Lazarsfeld & F. Stanton (Eds.), *Communication research 1948–1949*. New York: Harper.

Rogers, E. M. (1962). *The diffusion of innovation*. New York: The Free Press.

Ryan, B., & Gross, N. (1945). The diffusion of hybrid seed corn in two Iowa communities. *Rural Sociology, 8*, 15–24.

Sills, D. L. (1968). Diffusion. In D. L. Sills (Ed.), *International encyclopedia of the social sciences* (Vol. 4, 169–185).

Chapter 5

Children and Television

Hilde Himmelweit (1918–1989)*

As socializing agents, television, radio, film, and books teach, inform, amuse, titillate, and reduce or arouse tension. They also provide vicarious satisfaction, simulate companionship, signal sets of values, and indicate the permissible, the daring, and the disapproved of. The difference between media and other socializing agents—teachers, peers, and the neighborhood—is that the media have no *direct* power over the child.

Television can be ignored; moreover, it has no direct consequences because of its indirect relationship. That does not mean that the role of the media is negligible, just that we ought to set it in context. Thus, when it comes to evaluating research, we should really consider the media as *one* of the socializing agents and ask, "Under which set of conditions will they, as socializing agents, have the greater effect?"

I ought to note a difference between the British and U.S. broadcasting systems. In the late 1950s, I was a member of the United Kingdom's Committee on the Future of Broadcasting, a government committee set up to advise how broadcasting should be handled in the next 15 years. Our chapter on the British Broadcasting Corp. (BBC) called broadcasting "arguably, the single most important cultural organization in the nation." In contrast, Erik Barnouw, professor emeritus of dramatic arts at Columbia University, quoted the president of the National Association of Broadcasters on the 25th anniversary of U.S. broadcasting: "If the legend still persists that a radio station is some kind of art center, then the first official act of the second quarter century should be to list it along with other local dairies, banks, restaurants and filling stations." Both views are probably incorrect.

---

*Professor Emeritus in social psychology, University of London.

The expectations and views of broadcasting in the two countries are completely different. In Britain, the media have always offered the most desirable occupations; the ablest people enter the media, and they set very high standards for themselves. Of course, that influences a good deal of the expectations about children's television. There are differences in broadcasting structure as well. In the 1950s, when I started studying television in Britain, for example, we had something called the "Toddler's Truce": Between 6:00 p.m. and 7:30 p.m., there was no television, so that children could be put to bed. There was also a children's hour. Indeed, the statutes required particular care of children.

The godparents of research on children and television were the Payne Fund Studies in 1930 and the Eleanor Maccoby and the Riley and Riley (1955) studies, which brought out the interaction between television use, the child's cognitive stage, parent–child interaction, and peer interaction. These were very sophisticated—and they were the only studies that we could draw on in England.

Before I began my studies, I had seen television only once. I did not even own a television set, and I knew no one who did. But when the BBC approached the Newfield Foundation and said they would like a study of children and television conducted, I was asked to do it because I had been doing a study of children and leisure time.

At the time, most people in the United Kingdom did not own a television. But that did not stop many officials from making, with utter certainty, dire predictions about the effects of the new medium. These predictions of doom and gloom about every new medium of entertainment—be it comics, films, radio, or television—are very interesting. I think these prognostications represent the fear of change and a vast overestimation of the medium's attractiveness and a vast underestimation of the individual, in this case, the child. These three factors together seemed to produce a kind of gloom in every country—for example, Germany, Sweden, and Britain—countries with the mildest of television at the time. Of course, there was a lot of positive talk that TV would provide a window on the world, but the main concern was the harm it might do children. There was concern that TV would lead to delinquency and vile behavior and that school involvement would suffer.

My colleagues and I approached our first study like anthropologists. We spent 6 months doing nothing but talking to children, talking to parents, talking to teachers, going to families, and then watching television with them to learn more about the medium. We were heady with excitement because someone said that the results would matter: The BBC said they would actually adjust their programming according to our findings. From the start, we were mainly interested in how the child made a decision to fit this new foreign body—television—into his or her existing leisure time.

What did he or she give up? Moreover, how did he or she react to the medium?

Indeed, the initial three studies—ours (Himmelweit, Oppenheim, & Vince, 1958), Wilbur Schramm's (Schramm, Lyle, & Parker, 1961) and T. Furu's (1962), all done very closely together—had a broad canvas: They tried to find out as much as they could about television and the child. Although Schramm and I knew nothing of each other then, there was a similarity in our approaches that captures a way of conceptualizing the child within a television world.

We felt that the important factors to control during our studies were age, sex, social background, and intelligence. We had found that intelligence was an enormously important, almost overriding, factor: Intelligence determined the preferences for television as well as its consumption and effects. Because we thought television came within the context of leisure life, we tried to control the similarity in the children's leisure potential. Therefore, we matched each child who had television with a child who had no television and who also did not view television; in other words, an experiment child and a control child. We went to five different cities and examined 4,500 children in order to get 1,000 tightly matched pairs. (Both Schramm and Furu also had a large number of children.)

We settled on 10- to 11-year-olds because they could still be considered to be in primary school. Then we took 13- to 14-year-olds—the oldest age group in the secondary school. That dichotomy determined our study in many ways, but it is worth remembering that what usually determines a study is the expectation of the differences that are likely to emerge. In those days we did not have statistics, regression, or any programs on computers. All we had were tabulations. We were fortunate, though, to have a cross-sectional study and a before-and-after study; that is, following one city before the introduction of television and 1 year after. That meant testing 3,000 children because we did not know who was going to get television. It was a luxurious exercise. We could not farm it out to anyone because no one had actually done an exercise of that size before, so we had to recruit people as we went along. I think if I had known more about surveys, I probably would not even have attempted it. There is a lot to be said for total naïveté.

In the middle of our research, commercial television came on the scene. So we were able—and this turned out to be quite important—to examine a single-channel situation and a choice-challenge situation. In today's world, it is interesting to ask what actually happens when choice is increased, as with cable for instance (even though in many cities there is huge choice already). In our study, increasing the choice meant reducing the exposure to the novel.

As I noted, the focus of our studies was out-of-school leisure time and interests—whereas the focus of other studies was centered more on the media themselves. We wanted to try to hide the fact from our participants that we were interested in the media at all. In our study, as well as in Schramm's and Furu's, the children kept week-long diaries. We also had 3 half-day school days given to us in every school. There were 200 class-rooms, and we arranged it so that no teacher was present. However, like Schramm and Furu, we had teacher assessments. We gave the teacher a television child and his or her control counterpart and asked the teacher to assess who was more imaginative, more aggressive, and more involved in school.

We covered a whole range of items and found that the amount of television each child views seems to be a function of age, then intelligence, and then social class. It is the intelligence factor that makes the children impatient, at a certain stage, of the stereotype diet offered on televi-sion—relative to a more self-choosing diet that involves reading and other activities. Indeed, at the age of 9 or 10, the intelligent children consumed everything—radio, the movies, reading matter, and television.

We decided that if we wanted to understand a television addict, it would not behoove us to look at heavy and light viewers. That would have been a very crude way of doing it. So we had to consider the ability level, within the age level, and then take the ones who were at the extreme ends. We then contrasted them with cinema addicts—those who had no television but went to the cinema—relative again to their ability level. We found that the heavy TV viewers tended to be more insecure and to look for vicarious companionship. Had we considered the amount of viewing alone, I do not think we would have gotten quite such a clear picture. I think it is a pity that such controls, which are still possible within a television audience, are not applied quite as rigorously today as they were in initial studies such as Schramm's, Furu's, and ours.

The results of the three studies—ours, Schramm's, and Furu's—were striking in their similarity. For example, bedtime was delayed by 25 min-utes in the United States, Britain, and Japan—an extraordinary similarity. There was also the usual reduction in radio listening and movie attendance and an increase in vocabulary for the very young, specifically those words frequently used on television. (For his part, Schramm picked up a special vocabulary from television, and he showed that young children with heavy television viewing had more knowledge of this vocabulary.) There was less viewing, on the whole, among the higher social classes. Reading decreased in the recent viewers, then re-established itself but changed in type; there was, for example, a sustained reduction in reading comics and in escapist fare in general; other reading was not affected.

Such findings show up repeatedly in study after study. In our day, though, the average viewing time was 1 or 2 hours a day; today, the average is 3, 4, 5 hours. I would be quite interested in a new study today in which the emphasis would be on what is lost through the amount of time spent on television. Overall, I think parental control and example are as important today as they were then. Another constant is teachers' total indifference to television—their vain hope that the medium will disappear if they make no reference to it. I am not talking about special media education in schools; I am talking about the fact that teachers sometimes make no effort whatsoever to draw the attention of children to something worthwhile on television that they might subsequently discuss.

In the one-channel situation with us (and in Schramm's and Furu's studies as well) the child had a choice: Either the child had to turn the TV off or, alternatively, had to expose himself or herself to some activity that was unfamiliar. With us, *The Children's Hour* was very carefully built on not only adventure programs but also many educational and informational programs. So the minute they had the second channel, the children simply switched from channel to channel to find their adventure programs. As a result of this choice, the children's exposure to the novel decreased.

I think people actually ignored—or distorted—many of our findings. CBS, for example, ran an ad in the *New Yorker* on our study, "Television and the Child," and the Television Bureau of Advertising published 10,000 copies of the study. Although we addressed specific chapters to teachers, parents, and television producers, when the bureau published our findings, they curiously ignored the chapter on the broadcasters. But at least the other chapters were widely distributed.

I now turn to specific areas.

TELEVISION VIOLENCE

It seems to me that television violence is one field that is extremely well covered, so I note only one or two things about it. First, many researchers have an impossible task, which is to look at disinhibition about aggression, prevalence of aggression, and arousal and consequences of arousal. Such behavioral correlates are so difficult to do with a child population that I think all one can do is criticize every study. I am more inclined to be impressed by the sheer ingenuity of these studies, with the use of films, and observation and play observation of identical behavior, like the famous Bobo doll that has been criticized so heavily.

The J. L. Singer and D. G. Singer (1981) study is a beautiful longitudinal study with young children. Their study shows, I believe conclusively and in a way that cannot be faulted at all, that both aggression and imaginative play suffer not so much from total amount of viewing as from a preference for viewing aggressive content. And Singer and Singer clearly play up the role of the parents and parental control. Fortunately, none of the researchers made the mistake that many broadcasters make, which is to say, "Well, it is all the responsibility of the parents." After all, it is also the responsibility of the broadcasters to provide healthy fare.

Incidentally, all the research with children, and a special study that we carried out with adults, shows that the broadcasters' belief that if there is not violence in programs people will not watch them is wrong. Both children and adults make a very clear distinction between excitement and violence. And they clearly agree on the formulation. In our study, we had 11 action dramas that we asked approximately 800 adults to characterize by a number of attributes, such as "involving," "brutal," "informative," and "down to earth." There were 19 such categories and each asked for gradations (a lot, a little, somewhat, or not at all). There was great agreement on violence: The standard deviations were small indeed.

We also asked them, independent of how they ranked the violence, about their liking of these programs; we then did a rather complicated multidimensional scaling. It became absolutely clear that liking programs depended on whether the characters were involving or not. It was the traditional conception of drama—nothing to do with television. Out of the 11, I think there were 8 programs in which violence played no part at all in whether people liked the program or not. Of the remaining 3, 2 were disliked and 1 was liked; but all were characterized by absence of feeling involved with the characters.

It is interesting that although television companies mostly agree that there is evidence saying televised aggression is likely to have a harmful rather than a neutral effect, that agreement has not actually changed the amount of violence currently shown on TV. It was only when Nicholas Johnson realized the real pressure lay with the advertisers and showed them how their ads looked next to the violent programs, that there was some reduction in violence.

In the famous Lefkowitz, Eron, Walder, and Huesmann (1977) study on children and violence, what shocked me was that although the longitudinal study obtained a correlation of .3, in the book there is a long presentation showing that .3 does not actually account for much of the variants. Psychologists and sociologists know that when they get a correlation of .3 about any behavior that is not obvious, .3 is the standard correlation that one gets about an individual's behavior—and something else that is influencing that behavior. Therefore, I did not really like the two-page pseudostatistical explanation of why .3 was considered very low.

I was equally sorry that the study was based essentially on what I would call an incremental view, not on a threshold. For instance, all their children had already seen endless violent programs. And yet one is looking for an increment by giving them a film clip of 10 minutes or even a whole film. Such field studies, which try to be natural, are, in fact, somewhat unnatural.

That was really not very much discussed. In contrast is the 2-year Canadian study by Tannis MacBeth Williams (1986), a before-and-after study in a town with no television compared with a town that had one-channel TV, compared with a town that had two channels and therefore more violent programs. Williams found that there was indeed a threshold phenomenon. The children did, in fact, become more aggressive, both verbally and physically, after they left radio for television.

But there was no difference between the children who had one channel and access only to Canadian broadcasting versus the ones who had access to commercial channels. A criticism I have of many studies is that they place the violence out of context—they do not actually look at the extent to which the individual is involved in the violence. Of those that do, I am very much interested in those trying to establish whether it makes a difference if a subject is a judge or a protagonist in a violent situation. That is the work of Jennings Bryant, Rodney A. Carveth, and Dan Brown (1981), who found that something ending in injustice rather than justice leads to far greater anxiety in adolescents.

CHILDREN AND ADVERTISING

It has been very well discussed and the age-related studies show that children are unable, initially, to distinguish various properties of commercials and the intent of advertising. But they soon become quite sophisticated. What I think is of novel interest is the effectiveness of a pressure group. Peggy Charren's group, Action for Children's Television, in the United States is a case in point. A factor of great concern is that toy companies are now producing television programs that they sell cheaply to television companies both here and abroad. These programs are designed entirely to sell products. That is, I think, probably both a legal and a moral issue. The newest form of this is the interactive program, where in order to get something exciting out of the program, one has to buy a product that is quite expensive. Such developments within advertising are different from original U.S. advertising, excessive though that was, at least by European standards. By the way, one of the greatest concerns in Europe currently is TV deregulation and new satellites that will make an individual country's provisions and restrictions difficult to sustain.

In Britain, the current political regime is going to relax the maximum 6-minutes-per-hour advertising limit for cable television. They do not realize how badly advertising interruptions affect the construction of a drama and the development of plot and character. I think one of the reasons violent television does not have more of an impact in the United States is that it is continuously diluted by advertising—the tension and the buildup are taken away to some extent.

CHILDREN LEARNING FROM TELEVISION

The reason *Sesame Street* was not received with the same enthusiasm in Europe as in this country was that in Europe, there is already a long tradition of that kind of children's programs. On radio there was one called *Listen with Mother*, then *Playschool with Children*. So the approach was not so novel. What I see as the enormous gift of *Sesame Street* is the extent to which it is getting children interested in something that is very carefully constructed and in which social relationships among people are friendly. It is rather a pity that much discussion about the program has focused on the fact that the knowledge gap has not narrowed as a result of *Sesame Street*. It seems to me that middle-class children and adults, whatever they are provided, do better than the working class. However, it seems to me important to acknowledge the extent to which disadvantaged children have benefited from the program—irrespective of comparison with the advantaged children.

Admittedly *Sesame Street* has not worked at all in Mexico, in the countryside: The tempo of *Sesame Street* is too fast; there is a slower rhythm and tempo in the Mexican culture. That is one indication that educational programs cannot be easily exported to another culture. Otherwise, *Sesame Street* the world over has been a great success.

Another example of a television program from which children learned was a rather remarkable one on sex education that appeared as part of a series called *Merry Go Round*. This program, watched in schools in Britain, featured a live childbirth. It also named, explicitly, the sexual organs and their functions. Because the schools were free to choose whether or not to show it, there was no way to have a control group and an experimental group under such circumstances. However, we could do a before-and-after study in schools that agreed to show the program. The success of the program was remarkable for several reasons. First, it became clear that the children were already very knowledgeable—they just did not use the Latin terms. Second, it was really something for the children to watch a childbirth at that age. They took it completely in stride. After the children had a discussion with the teachers, we did a test; then, after a 3-month vacation, we tested them again to see if their impressions were transitory or lasting.

The effects were lasting. In fact, the children had replaced the names they themselves had given the private parts with the Latin names. But they also changed their attitude on two things: Childbirth was less painful than they had originally thought, and nudity was less wrong than originally thought. The interesting point is that there was no correlation between attitude change and knowledge change. In this case, it was important to gauge attitudes. Often, we ask specific knowledge questions without asking broader questions of impression holding or impression gaining—which is really how we build up our political knowledge. For instance, I would not bother to learn the name of any British minister at the moment because they all do what Margaret Thatcher wants; if they do not they are changed. If there were someone significant, someone who has made an impact, that person would come to the forefront. True, sometimes one wants general impressions rather than precise knowledge. (On that note, I think there has not, as yet, been enough research on the important areas of racial and sexual stereotypes.)

When I look at the initial research we conducted, I find that we spent a lot of time on attitudes and values. Of course, we did a careful content analysis for 5 weeks, but then, when we realized that a lot of foreign people were mentioned in the show, we asked questions about people's impressions. And we found, for example, that the viewers used less stereotyped judgments about foreigners than did the controls who had not watched.

And when we asked viewers how a rich family lives, they noted all the hallmarks of wealth that television drama upholds—and put them inside a single living room. In contrast, if they were asked about the living room of an ordinary family, they described what their own family had.

It is important to note what people gave up as a result of making time for viewing. There is a general principle that one creates a functional equivalent; now I would consider radio and cinema functional–physical equivalents of each other and of TV. Consider, for example, that because television is free, children would rather watch TV—and therefore their cinema viewing goes down. At the ages of 13 and 14, however, cinema means something quite different. It is a means to be away from home, to be with a girlfriend or boyfriend—activities that television does not satisfy. So in this case, they are functionally not the same. Also, cinema has made an enormous attempt to make itself dissimilar from television. Again, there is a gradual functional reorganization.

To understand how that works, we have to look at what is displaced and why. The stimulation effects are the content of television minus the content of what the other things no longer offer. If the other things were, say, just mooching around in the street or delinquent activities, one does not have to worry about what is on television. Television would be a pure plus. But it would be different if, for example, reading did suffer, if self-expression suffered, if the testing out of personal relationships in a real-life situation rather than in a fantasy situation suffered.

Another thing about attitudes and values: Where exposure to and involvement with the television medium is strong, where the message is repeatedly given in dramatic and involving form, we found it had an impact on the interests, outlook, and needs of the individual. The child is ready for such information even when it is implicit. For instance, when we asked TV-watching 13- to 14-year-olds in another study, "What is a well-paying job?" they mentioned the middle-class jobs—doctor, accountant, and lawyer. But those who had no television said the shoe industry—because the shoe industry in Norwich was the better-paying, skilled-workers industry. But in the case of 10- to 11-year-olds, to whom the information is not relevant and who are not about to leave school, there was no difference in answers. Again, the information we are discussing is not explicit: What one picks up and has to be ready for are attitudes, values, and behaviors not firmly anchored yet through direct personal experience.

If the information is too dissimilar, too out-of-touch with the subject's experience, it probably does not have much impact. Of the two theories I like very much on this matter, one says that all of us carry scripts and schema-types and social representations. We start with these from an early age and continuously change them and improve them. But by and large, the theory goes, we have a certain set that is momentarily not affected by everything that goes around. If new information comes in, it is first ignored, then discarded as irrelevant, but gradually, if it comes repeatedly, it becomes less of a cognitive strain to change our schema than it is to ward off such pieces of information. One can see now where the aggression side comes into it—a sort of George Gerbner's symbolic reality. (Whether Gerbner has been proven exactly right or wrong seems to me quite immaterial: the concept of a symbolic reality is, to me, a very rich one.) A similar view is expressed about personality development with the second theory that states, "assimilation if we can, accommodation if we must." I think that is very true—and one can see the principle as applicable to any repeated television content, whether it is about AIDS or crime. As Hanna Adoni and her colleagues point out (Adoni, Cohen, & Mane, 1984), social reality as experienced by the individual varies with direct experience with symbolic reality and with the existing scripts that the individual holds.

There has been a series of studies, largely started by Gabriel Salomon from Israel, in which he said: "Look, the interesting point is that there are certain properties inherent in the television presentation and format. To what extent do they have a spillover effect on the cognitive skills of the individual?" Hubbard Tiedhard did a recent study on teaching children how to use and edit film. Six weeks later, a different person came and tested a variety of cognitive skills and found that there was, in fact, a carry over from the editing process with regard to matching sequences of pictures and sentences, understanding picture stories.

It is not the content I am discussing now but the format. In the 1950s, the only study I could find about format was one carried out in Germany in the 1920s. The researchers showed a film of the story about the town mouse and the country mouse to children ages 5, 7, and 9 and asked them to reproduce the story. The 5-year-olds could only pick out individual incidents; the 7-year-olds barely a story; and the 9-year-olds the motivation.

Then the researchers did it again and introduced bits about Eskimos, which really were very different from scenes of the town mouse and the country mouse—just 30-second inserts. The 7-year-olds, who were just beginning to master the original story, ignored the Eskimos completely, because all that mattered was trying to get the gestalt right, whereas the younger and the older ones could master the story gestalt.

POLITICAL SOCIALIZATION

The work of Steven H. Chaffee and others shows, I think, the extent of political socialization. According to Chaffee, such socialization has much to do with parent–child relations and the mode of communication within the family. And the one absolute recurring theme that goes through all the studies to do with children and television is the immense importance of the parent–child relationship. The more strain there is, the more television watching there is. And the children are more influenced by aggressive material; their fantasies are full of aggressive material as well.

That finding is one example of looking at the broader canvas. Let me offer another example from my research. After 11 years, I did a follow-up study of some children whom I had observed before I started doing television research; I had looked at their leisure activities and their attitudes toward family and home. This time I wanted to test some theories about social-class differences. I also asked them about their media preferences and interests in general. What I found was that the most preferred medium among those with fewest resources, in adolescence and in adulthood, was the one most available. In adolescence it was the cinema, in adulthood it was television. (That was after marriage; before marriage, they did not watch television.)

Furthermore, the tastes established in adolescence—after due allow- ances for social background, intelligence, and type of occupation were made—played a part in linking up with taste in adult life. As such, it looks as if the development of a varied taste pattern and a varied set of hobbies in adolescence is crucial. Sadly, it may well be that we are doing nothing about that particular area even though children now view television 3 to 4 hours a day.

The Canadian before-and-after study by Tannis MacBeth Williams (1986) that was mentioned earlier is one study well worth reading. But the Swedish one is the most impressive of the lot. It is an 8-year media panel. They took both cross-sectional and longitudinal data and found that if a child was either unhappy about school or felt he or she was not getting on well with school or parents, he or she veered towards the peer group. The peer group would have a particular pattern of either viewing or music listening, for example. (This study included a range of leisure activities.) In any case, the initial reason for moving in the particular direction—be it TV viewing or music—had nothing to do with the content of the media. It was later that the media made their own impact and a sort of spiral of effects occurred, which also increased the alienation from family and school. The ethnographic interactional approach emphasized talking to families, listening to families, watching with families, and seeing how they manage to have television on all the time and still ignore it—rather like radio used to be ignored.

I would like to make one point about the future and the need for all of us to move, again, to the broad canvas. We should find out more about what makes some children immune from television and others extremely responsive to it. And we should look at deviant cases. In Europe currently, we may have to re-do studies on what is happening to leisure activities and how to reduce the amount of children's viewing time. Equally deserving of our attention is the impact of deregulation.

But, once again, I do not think we need more studies on violence nor, indeed, on television and pro-social behavior—we know television affects things. Instead, we ought to enable ourselves to look at how the child defines the world and what place television has in that world; so I would be interested, for example, in their response to news. Nor should we pretend that children's programs are actually much viewed by children and very much liked, because it is really the mixture of children's and adults' programs that makes up the diet. There is a lot to be said for detailed studies of carefully selected families and their children, studies that put television not in the center of the stage but consider it one element in understanding the leisure life of the children.

REFERENCES

Adoni, H., Cohen, A., & Mane, S. (1984). Social reality and television news: Perceptual dimensions of social conflicts in selected life areas. *Journal of Broadcasting, 28*(1), 33–49.

Bryant, J., Carveth, R. A., & Brown, D. (1981). Television viewing and anxiety: An experimental examination. *Journal of Communication, 31*(1), 106–119.

Charters, W. W. (1933). *Motion pictures and youth, a summary.* New York: Macmillan.

Furu, T. (1962). *Television and children's life: A before–after study.* Tokyo: Japan Broadcasting Corp.

Himmelweit, H. T., Oppenheim, A. N., & Vince, P. (1958). *Television and the child.* London: Oxford University Press.

Lefkowitz, M. M., Eron, L. D., Walder, L. O., & Huesmann, L. R. (1977). *Growing up to be violent: A longitudinal study of the development of aggression.* New York: Pergamon.

Riley, M. W., & Riley, J. W., Jr. (1955). A sociological approach to communications research. In W. Schramm (ed.), *The process and effects of mass communication.* Urbana: University of Illinois Press.

Schramm, W., Lyle, J., & Parker, E. B. (1961). *Television in the lives of our children*. Stanford, CA: Stanford University Press.

Singer, J. L., & Singer, D. G. (1981). *Television, imagination and aggression: A study of preschoolers*. Hillsdale, NJ: Lawrence Erlbaum Associates.

Williams, T. M. (Ed.). (1986). *The impact of television*. London: Academic Press.

Chapter 6

The Press as a Social Institution

Theodore Peterson
University of Illinois at Urbana-Champaign

Once when I spoke with Osborn Elliott, the editor of *Newsweek* for a good many years, he had just come from a talk that had obviously intrigued him. It was an analysis of how newsmagazine stories are put together. He was fascinated: "Here I am, learning about how I did the things I did all my life," he said. I know how he felt, because I feel very much the same way. For almost 40 years, it has struck me as natural to look at the press as a social institution. I had never bothered to figure out where I got the idea. Actually, I have one notion. I got a "C" in a basic statistics course because I could never distinguish between mean, median, and mode. I decided I was not cut out for quantitative research, despite the fact that the University of Illinois, when I was a graduate student and indeed when I was dean of the College of Communications, was one of the centers of quantitative research.

But there was another side at Illinois—that of looking at the press as a social institution. I had never tried to express this area of studies before, so I started tracking down what has been written about the subject. I went first to the *Encyclopedia of Social Sciences* and found nothing. Then I went to various books on introductions to communication research, and they too were mute. There was one voice—Wilbur Schramm's—in the introduction to a book edited by Ralph O. Nafziger and David Manning White, *Introduction to Mass Communications Research* (1963).

Schramm, first of all, dismissed the research that *Journalism Quarterly* had been doing before World War II. He said it would not be regarded as research today. At the time, most of the fruitful research was done not by journalism professors but by academics in other disciplines. But Schramm noticed and rejoiced in the fact that quantitative studies had begun to emerge from schools of journalism, which were developing their own research approaches. He listed three areas that schools of journalism had a particular obligation to study. He gave first place to mass communication: "Mass communication as a social institution, its organization, its social control, its place in the social structure, its content, its audiences, its responsibilities and performances" (p. 5).

What he was reacting against were the purely descriptive studies, studies that lacked dimension, studies that had been the chief contributions made by journalism schools to research. He wanted works with a context that permitted comparisons and understandings. As an example of institutional research, he cited *Four Theories of the Press* (1956), of which he, Fredrick Siebert, and I were coauthors and which sets down four political philosophies under which most of the world's press communication systems can be classified.

That book has had an interesting history, for it was never intended to last as long or travel as far as it has. It was a spin-off of Schramm's *Responsibility in Mass Communication*, which was published in 1957. But *Four Theories of the Press* tried to answer some basic questions: Why is the press as it is? Why does it apparently serve different purposes and appear in widely different forms in different countries? Why, for example, is the press of the Soviet Union so different from our own? In one question, I think, Schramm caught the essence of this institutional approach—"Why is the press as it is?"

I cannot speak for others who have studied the press as a social institution, but for me that study is more an approach than a methodology. Although it is just one way of looking at the media, it is an illuminating one. It looks at the mass media in their place in society and tries to answer at least three basic questions: What are the media like? Why are they that way? What do they do? If one uses this approach, one tries to check one's ideological baggage—one tries to look at the media as objectively and clinically as possible. One's view should not be monistic: one should try to look at the media from as many perspectives as possible. And one is always looking for relationships—between media and government, between media and society, and so on. Although the approach is essentially qualitative, it is not necessarily anti-quantitative. In fact, it may and often does draw on the results of quantitative study.

Neither is the approach merely historical, although it often draws from history to provide a context and to illuminate the present. It is sometimes akin to, but sometimes quite different from, social history. In short, many disciplines are drawn upon—history, geography, political science, law, economics, sociology, demography, and indeed even philosophy.

Four Theories of the Press, for example, drew very heavily on history, law, and philosophy. I suppose it wound up, in many ways, as much as a sort of bastard philosophy book as anything else. That is because it originated by trying to answer some very basic questions: What is the nature of man? What is the nature of truth and knowledge? And what is the relationship of man to the state? In fact, my conviction is that in order to understand the press, one must understand the two environments in which the press operates. One environment I grandiosely call the world of ideas; the other is the material environment.

One cannot understand the media in this country without understanding the classical libertarian theory of the press that goes back to Milton and was grounded in the assumptions and worldview of the 18th-century Enlightenment. That was a theory of negative liberty, of "freedom from," and it has been modified slightly over time. Certainly the right-to-know doctrine that was largely a product of the 1950s and 1960s is a modification of classical libertarian theory, which assigned certain tasks to the press: enlightenment and servicing the political, economic, and entertainment systems, and a few others. Then, in the world of ideas I would add challenges to classical libertarian theory. Among those contemporary challenges are the writings of the Commission on Freedom of the Press, informally known as the Hutchins Commission, especially its book *A Free and Responsible Press* (1947), and more recently, the Sean MacBride book, *Many Voices, One World* (MacBride, Abel, & International Commission for the Study of Communications Problems, 1980).

The other environment to understand is a much more obvious one: the material one—the social and economic forces that have changed the press from essentially a craft to a mass-production industry. Specifically I am thinking about the industrial and technological revolutions. The technological revolution, for one, has had tremendous implications for the press. The rise of democracy, the spread of education, urbanization and suburbanization, the sheer growth of the population, increases in disposable income and disposable leisure—these things are still affecting the press. I think the material environment has sometimes made it difficult for the press to carry out functions that were assigned to it by classical theory. Profit making, obviously, is sometimes going to collide with enlightenment. In the material environment, there is also a fractionizing of audience. This is not a recent phenomenon. But it has become intensified in recent years, so much so that even today electronic technology has made much communication individualized.

In schools of journalism, the institutional approach of looking at the press as a social institution within these two environments has been mainly a product of the post-World War II period. But it had its origins outside of schools of journalism. In fact, now that I have Schramm's criticism of early journalism research to remind me, I would say that the approach, at least at Illinois, was a reaction to the descriptive studies that had characterized it. For one example, I take the works of Frank Luther Mott. Mott wrote what I think is a definitive chronicle of U.S. magazines from 1741 through 1930 in five volumes, the last of which Harvard University Press published posthumously in 1968. His works are exceedingly valuable, and no one seriously interested in the story of U.S. periodicals can do without his contributions. Although Mott once denied it, it seems to me his works are very long on names, dates, and places, but short on the context in which magazines evolved. Even so, the details that he painstakingly tracked down can provide a foundation for those whose approach is different from his.

Recently, while cleaning out my files, I came across a sort of Illinois manifesto about journalism research. It appeared in *Coranto*, a little mimeo-graphed newsletter that Siebert and I brought out for four issues in 1950 and 1951. It dealt with historical research on the press, British and U.S. Issue No. 1, dated April 1950, acknowledged the descriptive studies that had characterized journalism research and was epitomized, I think, by Mott. But then it said:

> What we need now are interpretive studies utilizing the factual information that Mott and his predecessors have given us. A few writers, such as Sidney Kobre, with his study of the colonial press, have pointed the way. But only a start has been made. Where are the historians to give us social histories of the press in the dark ages of partisan journalism, in the Civil War period, in the age of industrialization? If they exist, *Coranto* would like to hear about them. If they don't, *Coranto* wants to help create them.

We received one answer to those questions from the University of Minnesota. Edwin Emery and Henry Ladd Smith were working on their book, another standard text, interpreting U.S. journalism in relation to the social, political, and economic settings of various historical periods. That text has endured under the title *The Press and America: An Interpretative History of the Mass Media* (1984). My first attempt at a similar approach was a 28-page paper I wrote in November, 1949, for a graduate course taught by Schramm. In this paper, I brashly tried to show how the *Kansas City Star* was a product of its civic-minded founder, William Rockhill Nelson, and his successors; a product of Kansas City in the 1880s, a town of grifters, grafters, gamblers, and suitcase businessmen and a product of politics and of its peculiar staff ownership.

Siebert, then director of the School of Journalism at Illinois, encouraged such an approach—not only in his own work but also in the curriculum and in the works of others. This institutional approach can be found in Siebert's monumental 400-page study of *Freedom of the Press in England,*

1476–1776 (1952). Siebert wanted to understand the Bill of Rights, so he turned to England for the origins and the background of U.S. principles and institutions. His aim was to write a history of not just an idea—press control—but also, as he put it, of the application and practical working of ideas.

The book was basically a study of institutions in conflict: the press on the one hand and the church and state on the other and the relationship between them. He saw the press as integrated, a social organism affecting and being affected by society. He considered it significant that the decline of government controls in the 18th century coincided with the growth of private enterprise capitalism. And from his study, he tried to set out a few principles that he thought had universal application. They are in the beginning of the book, he told me, because, "if I put them at the end, they may get overlooked; if I put them anyplace, I'll put them at the beginning and at the end."

Another advocate of this approach was Jay Jensen, who was a fellow graduate student, a fellow teacher, and head of our journalism department for 20 years before retiring in 1977. He published comparatively little, but his influence on graduate students was great. Of the pieces he did publish, one was important in this context: "A Method and a Perspective for Criticism of the Mass Media" (1960).

The perspective Jensen advocated was the institutional. Like other institutions, the media were created by mankind to deal with one aspect of human existence, in their case, social communication. From that detached perspective, one can see that the media tend to develop objective functions as contrasted to the normative functions of libertarian theory.

By the nature of things, Jensen said, the media do certain things whether they are intended or not. No one asks the media to enforce social norms, for example. They just do. He also noted that in the United States, the demands of the industrial order have largely, though not entirely, determined the policies of the media in a very broad sense. Correspondingly, in former Soviet Russia, the political order governed the media.

Jensen said that to be truthful, his sort of institutional approach should have certain characteristics. For example, this approach should be done objectively and take into account the contextual relationships of the media with their environment—the demands and values and the aspirations of the society in which they operate. Gertrude Robinson, a contributor to this volume, used this approach in her doctoral dissertation at Illinois. Robinson studied the Yugoslav press, which she considered in the context of the country's politics and economics; she analyzed its structure, taking into account geography, history, and other factors.

Although I have focused on Illinois, I would like to stress that the approach had its antecedents outside of schools of journalism long before

World War II. I should also acknowledge that it had a good many champions and enthusiasts in schools of journalism other than Illinois, in the 1940s, 1950s, and thereafter. Surely one of the antecedents must be Walter Lippmann's *Public Opinion* (1922), a work that anybody who studies communication ought to read. The book can still be read for new insights. Lippmann, in his dissection of the nature of news, demonstrated why the conventions of journalism have made it difficult—he thought impossible—for the newspaper to report the underlying social conditions. (Admittedly, that summary of Lippmann is a little like describing the Grand Canyon as a magnificent example of soil erosion.) Lippmann also had a great deal to say about stereotypes and about how man imposes a pseudoenvironment between him and the real physical environment.

There are also elements of the institutional approach in Robert Park's *Natural History of the Newspaper* (cited in Schramm, 1960). Park had a delightful term for the newspaper: It is a product, and despite all the efforts of the generations of men to make it something after their own hearts, it has continued to grow and change in its own incalculable way. Within schools, surely one early example of the institutional approach is Sidney Kobre's doctoral dissertation at Columbia University in 1944. Actually, Kobre's degree was in political science, but he was a one-time newspaper man and a long-time journalism teacher. His dissertation was called *The Development of the Colonial Newspaper*. Like Schramm and that *Coranto* manifesto, Kobre was dissatisfied with studies that were largely descriptive.

Kobre thought that the early histories of the colonial press had been bad. They were preoccupied with names, dates, and places. And what their authors did not see about the press, Kobre felt, was that it was an evolving social institution. So he set out an excellent summary of what he proposed to do. He wanted to show "how various population, economic, political, religious, cultural, and technological changes in the lives of the seaboard settlers produced the newspaper and then caused modifications in it" (Kobre, 1944, p. x). That dissertation was a brilliant, seminal job.

Also at Columbia, Paul Lazarsfeld and Robert Merton of the Bureau of Applied Social Research certainly contributed to the approach that I am talking about, especially in a paper called *Mass Communication, Popular Taste and Organized Social Action* (cited in Schramm, 1960). The bureau was not a school of journalism; neither was it affiliated with the School of Journalism at Columbia. But those of us with research programs at institutes of communication research certainly have regarded that bureau as a close neighbor, if not a blood brother. Lazarsfeld and Merton examined the social role of the press and then asked: What role can be assigned to the mass media by virtue of the fact that they exist? What are the implications of a

Hollywood, a Radio City, and a *Time–Life–Fortune* enterprise for our society?

They noted that the media perform many social functions, but they dealt with only three of them. One was a status-conferral function; that is, the media confer status on issues, people, organizations, and social movements. That sounds a little obvious when you think about it, but it was still an early statement of this point. Another function Lazarsfeld and Merton noted was that of enforcing social norms; by forcing each individual to take a stand, publicity that the media give to deviant social behavior closes the gap between, as they put it, private attitudes and public morality. The next function has a delightful name, almost a parody of academic jargon—the "narcotizing dysfunction." Very simply, they say that the flood of information may narcotize rather than energize the individual. Or, to put it in common language, people mistake reading about something or knowing about something with actually doing something about it.

Another figure in the history of treating the press as an institution was Ralph Casey, a long-time director of the School of Journalism at the University of Minnesota. The few touches of the institutional approach in Casey's writing appear in an essay "Communication Channels" (in Smith, Lasswell, & Casey, 1946) in which he saw the newspaper as an institution shaped by the rise of democracy, by the technological and industrial revolution, and by urbanization. The institutional approach is more apparent in the work of J. Edward Gerald, also of Minnesota. It is implicit in his study of the press and the U.S. Constitution. This approach permeates his book, *The Social Responsibility of the Press* (1963). Gerald had no patience with observers of the media who studied it apart from society. He thought one of the big mistakes was thinking that the media have an autonomous existence. That point of view was unreal and static to him. One could, for example, write the history of the Reformation and Renaissance as a history of writers and printers who made use of Herr Gutenberg's invention, but he thought that was a limited perspective.

Gerald saw the mass communication industries as important; in fact, he ranked them very high on the list of institutions, way up in social importance with the family, agriculture, business, the government, and language and writing. With that conviction he tackled the problem of social responsibility in the press.

Despite what I have said, some may still have the notion that the institutional approach is useful only in historical studies. That is not true; let me cite a personal example. A few years ago, I was asked to write a section on magazines for George Gerbner's multivolume *International Encyclopedia of Communications*. I was allotted 2,000 words on magazines. That was hard enough, but then the editor said that he wanted me to cover the international scene as well. I knew nothing about magazines abroad, but I made a slight bow in that direction. What I discovered is that little has been written about magazines abroad. They tend to get lumped with periodicals, and the people who are writing about periodicals are mainly people writing about newspapers. They throw in the name of a magazine or two here and there, but their focus is usually newspapers.

I was also struck by the paucity of available information. I spent about 3 days going through the University of Illinois' excellent library and found virtually nothing. Then Leo Bogart, a contributor to this volume, suggested I get in touch with the people at the international edition of *Reader's Digest*, who provided me with some information. I also got in touch with an executive at the periodical association in London. And from him, I got enough information to suggest something that fascinated me: The structure of the magazine industry in industrialized nations throughout the world is taking on very much the structure of the magazine industry in the United States.

I began to suspect that access to the magazine industry abroad is as easy (or as relatively easy) as it is in this country. And I think access to the magazine field is probably easier than access to any of the other mass media. I was also intrigued by some of the forces that apparently affect the health of magazines in different countries. One was the amount of advertising time available on television. Another was the number and popularity of Sunday magazines in newspapers. Another one was whether the press is national, as in Britain, or local, as in the United States. And still another was the competition from other countries—such as the competition from England in Ireland. The role of the publisher, as a dealer in audiences, is essentially the same abroad as it is here.

One more thing. Now that I have retired, I intend never to write another word about mass communication. Not even a letter to the editor. But if I ever should write anything, it would be in the broad area of popular culture. And were I to do that, I would write a history of Chicago jazz. Why was it that Chicago became a magnet for jazz musicians and so fertile a spot for the music to develop from the early 1920s until at least mid-century? There is no simple answer to that question.

At the outset, one would have to consider a good many factors, many of them institutions; the family, for example, and attitudes toward jazz and the life that jazz engenders. Howard Becker, in a book on deviance, has a chapter on the jazz musician showing that the jazz musician is essentially an outsider. That is just a starting point. One would have to understand black culture and its ambivalent attitudes toward jazz. One would have to understand the church, especially the Black church, because although it was the inspiration for a great deal of the music, it was also an inhibiting force, for to some people, jazz was an instrument of the devil. One would even have to consider transportation. The Illinois Central Railroad, between Chicago and New Orleans, was not simply a carrier of bodies—it was also a carrier of information and messages. Chicago was a wide open town when jazz developed, as was New Orleans earlier, as was Kansas City, in the 1930s, as was New York in the 1920s when jazz hit there. One would have to understand the political system that made Chicago such a wide-open town, as well as the part that organized crime played in operating the night spots where jazz was played.

There were also the unions, both Black and White. In Chicago, the White union staked out territory that Black musicians could not perform in. The reformers also played a role. Their attitudes came about because jazz originated and was played in disreputable places. If one wants to believe some of the reformers, more women had been seduced by jazz than by Errol Flynn. The record companies also played a role. They determined what the musicians would play and under which circumstances; in fact, the main artifacts we have now of Chicago jazz are those of the recording companies. This study would be a massive undertaking, but it would also be an exciting way to the approach that I have tried to describe and explain.

REFERENCES

Commission on Freedom of the Press. (1947). *A free and responsible press: A general report on mass communication, newspapers, radio, motion pictures, magazines, and books.* Chicago: University of Chicago Press.

Emery, E., & Smith, H. L. (1984). *The press and America: An interpretative history of the mass media.* Englewood Cliffs, NJ: Prentice-Hall.

Gerald, J. E. (1963). *The social responsibility of the press.* Minneapolis: University of Minnesota Press.

Jensen, J. W. (1960). A method and a perspective for criticism of the mass media. *Journalism Quarterly, 37,* 261–266.

Kobre, S. (1944). *The development of the colonial newspaper.* Published doctoral dissertation. Pittsburgh, PA: Colonial Press.

Lippmann, W. (1922). *Public opinion.* New York: Macmillan.

MacBride, S., Abel, E., & International Commission for the Study of Communications Problems. (1980). *Many voices one world: Communication and society, today and tomorrow: Towards a new, more just and more efficient world information and communication order.* Paris: UNESCO.

Mott, F. L. (1968). *A history of American magazines.* Cambridge, MA: The Belknap Press of Harvard University.

Nafziger, R. O., & White, D. M. (Eds.). (1963). *Introduction to mass communications research.* Baton Rouge: Louisiana State University Press.

Schramm, W. (1957). *Responsibility in mass communication.* New York: Harper.

Schramm, W. (1960). *Mass communications: A book of readings.* Urbana: University of Illinois Press.

Siebert, F. S. (1952). *Freedom of the press in England, 1476–1776: The rise and decline of government control.* Urbana: University of Illinois Press.

Siebert, F. S., Peterson, T., & Schramm, W. (1956). *Four theories of the press: The authoritarian, libertarian, social responsibility, and Soviet communist concepts of what the press should be and do.* Urbana: University of Illinois Press.

Smith, B. L., Lasswell, H. D., & Casey, R. (1946). *Propaganda, communication and public opinion.* Princeton: Princeton University Press.

PART II

EYEWITNESS ACCOUNTS

Chapter 7

Fashioning Audience Ratings— From Radio to Cable

Hugh Malcolm Beville (1909–1988)*

Media rating has come a long way in 60 years, from the rudimentary beginning to today, and I have been privileged to play a role in that field from the start. I went to NBC in 1930 because I needed a job. I had gotten out of Syracuse University in January knowing that there was a recession on the way. The stock market had crashed in 1929, and the job market was drying up. I felt that because I had completed all my course requirements, I should get out and find a job before the June graduates hit the field. That is how I happened to wind up at NBC, which gave me a job as a statistician in their station relations department. Coincidentally, the month that I joined NBC was the month that the first field work was started for the first ratings service by Arch Crossley.

Before discussing details, I want to point out that effective mass communication requires two elements: First, it needs a viable feedback system to report how the output is being received; second, it needs a strong financial structure of some kind either from subscribers or advertisers or both. These two elements go hand in hand; without one you do not have the other.

I think it is clear that these fundamental issues in the mass media frequently seem to be overlooked by people who talk about mass communication. There is often a sense that anything that gets into the commercial field is somehow to be hated, and therefore the academicians tend to go the other way.

---

*Former Executive Director of the Broadcast Rating Council (now the Electronic Media Research Council); Author, *Audience Ratings: Radio, Television, Cable (1985).*

But I want to offer a heavy dose of the real world here. To my knowledge, no one has pointed out that a major form of mass communication is something called advertising. Without advertising and its revenue, few newspapers, magazines, television networks, or radio stations would exist. Even on Channel 13, New York's Public Broadcast Station, viewers will notice that commercialism has crept in, something I think we are going to see a lot more of in the future. In other words, there is no way that mass communication can exist, at least in the United States, without advertising.

In 1985, about $95 billion was spent on advertising, of which about $27 billion went to the electronic media and $35 billion to the print media. That kind of money is not going to be spent unless the people who are spending it are getting something for it in return.

Advertisers, furthermore, are trying to communicate to the interests of the audience and to persuade potential buyers. That is mass communication. The successful use of the media brings buyers back again and again and has been largely responsible for the growth of the electronic media over the years. That means there has been a heavy reliance on the feedback system as embodied in ratings.

On the other hand, in the print media, we have seen the demise of such publications as the *Saturday Evening Post, Collier's, Life,* and certainly many metropolitan newspapers. I think that to some degree this has been due to the fact that they did not have an effective, current, and constant measure of reader interest. These publications lost their financial base, and even though in most cases the subscribers stayed with them, the advertisers did not. Without the advertisers, they could not make it.

I am inserting a plea here for communication research to pay more attention to the role of advertising as a form of mass communication. Better and faster feedback is the answer.

I want to place ratings in perspective, because after all, there are a great many other forms of research in a network's research department. Certainly audience measurement, which is what we always call the ratings activity, is only one research activity. There is also program testing, public opinion research, social research, and various other forms of intelligence and management guidance. I was told once that the network expenditures related to ratings were matched by the cost of program testing and other research done by the research department. The ratings work was just about half the total budget.

I think it is clear that there are a great many other activities going on in the area, including media research or media comparisons with competitive media policy research issues. When I was at NBC, we did some work on editorializing, and we tried to find out how people would react to it. NBC did a massive study on television's effect on children. We did a series of studies on the sales effectiveness of television and how to put that medium forward as a viable sales tool for advertisers.

This kind of activity is constantly being carried out in addition to ratings. But why do we have the ratings? Well, radio emerged in the 1920s like a shot out of the blue. Suddenly people found that there was a device by which they could get speech and music in their own homes through the airwaves. This was something that up to then had been in the province only of gods and ghosts, but now they could get this out of a little box. Advertisers were intrigued. After all, for centuries, selling had depended on the human voice for persuasion, and the written word was only a surrogate. So, when they suddenly found that they could have the human voice—and later, with television, the appearance and motion of the human body—the advertisers began to experiment.

In the early days, advertisers found that the medium was quite powerful, but they lacked any way to measure how many sets there were, how many families there were, what the size of the audience was, and where the audience was located. There was nothing for them to go on but sheer faith. Clearly, the medium could not develop fully under those circumstances.

Unfortunately, the medium at that time was not itself aware of the need for the kind of measurement later to be developed in the ratings system. The advertisers were aware of it, however; it was the advertisers who started the first rating system. Networks had very little to do with the first two rating systems. By 1930 there were more than 200 advertisers using the networks; total gross sales for that year were $22 million, not much more than the amount that advertisers spent in 1985 on the Super Bowl alone.

After some experimental work done by Crossley for individual advertisers, a telephone recall-measurement system was set up. It was called the Cooperative Analysis of Broadcasting (CAB) system and was established in 1930 with a 24-hour recall. CAB was sponsored by a few dozen advertisers, who originally kept the figures to themselves. In fact, the first year, they did not even permit the agency to see the list of subscribers. The second year, the agencies came in. Once they became sponsors of the service, the advertisers began to drop out, feeling that they could get the data from the agencies.

The second radio-rating service, supported by the Association of National Advertisers (ANA), was launched in 1934 in competition with the established CAB. C. E. Hooper, who started the second service, was therefore bucking the establishment. He got started because a group of magazines was suspicious of the size of CAB ratings and the recall system that was being used. They felt that the ratings were inflated and sought something better. They found that George Gallup, a pioneer in ratings in Iowa before he came to Young & Rubicam, had set up a system of making coincidental telephone calls for all of that agency's clients who used radio.

Hooper, who was in the magazine measurement business, knew about this. He and some of the magazine people took this system over, modifying it somewhat. They established a rating service that was not originally intended to be continuous or syndicated. However, they put out one or two reports, and they came out with lower ratings than CAB for various technical reasons. For example, they were on an average-minute basis, which was one of the reasons for the difference against the 24-hour recall.

Hooper came around to the networks with this service when the magazines had lost interest in CAB. The magazines were not necessarily interested in continuing, although Hooper wanted their support. He came around to the networks, and Frank Stanton at CBS and I both thought it was a very good system, much better than CAB.

We supported Hooper's system and got it going. The system began taking off with agencies and advertisers, so Hooper expanded the service, increased the sample, and provided a lot of features that CAB did not. He had a much faster delivery and was able to do customized research for particular clients and programs. He was also able to add questions about audience composition.

Hooper's coincidental service became the more predominant one and finally forced the people at CAB to change their method. They gradually reduced from 24-hour recall to once-a-day interviewing and then to three and four times a day. Eventually they gave up recall completely and went to coincidental. So we had two coincidental services competing with each other—CAB and Hooper's. Yet, the results were 20% apart. CAB was now lower than Hooper. Why? Hans Feisel did a study that showed very clearly that the reason for the disparity was that CAB was only letting the telephone ring four times before hanging up, labeling it a "no listener"; Hooper let the phone ring six times. Other differences included the fact that CAB was also using a very artificial method of taking care of some of the "no answers." When all of this was put together, it accounted for the difference between the two ratings, and that was the end of CAB. The ANA and all the fat cats that were in it went down the drain.

Originally it was the advertisers and then the agencies who supported the rating service. Then when the networks got in, year by year they raised the price to a degree that the networks controlled it. So when it got to the point of whether CAB would continue, the networks went with Hooper, and CAB went under, just like that. That was about 1946.

By then television was coming into the picture. Some of us at NBC had started research on television by 1939 or 1940, when the first television station went on the air in New York. We were sending out double postcards to people in New York with a weekly schedule on it and a return card for people to check what programs they had listened to. The result was that we were getting some kind of ratings through the war years. This kept up, and after the war I tried to get Hooper to start a service. However, he was not very interested in television.

Finally, I offered Hooper the NBC mailing list of television homes. Television had a very limited concentration. Hooper would pick up some television homes in his radio listening surveys, but the number was pretty small. Still, I thought that he ought to be able to get hold of a New York list, so I set up a system whereby he could get the names of a New York RCA dealer/distributor for new owners' warranty cards.

We finally persuaded Hooper, but only after he had seen a baseball game on television. This helped to show him that television might amount to something, although he was never really sold on the idea. That was very bad for him, because when he made a deal to sell his service to A. C. Nielsen, he ended up selling out not only his radio service but his television service as well. In fact, he said he threw in the television service to make the deal. He just did not realize what he had or what it was going to be.

Nielsen was just trying to get started. He had a few hundred homes, such a small sample that it did not amount to much. He had also become involved in the field way back, although he did not invent the Audimeter, as many people think. It was invented by two professors at the Massachusetts Institute of Technology in 1934. Several studies had been run in New England using the original audimeter device before Nielsen took it over. Nielsen took control in 1936, made a deal with the inventors, and spent six or seven years developing it.

Nielsen was a very shrewd and smart operator. He was an electrical engineer; the last I was able to determine, he still had the highest average ever achieved by an electrical engineering student at the University of Wisconsin. When he first went into business he was in electrical engineering. Later he switched to market research. He recognized that the audimeter was only going to be good if it could be turned from a mechanical device into an electronic device.

He found that one of the biggest problems was the timing. He recorded that 40% of the households averaged some kind of a power outage every 4 weeks (that is the kind of electric service that was available in 1935). He had to devise some way to overcome this problem and come up with a more precise timing device to get minute-to-minute data. He had to develop procedures for handling the tape and for speedily editing and processing the data. So between 1936 and 1938, he did only experimental work. In 1938, he did a pilot study in the Chicago area; by 1942, he had launched an 800-home sample in the Midwest. His study was expanded in 1946 and eventually went to total U.S. coverage. Nielsen stated that he had spent 10 years and $2 million to bring the service to completion.

There were a great many advantages to the meter, including continuous measurement, minute-by-minute data, unlimited geography, and, for the first time, projectable ratings. Up to that time the ratings had only been indexes, just numbers. It was never possible, because of the limited sampling being done, to project the ratings. Of course, everyone did project them, because that was the only thing we had. We used some kind of an estimation procedure to project ratings from the limited number of cities to a national basis. Nonetheless, one big advantage of the Nielsen system was that it gave us projectable ratings for the first time. He also developed a great many analytical possibilities using duplication-of-frequency studies.

His system had a disadvantage, of course, in that there were unattended sets, estimated to be between 2% and 3% of all sets that were on at a given time. The biggest disadvantage was the very slow delivery (12 weeks), because the meters had a paper tape in them. The Nielsen field man had to go around to these households every 2 weeks, collect the tapes, and send them back to Chicago, where they had to be decoded and analyzed. So it was a very slow and cumbersome process.

Later, Nielsen developed the mailable tape audimeter in the early 1950s using 35-millimeter film. The mailable tapes were sent to the householder, who put the cartridge in. When he put the cartridge in, two quarters came out into his hand, which was how he was paid. Later, he took out the exposed tape and sent the other part of the cartridge to Nielsen. That cut down the time by several weeks.

The big breakthrough came in 1973, when Nielsen installed the storage-instantaneous audimeter, which in those days provided for all the Nielsen households to be linked by a dedicated telephone line to the central Nielsen computer. This way the information from the meter was translated and transmitted every 24 hours (between 2 a.m. and 6 a.m.). During most of this period the Nielsen service had about 1,250 households in the sample, but in 1983, the number was increased to 1,700 to take care of the problem of rating cable programs.

Other meters have been tried over the years. There was one in 1948, which we supported very heavily. It used dedicated telephone lines in Philadelphia, and it rated both television and radio stations in the market—seven radio and three TV stations at the time. Daily reports were teletyped to clients.

In spite of these competing systems, Nielsen was shrewd enough to keep competition out. He had two ways of doing it. One way was through his patent situation. He had established the electronic laboratory headed by Henry Rahmel where they continued to work on every conceivable form of meter. They got patents on every possible device. When anyone came up with another meter, it turned out Nielsen already had a patent or a patent pending on that device.

Nielsen had another ploy, which was to go after the finances of the competition. This was important in the case of Radox, because Radox had little money. However, a group of investors was very much interested in putting money into Radox's system. Unfortunately, these investors happened to be in Chicago, where Nielsen had pretty good entrée to them. Nielsen persuaded these potential investors that the patent would not hold up and that they were putting their money on a dead horse. So Radox was unable to get the thing going. He sued Nielsen, winning $75,000, which he used to establish himself in another business.

Radox's was just one of the early efforts. Another was that of James Seiler of the American Research Bureau. Seiler pioneered in the diary field. In 1957, he established a 300-household simultaneous meter system in New York called Arbitron. In this case, Nielsen was unable to do anything about Seiler's money, because Seiler was fairly well financed. Nielsen, however, was able to start his own New York service in 1959. He was also able to get the company that owned the Arbitron service to pay Nielsen a 5% royalty on the use of its meters. The result was that Nielsen continued to operate, and the Arbitron service folded up in 1972. However, in 1976, Arbitron was reintroduced with a completely new and different meter. I do not know what their patent situation is. However, the president, Ted Shaker, told me that one of the reasons his company originally folded was because he wanted to stop paying a royalty to Nielsen, who was his archrival.

Turning to diaries, I believe they have been a significant factor in the field in recent years. For a long time, the use of diaries was a stepchild technique. It was used intermittently in the 1930s, but it was never considered on a par with telephone coincidental, telephone recall, or the meter. Frank Stanton and his staff at CBS did much of the early work in the 1940s. Stanton was particularly interested in getting local ratings on CBS-owned stations in markets like New York and Chicago. He was unhappy with the fact that all they had were metro ratings or coincidentals from Hooper.

He was interested, of course, in getting early-morning, late-night, and area ratings for the total coverage area of the station, rather than just New York or the New York metropolitan area. So CBS began using the diary for that purpose and also for analytical work, with the same household keeping the diary for weeks. But nothing really came of it, and no one started a syndicated service. Hooper did some work with the diary when he was trying to fend off Nielsen. He tried to use it to make projectable national ratings.

The diary really had not gotten very far until Seiler, who worked for NBC in Washington, started a diary service in 1947–1948. Seiler was doing surveys on a quarterly basis. The other stations in the market became interested and agreed to a cooperative arrangement. After some months of that, Seiler decided to split off from people in Baltimore and Philadelphia to start his own company called the American Research Bureau, which I mentioned earlier, with an office in the National Press Building in Washington. He and his wife were the only employees of the company. Still, by 1951 it had expanded to the West Coast and the service was nationwide by 1955. He took over the Hooper local coincidental TV service at that time.

By 1961, Seiler's system, Arbitron, was measuring every U.S. television market and had begun to conduct the national sweeps. Most people have heard about the national sweeps, but they may not really know what they are, so I briefly define them. In many markets, the local diary service reported ratings three, four, or five times a year. These would be the major markets, like New York, Chicago, and so on. In many of the smaller markets, they often reported only once a year, because of the cost of the service. Arbitron eventually got all of the smaller markets to agree to twice-a-year reporting. That way reports for all of the markets in the country coincided for a certain four-week period for what is called the sweep. In that sweep, all 200 television markets were measured simultaneously.

The importance of the sweep is that it provides the principal figures the advertising agencies use for buying national advertising spots on television. The sweeps are of great importance because they also affect the kind of programming that takes place. The reason has nothing to do with the networks. It has to do with the affiliated stations of the network who want to make sure that they have the best possible chance to show well during the sweep week. So every network is under pressure from its affiliates to offer its best programming during the sweep weeks, which is why the sweeps get so much attention and prominence.

Nielsen had started up with diaries some time after Seiler. I think it was in 1954 when he introduced his own method of diaries, which I will not go into here. By this time, Nielsen had lost interest in radio. He realized that the home radio audience was declining in importance, because radio went out of the home with automobile radios and portable radios. Also, it was becoming much more difficult to meter radio activity. So over a 2-year period (1963–1964), Nielsen dropped both the local and the network radio measurements. This meant that, after that there was not very much available until we at NBC did some experimental work.

Bill Rubins was very much involved in setting up a new service known as Radio's All-Dimension Audience Research (RADAR) that has now been in operation for a number of years. I think that the first study was done in 1967, but that was after NBC had done its own study. What is used there is a telephone recall technique in which an individual is recruited within a household on a randomized basis. The person reports each day for 7 days what his or her radio listening is, and the interviewer calls each day at a time that is agreed on and gets the report from that person. That is a form of aided recall. It has served the network radio industry very well and is still very much in vogue.

The American Research Bureau went into radio audience measurement in 1966. Up to that time it had been doing only television audience research. When ARB went into radio, it went in with the concept of the personal diary. The idea of the personal diary was that an individual would keep an open-ended diary of his or her radio listening. This is quite different from the television household diary in which there is a diary for every television set, not every person. So we find ourselves moving into the person basis at this point. Indeed, this is the system that still dominates in radio.

Chapter **8**

Stanton, Lazarsfeld, and Merton— Pioneers in Communication Research

David L. Sills
Social Science Research Council,
New York

In writing about Frank Stanton, Paul F. Lazarsfeld, and Robert K. Merton, I have the advantage of having known all three. Many of the events I relate, however, took place before I came to Columbia in January 1951.

Because all three of these pioneers were immigrants to New York City[1] and were closely associated with each other for many years—largely on various projects in communication research—there is a great deal of logic in discussing them together in one chapter. Although I focus on them, it should not be forgotten that they often worked closely with many colleagues. They were true pioneers, but there were others as well who are celebrated in other chapters in this volume.

The circumstances surrounding their first encounter and their collaboration in communication research constitute an important part of the history of their relationship. Planned and unplanned research efforts often take unanticipated directions, and the importance of personality and intellectual entrepreneurship can best be seen in relation to events and their social context.

---

[1]Frank Stanton was born in Muskegon, Michigan, in 1908. Paul Lazarsfeld was born in Vienna in 1901 and died in New York City in 1976; Robert Merton was born in Philadelphia in 1910. This presentation was made at the Freedom Forum Media Studies Center in 1995.

FRANK STANTON

Stanton was the first of the three to arrive in New York City. Recalling his youth, he once reported that he had built his first short-wave radio when he was still in grade school. This must have been around 1920, early in the history of radio and certainly early in his career. What is astonishing is his claim that he was always interested in radio, although radio hardly existed as a national institution in those years. In 1930, his family's reduced financial circumstances canceled his plans to study medicine. He obtained a teaching assistantship at Ohio State University, where the dean of the business school advised him to stay away from radio, saying, "Nothing is going to ever happen with that." The department of industrial psychology was more tolerant of his interests, and he began to invent audience measurement techniques as a start toward inventing himself as a founding father of radio research.

Stanton received his PhD in psychology from Ohio State in 1935 and soon went to work for the Columbia Broadcasting System (CBS), which at that time did not even have a research department. In effect, he *was* the department. His rise to the top at CBS was meteoric. For 10 years, he invented ways to study radio audiences, building a research department and employing more than 100 people in the process. Then one day in 1946—when he was 38 years old—he was asked by William Paley, the founder of CBS and the chairman of the board, to become president of the company. He remained president until 1971.

For approximately 30 years—that is from their first meeting in the mid-1930s until Lazarsfeld effectively left the communication research field in the mid-1960s—Stanton and Lazarsfeld had what appears in retrospect to have been for both of them a truly rewarding symbiotic relationship. Stanton, through CBS, provided both funds and data for much of Lazarsfeld's research program at Columbia University's Bureau of Applied Social Research (formerly the Office of Radio Research); he provided his share of ideas for research as well. Lazarsfeld directed research that often proved to be beneficial to them both. The Lazarsfeld–Stanton Program Analyzer was jointly developed and used; in fact, at CBS it was called the Stanton–Lazarsfeld Program Analyzer. Three of the major collections of papers resulting from the research at the Columbia bureau are jointly edited books (Lazarsfeld & Stanton, 1941, 1944, 1949). There seems never to have been any significant misunderstandings between them.

But they were quite different people. Stanton worked in a corporate environment, and his reference groups were business colleagues and clients. He published very few research reports on his own. Lazarsfeld worked with professors and students, who constituted his reference group, and he published voluminously. My own impression of their relationship during these early years is that Stanton was much more than a funder of Lazarsfeld's research but less than a full partner in that research—a "middleman" or "facilitator" perhaps, but one who helped change the face of communication research in just a few decades.[2]

PAUL F. LAZARSFELD

It was during the decade that Stanton directed the research department of CBS that his productive relationship with Lazarsfeld began. Lazarsfeld was a young Austrian mathematician and psychologist whose research institute in Vienna had caught the eye of the Rockefeller Foundation. He came to the United States in 1933 on a Rockefeller fellowship; when the fellowship ended in 1935, he decided to remain. He might well have remained anyway to advance his career, but the suppression of the Austrian Social Democrats by Engelbert Dollfuss in 1934 took the decision out of his hands. With the wisdom of hindsight, David Wallace (1959), in his presidential address to the American Association for Public Opinion Research, archly described Lazarsfeld's coming to the United States as "an aid-to-underdeveloped-areas kind of thing" (p. 314).[3]

In 1937, the Rockefeller Foundation made a grant to Princeton University for Stanton and Hadley Cantril, a Princeton psychologist, to conduct a study of the psychological effects of radio, largely through laboratory experiments.

Fortunately for everyone concerned, Cantril soon decided that he preferred to continue with his own research, and for his part, Stanton was overwhelmed with his work at CBS. On the recommendation of Columbia sociologist Robert Lynd, Lazarsfeld was recruited to be director, with Cantril and Stanton serving as associate directors. Because Cantril and Lazarsfeld had a major falling out over financial and management issues, and because Stanton was always busy with CBS research, Lazarsfeld had a great deal of freedom. One of his first decisions was to undertake studies of real audiences as well as conduct laboratory experiments.

Lazarsfeld met often with Stanton, usually on Sundays, and consulted regularly with him by phone, frequently in the middle of the night. Much of the data used by the Princeton radio project came from CBS. But the radio project was only a beginning: It grew into the Office of Radio Research,

---

[2]For another discussion of Stanton's career and influence, see Rogers (1994).

[3]For discussions of Lazarsfeld's career and influence and bibliographies of his publications, see Merton, Coleman and Rossi (1979) and Sills (1987). For two autobiographical accounts of his career, see Lazarsfeld (1969, 1975). For reviews of his work in mass communication, including unpublished materials and correspondence, see Converse (1987), Hyman (1991), Pasanella (1994), and Rogers (1994).

which moved in 1940 to Columbia University where it became the Bureau of Applied Social Research in 1944. (It survives today with a quite different mission as the Center for the Social Sciences.)

From 1937 until he more or less abandoned the field of communication research in the early 1960s, Lazarsfeld and his colleagues carried out a large number of studies. There were, of course, interactions with and influences from scholars at such universities as Chicago and Michigan, but the world of commercial radio research, centered in New York City, contributed the lion's share of both funds and practical problems to be solved. It seems fair to conclude that the empirical study of the mass media—largely, but by no means entirely, the study of their effects on audiences—initially grew out of the Princeton radio project and flourished at Columbia's Bureau of Applied Social Research during this momentous quarter century.

Only a fraction of this research, only some highlights, can be mentioned in the space available. Much of this research was conducted by Lazarsfeld's students and colleagues at the bureau. In this review, I have only included studies in which I know that Lazarsfeld played a key role. In order to give some semblance of order to this vast array of studies, I have sorted them into three somewhat arbitrary groups: the effects of the mass media, "uses and gratifications" studies, and methods of research.

The Effects of the Mass Media

• Joseph Klapper's 1949 dissertation at Columbia, a summary of what was then known about media effects. This was widely distributed by the Bureau of Applied Social Research in mimeograph form and subsequently revised and published as a book (Klapper, 1960).[4]

• Lazarsfeld's coauthored analyses of two nationwide surveys of radio listeners that had been carried out by the University of Chicago's National Opinion Research Center in 1945 and 1947 (Lazarsfeld & Field, 1946; Lazarsfeld & Kendall, 1948).

• Specific studies of the effects of radio published in two special issues of the *Journal of Applied Psychology* (Lazarsfeld, 1939, 1940a) and in three volumes of essays edited by Lazarsfeld and Stanton (1941, 1944, 1949). These five volumes contain many examples of Lazarsfeld's innovative methodological ideas and approaches to the study of mass communication.

• Hadley Cantril, Hazel Gaudet, and Herta Herzog's study of the radio listeners who perceived as a live newscast Orson Welles' now-famous 1938 broadcast of a fictional invasion of the Earth by Martians (Cantril, Gaudet, & Herzog, 1940; Herzog, 1955).

---

[4]For a useful summary, see Klapper (1968).

• Merton's 1946 study of the impact of Kate Smith's war bond broadcasts—described later.

• Lazarsfeld's study (1940b) of the differential effects of radio broadcasts and the print media.

• Lazarsfeld and his colleagues' studies of the 1940 and 1948 U.S. presidential elections (Berelson, Lazarsfeld, & McPhee, 1954; Lazarsfeld, Berelson, & Gaudet, 1944), which demonstrated the relatively limited role that the mass media then played in forming election decisions during presidential campaigns.

Uses and Gratifications

• Herta Herzog's (1944) and Rudolf Arnheim's (1944) studies of the content and audiences of daytime radio soap operas, analyses that examined these oral products of popular culture as literature.

• Bernard Berelson's study of "What 'Missing the Newspaper' Means" (1949), which used the occasion of a 1945 newspaper strike in New York City to discern the functions that newspapers serve for their readers.

• T. W. Adorno's studies (1941, 1945) of the roles that popular and classical music play in the lives of listeners. Adorno, a German philosopher, musicologist, and sociologist, was among the many European refugees befriended by Lazarsfeld. But in spite of Lazarsfeld's efforts to recruit him as a collaborator, it could not be: Adorno was an archetypical example of the European intellectual who could not adjust to U.S. research methods. Years after his brief association with Lazarsfeld on the Rockefeller radio project, he wrote that "when I was confronted with the demand to 'measure culture,' I reflected that culture might be precisely that condition that excludes a mentality capable of measuring it" (Adorno, 1969, p. 347).

Methods of Research

• The Lazarsfeld–Stanton Program Analyzer, a machine developed to record simultaneously the expressed likes and dislikes of 10-person test audiences to specific parts of a program. It was also used to aggregate responses, so that the number of "likes" and "dislikes" for each portion of a program could be ascertained. The nature, history, and use of this perhaps premature machine have been reviewed by Mark R. Levy (1982).

• Content analysis, the technique of analyzing the content of a document by classifying and counting phrases and words, was named and first used systematically by Harold D. Lasswell at the University of Chicago. At Columbia, at Lazarsfeld's suggestion, a manual for its use in communication research was written by Bernard Berelson (1952). The technique was used at Columbia primarily for the analysis of responses to open-ended survey questions. Content analysis was also used in Leo Lowenthal's classic analysis (1944) of the biographies of culture heroes published in popular magazines, which demonstrated the transition during a few decades in the type of persons generally written about, from "idols of production" (e.g., Henry Ford) to "idols of consumption" (e.g., movie stars).

• So-called "snowball sampling" was developed by Lazarsfeld and his colleagues in order to trace patterns of influence from person to person. Sample members are asked to identify persons who had influenced them in the formation of an opinion. Subsequently, these persons are interviewed about the discussion reported by the first respondent. The method makes possible the identification and analysis of interpersonal networks. Examples of its use by the Columbia bureau include Merton's (1949) study of interpersonal influence in a small city, in which two kinds of locally influential individuals were identified. "Local influentials" are people whose interests and influence are largely limited to the town or city in which they live, whereas "cosmopolitan influentials" are interested in the nation and the world and thus have a much broader influence. Also included are the Elihu Katz and Lazarsfeld (1955) study of interpersonal influence, which describes the "two-step flow" of communication messages from the media to influential people and then to others in the community, and the Coleman, Katz, and Menzel (1966) study of doctors and new drugs, which shows how the adoption of new drugs by physicians in a community is accelerated after particularly influential physicians begin to prescribe them.

• Deviant case analysis, a method of examining the attributes of respondents to a survey who do not conform to the normal pattern; examples are working class people who vote Republican and college graduates who depend on the radio or television for most of their knowledge of news events.[5]

This listing shows an impressive array of accomplishments by Lazarsfeld, his students, and his colleagues, particularly when it is remembered that initially he had no grandiose plan to establish a communications research program. He really cared little for the substance of mass communication; he chiefly sought research funds to learn how people make decisions in their lives and to train others to do research on this and similar problems. Mass communication research provided many fortuitous opportunities to achieve these purposes.

---

[5]Deviant case analysis was first presented in Lazarsfeld's classroom lectures; an early discussion in print is Kendall and Wolf (1949).

ROBERT K. MERTON

The meeting of Lazarsfeld and Stanton might be described as accidental: Two young men on quite different career trajectories arrived in New York from Vienna and from Columbus, Ohio, with only a need for a job and an interest in research in common. The meeting of Lazarsfeld and Robert K. Merton, in contrast, was inevitable, because they both joined the Columbia faculty at the same time. The Columbia sociology department had a vacant professorship, and the empiricist Lynd and the theoretical sociologist Robert M. MacIver were in conflict over whom to appoint. Lynd, who had found several positions for Lazarsfeld after his arrival in New York, proposed Lazarsfeld, and MacIver proposed Merton. In the end, University President Nicholas Murray Butler resolved the dispute by authorizing the appointment of two junior-level professors, one in methods and one in theory. It seems that he was not called Nicholas "Miraculous" Butler during the 45 years of his presidency for nothing.

Merton came from a poor immigrant family in Philadelphia, where he attended Temple University. A private university now, it was then the Philadelphia equivalent of City College in New York City. Merton obtained a fellowship for graduate study at Harvard, where in 1936 he received a PhD with a pioneering dissertation on the emergence of modern science in 17th-century England. The sociology of science has remained a major interest; in fact, he virtually created this field, although he published widely in many others.

After 3 years as an instructor at Harvard, Merton was appointed an associate professor of sociology at Tulane University in New Orleans. He soon became, at age 30, a full professor. But when Columbia offered him an assistant professorship, he wisely accepted.

Lazarsfeld and Merton did not know each other before they were appointed at Columbia; in fact, they barely knew of the other's existence. Lazarsfeld knew why he came to Columbia: to provide a more secure and stable base for his still-struggling Office of Radio Research. And Merton knew why he came: to pursue his interests in sociological theory and the sociology of science in the supportive atmosphere of a great university. By his own admission he had never heard of radio research at the time he arrived in 1941.

Merton and Lazarsfeld must have had brief discussions during Merton's first months at Columbia, but their first meaningful meeting has subsequently assumed the stature of a mythic event. The story has been told a number of times,[6] but the canonical version is probably that provided by Morton Hunt (1961) in his *New Yorker* profile:

[6]See Lazarsfeld (1975). For two other accounts of Merton's career, see Crothers (1987) and Hunt (1961). For two autobiographical accounts, see Merton (1994, 1995).

In November of 1941, Lazarsfeld felt that, as the older man, he ought to do the graceful thing and acknowledge the existence of his opposite number. He invited Merton to dinner, but on the afternoon of the engagement he got an urgent call from the Office of Facts and Figures (the predecessor of the O.W.I. [Office of War Information]), requesting him to conduct an audience-reaction test that evening on a new radio program that had been devised as part of the agency's pre-war effort. When the Mertons arrived Lazarsfeld met them at the door of his apartment and said, as the guests recall it, "How nice, how nice that you are here at last. But don't take off your coat, my dear Merton. I have a sociological surprise for you. We will have to leave the ladies to dine alone together, and we will return as soon as we can." Then he hustled off with Merton to a radio studio where a score of people were listening to a recorded broadcast of "This is War." . . . After the program, when an assistant of Lazarsfeld's questioned the audience on the reasons for its recorded likes and dislikes, Merton perked up; he detected theoretical shortcomings in the way the questions were being put. He started passing scribbled notes to Lazarsfeld . . . . As a second batch of listeners entered the studio, Lazarsfeld asked Merton if he would do the post-program questioning. Merton did, and his errant host said afterwards, "Marvelous job. We must talk it all over. Let's phone the ladies and let them know we're still tied up." . . . This they did, went down to the Russian Tea Room, and talked sociology until long after midnight. (pp. 39–63)

This episode reveals many characteristics of these two individuals and their pattern of work. The visit to the radio research site was hastily planned and they arrived late, when the research had already begun; haste and lateness were two constants in Lazarsfeld's daily life. The research itself was conducted by using the Lazarsfeld–Stanton Program Analyzer. Lazarsfeld played the role that characterized his entire career: the promoter enlisting others to help him carry out his own research interests. Merton instantly detected flaws in the work of others and corrected them himself. And the two of them talked until long after midnight. A truly mythic event, because from this unplanned episode, a lifetime of fruitful collaboration emerged.

Lazarsfeld enlisted Merton that night not only as a communication researcher but also as a friend and ally, and for the next 35 years they informally ran both the department of sociology and the Bureau of Applied Social Research. All during those years, Merton also pursued his own research interests in science, in the professions, and in social theory, and his publications in the field of mass communication are few in number, if judged by the number of his publications in other fields. But they are consequential, still cited and used 50 years after their first appearance. Publications and their use by others are of course the tokens of enduring importance in science.

Charles R. Wright (1975), a mass communication researcher and former student of both Lazarsfeld and Merton, summarized Merton's contributions and added this evaluation: "Less visible . . . but nevertheless important to the field are Merton's many indirect contributions made through his influence on past and present colleagues, former students, their students, and *their* students (thereby the intergenerational continuity of science!)" (p. 379).

Both of Merton's major papers on mass communication were coauthored with Lazarsfeld. The first, a wartime study of propaganda (Lazarsfeld & Merton, 1943), is in effect an outgrowth of the evening when Lazarsfeld and Merton first met. It is a summary and reconceptualization of many studies of the impact of radio broadcasts and propaganda films on their listeners and readers.

The second joint publication (Merton & Lazarsfeld, 1948) is an analysis of what today are called "culture wars," then largely limited to conflicts between advocates of popular culture and high culture. The core of the article was written by Merton, who, using his skills as a sociologist, pointed out that the mass media often perform three functions for society. They confer status on individuals whether deserved or not: O. J. Simpson, the sports commentator and former football star who was tried for the murder of his ex-wife and her friend, is an excellent contemporary example. They help enforce social norms; until recently, I suppose, a major lesson taught by the mass media is that crime does not pay, as the bad guys always get caught. And they perform what Merton called a "narcotizing dysfunction"; they degrade listeners and viewers into passivity, into becoming what are today called "couch potatoes." I have deliberately used contemporary examples and vocabulary to emphasize the continuing relevance of an analysis published nearly 50 years ago.

Merton's book (1946) on a radio war bond drive is a classic example of what is known at Columbia, and elsewhere, as "firehouse research." Something happens in the world, often an unscheduled event such as a disaster that calls for research, and with little time for adequate preparation, a research plan is made and carried out. Lazarsfeld (1975) himself provided an account of the origins of *Mass Persuasion:*

> On one occasion, Merton carried out a full study in which the linkage between a public relations effort and the reaction of the audience was examined in detail and its general implications extrapolated. During the war, great efforts were made to sell war bonds. One of the more specialized efforts was staged by CBS. The popular entertainer Kate Smith [the singer who made "God Bless America" the nation's unofficial national anthem] remained on the air for twenty-four hours and returned every fifteen minutes, urging people to buy war bonds. The episode seemed almost as bizarre as "The Invasion from Mars" five years earlier, and again I obtained from Frank Stanton the necessary funds to arrange for a hundred interviews with people who had pledged over the telephone to purchase war bonds. Why had they done so? (p. 50)

(Lazarsfeld described this event as bizarre because he believed that nothing like it had ever taken place before on radio. This Kate Smith fund-raiser and a few others of its time were to serve as the models for what became in the television era the "telethon.")

Merton derived a great deal of sociological relevance from his analysis of these qualitative interviews. His major finding concerned the importance of perceived sincerity: Listeners who perceived Kate Smith to be sincere responded positively to her appeal. Related to this is Merton's concept of "pseudo-*Gemeinschaft*," a feeling created by Kate Smith that her listeners were intimates, members of a community, not members of a manipulated mass audience. This finding alone has stimulated considerable research.

Ironically for a scholar who was brought to Columbia to teach social theory, Merton coauthored a 1946 journal article on interviewing that was subsequently expanded into a book (Merton, Fiske, & Kendall, 1956). The method described, the focused interview, was first developed in the course of Merton's work with Lazarsfeld on the effects of indoctrination films shown to U.S. soldiers during World War II. Briefly, the technique is to relate specific moments or episodes in the film to specific reactions of individual members of test audiences, with the ultimate goal of changing, enhancing, eliminating, or improving those episodes found to be more or less effective. The term *focus group* is now widely used by commercial and political researchers to designate pretests of products or political ideas in small groups recruited for this purpose.

This has been a hasty review of the history of communication research at Columbia University. My account, in focusing on three individuals, has necessarily slighted the contributions of others; it is obviously both parochial and insular, in the sense that I have not related these developments to those in other research centers. But it is fair to say that there were not many significant developments elsewhere at this time. Stanton and Lazarsfeld arrived in New York at a moment when audience research really did not exist until they created it, and certainly no sociologist had paid any attention to radio audiences until Merton did. After all, that is what pioneers are for.

ACKNOWLEDGMENTS

An earlier version of this chapter was presented at The Freedom Forum Media Studies Center, Columbia University, on February 13, 1995. The author is deeply indebted to Albert E. Gollin for substantive and editorial suggestions.

REFERENCES

Adorno, T. W. (1941). The radio symphony: An experiment in theory. In P. F. Lazarsfeld & F. Stanton (Eds.), *Radio research 1941* (pp. 110–139). New York: Duell, Sloan & Pearce.

Adorno, T. W. (1945). A social critique of radio music. *The Kenyon Review, 7,* 208–217.

Adorno, T. W. (1969). Scientific experiences of a European scholar in America. In D. Fleming & B. Bailyn (Eds.), *The intellectual migration: Europe and America, 1930–1960* (pp. 338–370). Cambridge, MA: Harvard University Press.

Arnheim, R. (1944). The world of the daytime serial. In P. F. Lazarsfeld & F. Stanton (Eds.), *Radio research 1942–1943.* New York: Duell, Sloan & Pearce.

Berelson, B. (1949). What "missing the newspaper" means. In P. F. Lazarsfeld & F. Stanton (Eds.), *Communications research 1948–1949* (pp. 111–129). New York: Harper & Brothers.

Berelson, B. (1952). *Content analysis in communication research.* Glencoe, IL: The Free Press.

Berelson, B., Lazarsfeld, P. F., & McPhee, W. (1954). *Voting: A study of opinion formation in a presidential campaign.* Chicago: University of Chicago Press.

Cantril, H., Gaudet, H., & Herzog, H. (1940). *The Invasion from Mars: A study in the psychology of panic.* Princeton, NJ: Princeton University Press.

Coleman, J. S., Katz, E., & Menzel, H. (1966). *Medical innovation: A diffusion study.* Indianapolis: Bobbs-Merrill.

Converse, J. M. (1987). *Survey research in the United States: Roots and emergence 1890–1960.* Berkeley and Los Angeles: University of California Press.

Crothers, C. (1987). *Merton.* New York: Methuen.

Herzog, H. (1944). What do we really know about day-time serial listeners? In P. F. Lazarsfeld & F. Stanton (Eds.), *Radio research 1942–1943* (pp. 3–33). New York: Duell, Sloan & Pearce.

Herzog, H. (1955). Why did people believe in the "Invasion from Mars"? In P. F. Lazarsfeld & M. Rosenberg (Eds.), *The language of social research* (pp. 420–428). Glencoe, IL: The Free Press.

Hunt, M. (1961, January 28). How does it come to be so? *The New Yorker, 36,* 39-63.

Hyman, H. H. (1991). *Taking society's measure: A personal history of survey research.* New York: Russell Sage Foundation.

Katz, E., & Lazarsfeld, P. F. (1955). *Personal influence: The part played by people in the flow of mass communication.* New York: The Free Press.

Kendall, P. L., & Wolf, K. M. (1949). The analysis of deviant cases in communications research. In P. F. Lazarsfeld & F. Stanton (Eds.), *Communications research 1948–1949.* New York: Harper & Brothers.

Klapper, J. T. (1960). *The effects of mass communication.* Glencoe, IL: The Free Press.

Klapper, J. T. (1968). Communications, mass: Effects. In D. L. Sills (Ed.), *International encyclopedia of the social sciences* (Vol. 3, pp. 81–90). New York: Macmillan and The Free Press.

Lazarsfeld, P. F. (Ed.). (1939). [Special issue]. *Journal of Applied Psychology, 23,* 1–219.

Lazarsfeld, P. F. (Ed.). (1940a). Progress in radio research [Special issue]. *Journal of Applied Psychology, 24,* 661–870.

Lazarsfeld, P. F. (1940b). *Radio and the printed page: An introduction to the study of radio and its role in the communication of ideas.* New York: Duell, Sloan & Pearce.

Lazarsfeld, P. F. (1969). An episode in the history of social research: A memoir. In D. Fleming & B. Bailyn (Eds.), *The intellectual migration: Europe and America, 1930–1960* (pp. 270–337). Cambridge, MA: Harvard University Press.

Lazarsfeld, P. F. (1975). Working with Merton. In L. A. Coser (Ed.), *The idea of social structure: Papers in honor of Robert K. Merton* (pp. 35–66). New York: Harcourt Brace.

Lazarsfeld, P. F., Berelson, B., & Gaudet, H. (1944). *The people's choice: How the voter makes up his mind in a presidential campaign.* New York: Duell, Sloan & Pearce.

Lazarsfeld, P. F., & Field, H. (1946). *The people look at radio*. Chapel Hill, NC: University of North Carolina Press.

Lazarsfeld, P. F., & Kendall, P. (1948). *Radio listening in America: The people look at radio—again*. New York: Prentice-Hall.

Lazarsfeld, P. F., & Merton, R. K. (1943). Studies in radio and film propaganda. New York Academy of Sciences, *Transactions* (Series 2, 6), 58–79.

Lazarsfeld, P. F., & Stanton, F. (Eds.). (1941). *Radio research 1941*. New York: Duell, Sloan & Pearce.

Lazarsfeld, P. F., & Stanton, F. (Eds.). (1944). *Radio research 1942–1943*. New York: Duell, Sloan & Pearce.

Lazarsfeld, P. F., & Stanton, F. (Eds.). (1949). *Communications research 1948–1949*. New York: Harper & Brothers.

Levy, M. R. (1982). The Lazarsfeld–Stanton program analyzer. *Journal of Communication, 32*, 30–38.

Lowenthal, L. (1944). Biographies in popular magazines. In P. F. Lazarsfeld & F. Stanton (Eds.), *Radio research 1942–1943* (pp. 507–548). New York: Duell, Sloan & Pearce.

Merton, R. K. (1946). *Mass persuasion*. New York: Harper & Brothers.

Merton, R. K. (1949). Patterns of influence: A study of interpersonal influence and communications behavior in a local community. In P. F. Lazarsfeld & F. Stanton (Eds.), *Communications research 1948–1949* (pp. 180–219). New York: Harper & Brothers.

Merton, R. K. (1994). *A life of learning* (Occasional Paper No. 25). New York: American Council of Learned Societies.

Merton, R. K. (1995). *Working with Lazarsfeld*. Unpublished manuscript.

Merton, R. K., Coleman, J. S., & Rossi, P. H. (Eds.). (1979). *Qualitative and quantitative social research: Papers in honor of Paul F. Lazarsfeld*. New York: The Free Press.

Merton, R. K., Fiske, M., & Kendall, P. L. (1956). *The focused interview*. New York: The Free Press.

Merton, R. K., & Lazarsfeld, P. K. (1948). Mass communication, popular taste, and organized social action. In L. Bryson (Ed.), *The communication of ideas* (pp. 95–118). New York: Harper & Brothers.

Pasanella, A. K. (1994). *The mind traveller: A guide to Paul F. Lazarsfeld's communication research papers* (Special report). New York: The Freedom Forum Media Studies Center.

Rogers, E. M. (1994). *A history of communication study: A biographical approach*. New York: The Free Press.

Sills, D. L. (1987). Paul F. Lazarsfeld: 1901–1976. National Academy of Sciences, *Biographical Memoirs* (Vol. 56, pp. 251–282). Washington: The National Academy Press.

Wallace, D. (1959). A tribute to the second sigma. *Public Opinion Quarterly, 23*, 311–325.

Wright, C. R. (1975). Social structure and mass communications behavior: Exploring patterns through constructional analysis. In L. A. Coser (Ed.), *The idea of social structure: Papers in honor of Robert K. Merton* (pp. 379–413). New York: Harcourt Brace.

Chapter 9

A Conversation
With Frank Stanton

The following interview with Frank Stanton was conducted in 1976 for the Advertising Research Foundation's film *The Founding Fathers of Advertising Research*, which was produced in commemoration of the foundation's 40th anniversary. The interview, conducted by Rena Bartos, is reprinted here from pp. 43–46 of the 50th anniversary issue of the *Journal of Advertising Research* Copyright © 1976, by the Advertising Research Foundation, by permission.

FRANK STANTON served as president of the Columbia Broadcasting System from 1946 to 1971. He is associated with some of the country's top corporations as a director and trustee, including Pan American World Airways, Atlantic Richfield Corporation, New York Life Insurance Company, and the Rand Corporation. He has also contributed to the work of such charitable organizations as the Rockefeller Foundation and the American National Red Cross, of which he is chairman. Born in Muskegon, Michigan, he received his BA from Ohio Wesleyan University and a PhD from Ohio State University.

RENA BARTOS is a consultant on communications and consumer issues. A veteran in the field of advertising and marketing research, she has authored five books, including the internationally published *Marketing to Women Around the World*. Formerly a senior vice president at J. Walter Thompson, she also became the first woman to chair the Advertising Research Foundation in 1985. She is currently the president of the Rena Bartos Company. She is also an associate of The Freedom Forum Media Studies Center.

RENA BARTOS: How did you get into research?

FRANK STANTON: I was a product of the Depression in the 1930s, and I had been a pre-med student but dropped out because I didn't have enough money to see my way through the first year of medical school. I decided that I would do something other than medicine and applied for scholarships and fellowships and got a response from one university, where I was offered an instructorship in industrial psychology.

I started down that road and became interested in the field of communications—how people knew whether the information was hitting the target and what kind of response they were getting. And in those days that led me right into radio because radio was just starting. Radio had begun earlier but wasn't a successful commercial venture until the very early 1930s. I was concerned and very curious about how you knew who was listening, what they listened to, and what they liked and didn't like. When I was still in graduate school I developed an automatic recorder, a poor man's version of today's Nielsen device, and trundled around Columbus, Ohio, installing these devices and getting measurements on how much people listened and what stations they listened to.

I'm sure people today don't realize that in the most primitive stages of market research, you called the next morning to find out what happened the night before and the composition of the audience the next day wasn't the same as it was the night before, which led to a lot of errors. I wanted to quantify those errors and did some work on checking the various techniques—the telephone coincidental, the hear recall, and the personal interview.

This introduction to research led me closer and closer to social research of the political nature of public opinion polling. In about 1935, when I had completed my doctorate, I was offered an opportunity to go to work for the Columbia Broadcasting System. I started there in the fall of 1935, and that's the only job I ever had—I was afraid to go anyplace else. But I started there in '35 and organized what essentially was their research department in listening research. They had some rudimentary market research in those days, but the research department became the repository for almost all of the research that was being done in radio. In the early days we not only didn't know who was listening, we didn't even know who had a radio!

Today, with over 250 million sets in use in this country and with the CB rage, it's difficult to believe that there was a period when research started out by just finding out who had radios and the demographics of the radio audience. And there was some early research that I had to do to find out whether the AT&T lines actually delivered the program to the city where the program was supposed to be broadcast. That's the kind of research we were doing in those days.

I got interested in polling and worked with Elmo Roper a lot. In fact, I almost left CBS to become a partner with Elmo. A little later I got involved in the program analyzer and measurements of where people listened, not necessarily to the programs, but where they could receive the signal. I was involved in an FCC hearing in the 1930s having to do with some engineering measurements that were being made on a station that operated in Scranton, Pennsylvania, on the same frequency that our station in New York City operated on. There was some interference. The engineers were fighting about the interference, and they had drawn circles and said this is the way it should be. I got in my Model A, drove over to Lycoming County, went around, and looked at the radio sets to see where they were set. I talked to the people about their listening habits, trying to elicit comments about interference, and then took my data, which were based on field interviews, and went down to the FCC and said, "This is what the listener really does." I was discredited as a witness and wasn't allowed to testify because I was neither a lawyer nor an engineer, and anyone from research, from the audience side, was ruled out as a witness. I sat on the stand the better part of a day while the lawyers haggled over whether or not my evidence could be introduced. Today, of course, that's the basis for a lot of policy decisions. But in those days audience research was frowned upon.

BARTOS: How would you describe the state of research in those days as you recall it? How would you say it compares to research today?

STANTON: Research was not as precise, not as sophisticated in techniques. It was not as easy to do the variety of cross tabulations that can be done today with computers and mechanized tabulating services. It was much slower in terms of development of reports, although I think most management people always wanted the answer the next day. In those days, you know, you would give a timetable for a report that today you couldn't get away with at all. It was fun in those days, though.

I think the fun of any business is when you're in the formative stages, when you don't know that things can't be done. Experience gets in the way of an awful lot of innovation. And we didn't know things couldn't be done. I didn't know anything about engineering, but I had to learn a lot about it and we had to improvise; we had to develop techniques. Panel studies were just becoming an idea that was being talked about in some of the literature but not used by agencies or producers of goods. The idea that you would set up a panel probability sampling hadn't even been talked about. Small-sample theory was just beginning to be used in those days. This was a time when George Gallup and Roper were just picking up after *Literary Digest* had made its horrendous error about Alf Landon's election.

BARTOS: What would you say were the main issues and problems facing researchers in those days?

STANTON: Budgets. Getting an understanding on the part of management that this was an important tool. I had a very enlightened management when I came into CBS. I was encouraged to try things, to participate in senior management decisions based on what the audience really did.

For example, it was research that led us to put daytime serials back-to-back in the early days. When I first came into the industry, daytime serials were interspersed with music and poetry and things of that kind, and you'd get high points on the serials and low points on the poetry. I came up to management one day and said, "Why don't we put these things back-to-back?" I did the same thing with the news. In the early evening hours we had the news interspersed with other kinds of programming. I said, "Let's put all three of these news broadcasts back-to-back," and management said, "Oh, you can't do a thing like that; the audience won't accept that kind of programming." I was pretty confident that the audience would because I did some experimenting. And, of course, when we did it, we got higher ratings, and whenever you can deliver circulation, that makes management sit up and take notice.

BARTOS: In your judgment, what would be the key problems and issues facing researchers today? Are they different?

STANTON: Well, I'm far removed from research today. But I wouldn't think the problems would be a lot different. I know that costs are higher today than they were when I went out and organized field forces to do personal interviews and telephone interviews. One of the problems that research faces today, and this was true earlier as well, is that the end use of the research is not necessarily thought of by the researcher. And there are other kinds of research. There's research for its own sake, and that's very valuable. But in the applied research, sometimes the researcher gets carried away with methodology and loses track of some of the applications of the information. It's a difficult line to draw because you don't want the end use to bend the findings. But you've got to think in terms of how that research is going to be fitted into the matrix of management. I also think that people get carried away with decimal points and refine things in statistical terms beyond the credibility of the original data. This is dangerous.

BARTOS: If a young person were entering the research field today and came to you for advice, would you have any general thoughts about what he might do or what the future might be in research?

STANTON: I would urge that individual to be thoroughly saturated in mathematics and statistics. I would also stress that the individual be exposed to journalism because I think it is important to know how to get a story of a journalistic nature, how to write a report, and how to frame questions.

BARTOS: Do you have any thoughts as to the future of research? Do you see any changes?

STANTON: I'm not sure that I can give you a very profound answer on that because I have been far too removed from it.

BARTOS: I know that you were involved in some projects with Paul Lazarsfeld at some point in your career. Would you care to share any recollections you have about his role and his contributions?

STANTON: Paul was one of the giants in the social sciences, the most innovative man I've ever known in the field of research and analytical work. He's absolutely without peer as I would judge him and, I think, as history will judge him. Paul and I knew each other quite intimately. I was one of two who brought him to this country and put him in charge of the Office of Radio Research at Princeton University. Our paths crossed frequently. I helped start the Bureau of Applied Social Research at Columbia University, which, of course, was Paul's dream. Paul and I were involved, just before World War II, in some planning and writing that led to the Ford Foundation starting the Center for Advanced Study in the Behavioral Sciences. I was chairman of the board when that institution was founded, so Paul and I had been in and out of each other's lives for, I guess, the better part of 40 years.

I spent a lot of time with Paul when we were starting the Office of Radio Research at Princeton. That didn't last very long. Hadley Cantril, then in the psychology department at Columbia, and I thought that there ought to be some work done on methodology in radio research, work removed from the pressures of developing reports on a time schedule and so forth. We went to the foundation for a grant. Both of us were dedicated to running the project as a joint venture if we got the grant. But it took quite a while before the foundation made up its mind. In the meantime, Hadley had become a professor at Princeton, and I moved on into more work at CBS and got involved in broadcasting to the point that I didn't want to interrupt my career as I saw it then to head this project. Both of us got our heads together and said, "If we could go anyplace in the world to find the most competent person to run the project, just who would it be?" We decided that we would get Paul to do it.

We sent Paul a cable and asked him if he would be interested and if he would come over and be interviewed for the job. We gave him the outline that we had sent to the Rockefeller Foundation describing the project. Paul accepted the job, obviously, quickly discarded the proposal we had written, and said that he wanted to write a new testament. And so the Office of Radio Research started pretty much in the image of what Paul wanted to do, although there were some projects that, in the early days, Hadley and I had originally proposed.

Princeton just didn't appreciate Paul. I don't think that the then-president of administration at Princeton was even sure that radio was ever going to amount to anything. It was an embarrassment to have the Office of Radio Research at Princeton, so we moved it to the University of Newark, and then to an office in Union Square. Frequently, Paul and I worked together down there late into the night.

Then Paul persuaded Columbia to allow us to have some space at 15 Amsterdam Avenue. And even Columbia wasn't quite ready to accept

Paul. But the Bureau of Applied Social Research has, I think, brought a lot of distinction to Columbia. And there are little bureaus all over the world now in the image of Paul's work.

BARTOS: What do you feel is your most unique contribution to the field of research?

STANTON: I don't know that I've really been that innovative. I think the marriage of research to management in broadcasting is something that I would point to with considerable pride. The emphasis that was put on the listener as against the engineer in research would be one that I would be happy about. I believe that the program analyzer has been a contribution to the creative people to give them a better feel of how the audience perceives a broadcast. I am also proud of my early work with the automatic recorder, which paralleled the work that was being done elsewhere in the country. But when I became a management person at CBS and could throw my weight behind a national service based on the automatic recorder as against the memory techniques or the recall techniques, I think, perhaps this was something that was worth noting.

BARTOS: Is there anything else you'd like to say on the subject of research?

STANTON: I've been the champion of research in a variety of places because when I've served on boards and things, whether it be in government or in public service activities or cultural activities, I have always stressed the importance of getting the facts and having some hard data before making a policy judgment. And I think that that's interesting because 15 or 20 years ago they used research on a technical basis—that is, technical research, laboratory research, and so forth—but didn't make the bridge to the consumer. And I think this is going on today even in connection with nuclear power plants and some of the environmental problems that the people in the utilities field are facing. They are making elaborate technical studies of the conduct of the energy but are not relating it quickly enough to the human side of the field.

This is true even in medical research. I sat on a committee of the National Academy of Science having to do with biomedical research in the veterans' hospitals, and I remember at one of the early meetings I said, "Well, what about the patient; what's the patient's attitude toward this?" A couple of the medics said "the patient?" as though he wasn't important. And I think it tends to happen too frequently that the consumer or the ultimate user of the product is neglected until the very last minute. A lot of disasters happen as a result of that—not disasters necessarily in the way of health, but economic disasters in terms of marketing products.

BARTOS: I think that that brings us back to the fundamentals of what research is all about.

STANTON: It certainly does.

Chapter 10

The Master Teachers

Wilbur Schramm (1907–1987)*

Let me begin with a story Paul Lazarsfeld told me 35 years ago.

One of the first field research contracts outside New York for Columbia University's Bureau of Applied Social Research was Iowa State College, which wanted its radio audience surveyed. The college-operated station was one of the few educational stations supported by commercial advertising. Needing audience information, it sought out the bureau. Lazarsfeld's assistants did the field work and analyzed the data. Then Lazarsfeld went to Iowa to deliver the report. He had never been in the Midwest before and was not accustomed to being greeted by the president of a college in a long, black automobile. As they rode through the beautiful campus, Lazarsfeld made nervous conversation, asking about the buildings they were passing. Then he saw a steel tower in the middle of campus and in absolute horror heard himself say, "Oh, you have a broadcasting station." The station was the subject of the report he was there to deliver. He would have given anything not to have uttered that exclamation. Fortunately, however, the president took it as a joke and laughed.

Telling me about the incident, Lazarsfeld said he spent his entire visit thinking about his embarrassing slip until he finally came up with a satisfying Freudian explanation. He concluded that perhaps radio as an entirety, from production to reception, was not quite real to him. Radio was something that came out of a horn. People listened to it, and we asked them questions about what they heard, but Lazarsfeld had never spent much time thinking about what happened before the horn.

---

*Director of the East-West Center, Honolulu, Hawaii. Schramm founded institutes of communication research theory at both the University of Illinois and Stanford University.

Lazarsfeld used that anecdote to make a point, for he was giving advice
to me as I became a new institute director; I had just started a communication research institute at the University of Illinois. Lazarsfeld said, "This is
what we most envy you and your colleagues. Most of you have worked in
the media. Most of you know what happens inside a newspaper office or
inside a broadcasting station. We have more experience than you with field
research but perhaps a little less with media operations." Then, in the
fatherly tone of an experienced director, he added: "Don't let the university
get too far from the media."

During the years I have spent in universities, I have come to see communication history as consisting of three main waves: the appearance of
mass communication as a major topic of social science; the influence of
those men we call the "fourfathers"—Lazarsfeld, Harold Lasswell, Kurt
Lewin, and Carl Hovland; and, finally, the development of journalism.

The waves came late, 400 years after printing and 300 years after the first
printed media. However, I do not mean to suggest that communication
studies began in 1900. The Greeks had the study of rhetoric, named after
their word stem *rhetor*, and the Romans had studies based on their verb
communicare. Remember Aristotle and Plato; and in Asia, remember Con-
fucius, the Hindu Bhaskara, and the authors of the Upanishads. Some of
the questions Abelard posed for his students were clearly based on his own
thinking about communication. And communication research emerged as
a significant intellectual interest of universities in the 16th and 17th centuries after the birth of the mass media and the appearance of a newly literate
and affluent middle class.

But when scroll writing gave way to book publishing and news sheets
gave way to newspapers, communication became a matter of broad social
importance. However, it was only in the last decade of the 19th century and
in the first decade of the 20th that communication became a separate and
respectable focus of university study. In this country, the impressive Chicago School showed the way.

Most scholars remained outside communication, coming into the field
briefly, bringing valuable tools and insights, and then going back to the
more central concerns of their own disciplines—scholars like Robert E.
Park, Charles Cooley, and Edward Sapir. Common to all of them was time
spent outside university study and outside university-directed teaching.

Park is a good example. Park's chief teacher at Michigan was John
Dewey. Dewey introduced Park to Franklin Ford, with whom Park conceived the idea of a newspaper to be called *Thought News*. This newspaper
would report changes in public opinion as other newspapers reported
changes in prices or results of elections. But the time was not yet right.
Polling and survey research would not be ready for another 30 years. So
instead of becoming editor of his own paper, Park reported for existing

dailies in Minneapolis, Detroit, Denver, New York, and Chicago. Then he went to Harvard to work on a master's degree under William James and Hugo Munsterberg, then to Heidelberg for a doctorate under Georg Simmel.

When Park returned to the United States, however, he still was not ready to go into academia. So he became, somewhat informally, secretary to Booker T. Washington, and he is thought to have been helpful to Washington in the writing of *The Man Farthest Down*. For a time, Park studied the condition of U.S. Blacks in the South. Only at the age of 50, in 1914, 10 years after he got his PhD, did Park join in building the great social science division at Chicago. A skillful writer and a beguiling lecturer, he not only wrote *The City*, the most popular textbook in sociology of his time, he also inspired several generations of students to investigate racial problems and, needless to say, human communication.

A great deal of his experience, then, was outside the university. To a certain extent, so was that of Cooley and Sapir. Cooley studied engineering at Michigan and taught sociology. Sapir was halfway through an MA at Columbia in Germanics when he met Franz Boas, and from that moment on, he was a linguistic anthropologist. He founded the Department of Anthropology at Yale. These three men, Park, Cooley, and Sapir, kept the idea of human communication studies before university scholars and advanced students until the second wave of communication study, the Lasswell–Lazarsfeld wave, broke on the shores of U.S. scholarship.

Lasswell, Lazarsfeld, and their colleagues Lewin and Hovland were four vastly different scholars, but they were united in their determination to explore the causes and effects of communication. I have sometimes called them the fourfathers of U.S. communication, but such a term is not quite fair, because it does injustice to the Park–Sapir generation and to others. Still, it is unlikely that in any comparable period of time any other four people ever had such a spectacular effect on the development of communication research in the United States or produced so many able and influential scholarly offspring.

In any case, several of the second wave of founders were strongly influenced by Freud in Vienna. A psychology seminar at the University of Vienna was Lazarsfeld's jumping-off point from a graduate degree in mathematics (and a dissertation on Einstein) into market research and later communication research. Psychology at the University of Berlin provided both a home and stimulation for Lewin's research in communication. One of the reasons Lasswell went to Europe was to study psychoanalysis; when he returned to Chicago, he gave a remarkable series of lectures on Freud and Marx. We would do well today, I think, to pay more attention to European communication developments of that period.

Each of these founders had a sharp career change that brought him to communication studies. For example, Lasswell, after only a little more than a decade teaching at Chicago, during which time he had a profound effect on graduate students like Ithiel de Sola Pool, was denied a promotion, because, it was said, Robert Hutchins simply could not stand social science—or at least Lasswell's kind of social science. Lasswell left the university. Barely out of town, his truck caught fire and burned, and with it all his books, research notes, writing notes, and lectures. At age 35, he had just lost an academic position and many of the tools that an academic scholar needs. Whatever influence he exerted on young graduate students was achieved through his writing. When he finally got his professorship, it was at the Yale Law School, rather than in one of the great political science departments. But he was certainly one of the most productive social scientists who ever lived; when he died, the University Press at Hawaii had three books in print by him. Still, there were no more students like de Sola Pool in his graduate classes.

When Lazarsfeld spoke at the University of Colorado in the late 1960s, he said he thought he could identify four historical phases in the growth of organized social research in the United States. The first began before World War I with community studies, which was largely done by social workers. In the early 1930s, there was a second trend, originating with data rather than with problems—consumer survey, public opinion polling, and radio audit studies. These studies became the raw material for the new field of communication and opinion research. At the time, a few institutes were created to conduct social research for its own sake, most typically the Bureau of Applied Social Research at Columbia.

After World War II, there was a third wave of new institutes. These came out of the government's use of empirical social research in the war. Among these were Hovland's program at Yale and Samuel Stouffer's Harvard Laboratory on Social Relations. Then in the late 1940s and early 1950s, still another wave of institutes came into being when some universities felt the need to have organized social research but wanted that research to take place within or close to existing departments. This impetus led to the institutes of communication research at Illinois and Stanford, the research programs at Wisconsin and MIT, and perhaps the Annenberg Schools. But it is well not to forget that these fourfathers were both great teachers and scholars. Rose Goldsen, describing some of the early meetings of Lazarsfeld's group, said there was always "the exhilaration of watching a creative thinker think, of rising to the occasion, and of using yourself to your greatest capacity."

Of these great teachers, Lewin may be the least familiar. He was the one I knew very well. Lewin viewed the world and this profession with an excitement and wonder that never dimmed. He was the Francis Drake, the Captain Cook, the Edmund Hillary of social psychology. The excitement of exploration came through everything he did and said. None who saw him then will forget his thin, intelligent face flushed with excitement, eyes shining behind his glasses, arms flailing as he paced back and forth in front of the chalkboard asking, challenging, demanding of the student audience: "What have we forgotten?"

Lewin was another refugee from Hitler who brought his gifts to U.S. scholarship. In Berlin, his psychology program was one of the best in Europe, and his students were among the finest. In this country, he settled down after a couple of years at the seemingly unlikely location of the Iowa Child Welfare Research Station. But Lewin kept on doing exactly what he had done before, except that now he had disciples like Leon Festinger, Alex Bavelas, and Seymour Lipsett. Because he was worth talking with, his students began to meet with him on Saturdays.

In Berlin, these all-day sessions were called *Ouasselstrippe*. (*Ouassel* means to ramble on and *strippe* means a string; according to the German-English dictionary, the whole word means "prattler" or "telephone.") When Lewin came to Iowa, these sessions were renamed the "Hot Air Club"—a more Iowan term, one must agree, than *Ouasselstrippe*. These meetings were held in the upper floor of a restaurant whose kind proprietor let Lewin and his students sit all day talking, provided they bought coffee. These sessions would go on for 8 hours or so. Norman Maier of Michigan said of these meetings: "The interaction between Lewin and his group of students was so free and the disagreements sometimes so intense, I remember them as one of the most stimulating experiences I ever had." One of Lewin's students said: "I could hardly wait to come to those meetings on Saturday. And then I could hardly wait to dash out and run an experiment."

Like the careers of other founders, Hovland's career came to an abrupt turning point. In 1942, at age 30, he was one of the most promising experimental psychologists in the country. He had been Clark Hull's research assistant and coauthor. Then he was called to Washington, where he found himself chief psychologist and director of experimental studies for the Research Branch of the War Department's Information and Education Division. His assignment was to study the nature and causes of morale in the army and, more specifically, to examine the effectiveness of a series of army orientation films titled *Why We Fight*.

As soon as the war ended, Hovland and Stouffer loaded their data into a truck. They took part of it to New Haven, where Hovland became head of the Department of Psychology and head of the Yale Program on Communications and Attitude Change. They took the rest of the data to Cambridge, where Stouffer became head of the Harvard Laboratory of Social Relations.

After 15 years, cancer cut short the second career that Hovland had built at Yale, but only after he had established the Center for the Study of Communications. The Center was an exciting place of discovery and scholarship, and it prepared a number of young scholars to be leaders in communication research. Hovland did all this quietly, for he was a quiet man. Phil Zambarga called him "the world's most nonauthoritarian leader."

The influence of these founders on communication research within universities can hardly be overestimated. They trained dozens of leaders who went into social science or communication departments and who continued the kind of study they learned from the masters. This generation was more directly committed to the study of communication than the generation of Park, Cooley, and Sapir. Whereas the earlier generation represented analytical research, the latter did more quantitative research. Perhaps Lasswell was the least quantitative of the four, and yet he contributed considerably to the study of content analysis. Lazarsfeld worked chiefly with survey research, Hovland with experiments, and Lewin with controlled observation and experiment on small groups.

But these four scholars also pointed the way for other research programs, many of them outside universities. For instance, beginning in the 1930s, there were centers of public opinion, such as Gallup and Roper in the private sector and Michigan and Chicago universities in the public sector; and commercial media and advertising agencies had begun to establish their own programs of audience study. Educational institutions and government agencies concerned with education built their own programs based on these. Communication had become enormously visible and more attractive as an academic subject.

In my early years as director of a journalism school, I distributed a number of books and papers by Hovland, Lazarsfeld, Lewin, and Lasswell to my students. After a while, students began to come to me with a leading question: "Isn't this something we should be doing?" That, of course, was exactly what I wanted them to ask, and so we started to do audience studies. This is what I want to call the third wave of growth: the incubation and development of communication research within universities themselves.

The Park–Cooley–Sapir generation had studied communication as a part of the great social disciplines. Lazarsfeld's generation had studied it from the vantage point of research centers, outside universities and their disciplines. Now universities began to respond to the challenge Lazarsfeld put to me at Illinois in 1949: Should not universities be more interested in the study of the media? Of course, that challenge was not only directed at departments of journalism but also at speech and education and other departments concerned with economic and social development.

Journalism education in this country dates back more than a century. Some of the names in its early chapters may seem surprising, for example, that of Robert E. Lee, a great hero of the Confederacy who became president of Washington University (later renamed Washington and Lee). He was perhaps the first prominent academic leader to use his prestige and position to back the training of a number of students in "printing and journalism," along with the creation of 50 scholarships to support them. That was in 1869. The program itself did not prosper, but Lee's name was magic and his ideas were widely talked about.

Editors were divided. Henry Watterson of the Louisville *Courier–Journal* declared firmly, "There is but one school of journalism and that's a well-conducted newspaper office." Edwin L. Godkin of *The Nation* and Horace Greeley of the *New York Tribune* lined up with Watterson. Joseph Pulitzer of the *New York World* and Whitelaw Reid, like Lee, supported the idea of formal training.

Missouri gave a course on the history and materials of journalism in 1878. The Wharton School of Business at the University of Pennsylvania offered a journalism major from 1893 to 1901, under Joseph French Johnson who had been financial editor of the *Chicago Tribune*. The first separate school of journalism was founded at the University of Missouri in 1908 with long-time journalist Walter Williams as dean. But some of the most interesting developments were initiated by Pulitzer. He stirred up considerable dis-cussion with his proposal to establish an endowment of $2 million for a university school of journalism. He sought the advice of Charles William Eliot, president of Harvard, a venerable figure whose advice was generally heeded no matter what the subject. Eliot suggested that the curriculum teach students about, first, the organization of a newspaper office and function of various departments and services; second, printing presses and other mechanical devices used in publishing; third, the law of journalism; fourth, the ethics of journalism; fifth, the history of journalism; sixth, the literary form of newspapers, by which he said he meant punctuation, spelling, typography, and so forth; and finally, and this was his big point, background courses in various departments, all coordinated with journal-ism. In some ways, the program's practical tone belied its Harvard origin.

Pulitzer endowed the Pulitzer School at Columbia in 1912 under Talcott Williams and John W. Cunliffe. Eliot's plan cast a long shadow. The majority of the schools and departments that came into being in the first decades of the century followed the practical example of the Eliot program. Development was rapid. In 1910, there was only one school, at Missouri, and four departments. In 1917, 84 institutions were offering work in jour-nalism. In 1934, there were 455 institutions and about 812 teachers. By about this time, there were stirrings of change in curricula.

For one thing, a generation of strong directors was, or soon would be, in charge of the programs. Among these were Eric Allen of Oregon, Carl Ackerman of Columbia, Willard Bleyer of Wisconsin, Ralph Casey of Minnesota, Frank Mott of Iowa and later of Missouri, Theodore Olsen of Northwestern, Chilton Bush of Stanford, Lawrence Murphy and later

Fredrick Siebert of Illinois, John Drewry of Georgia, Nelson Antrom Crawford of Kansas, and Ralph Nafziger, who became director at Wisconsin and was an important figure in the national journalism organization.

Who were these leaders? Their educational backgrounds varied from only high school (Walter Williams) to PhDs. Their discipline was most often English, and later, political science. Their newspaper experience varied from a year or 2 on a copy desk to years as an editor or foreign correspondent. The average time they had spent on newspapers was about 6 years. But perhaps the most important thing about them is that they won the confidence of both professionals in the field and academics.

By 1924, there was even a scholarly journal: *Journalism Bulletin*, which 6 years later became *Journalism Quarterly*. In the first 5 years, the chief articles were typified by "Proof Errors Analyzed" and "Comparing Notes on Courses." But beginning in 1930, when Mott took over and established stronger standards, the publication underwent real change. The number of articles on the teaching of journalism was halved; the number of articles on international communication and the foreign press tripled. Shortly after, the publication acquired some real competition with the advent of *Public Opinion Quarterly*.

During its first 21 years, *Journalism Quarterly* published not a single article on communication theory. In the next 9 years, however, it published 21 and between 1964 and 1970, 119. Only five articles on content analysis appeared in the journal in its first 10 years and only 50 in the first 40 years, but there have been 106 in the 10 volumes between 1974 and 1983.

Clearly, the academic face of journalism was changing. I think that can be traced to the influence of Willard G. Bleyer, who came from a journalistic family, but had relatively little practical experience with journalism. He majored in English at Wisconsin, then taught English in high school. He returned to Wisconsin for a PhD in English. In 1905, responding to his own long-standing interest in how journalism should be taught, he offered Wisconsin's first journalism course. In 1906, he outlined a junior–senior program that he described as possibly "the first attempt to carry out Pulitzer's and President Eliot's proposals for combining instruction in social science with that of journalism, for . . . broad background and some technical training." Journalism became a separate department at Wisconsin in 1910, with Bleyer named chairman in 1913. That same year a graduate program in journalism was established.

Bleyer demanded quality in everything he did. His first graduate fellowship was given to Louis P. Lochner, his first PhD to Ralph Casey. When journalism changed from a department to a school, Bleyer became dean. He introduced his students to content and readership studies. Throughout his 30 years of journalism leadership at Wisconsin, Bleyer maintained extremely close and helpful relationships with his students. When I came into the field, 10 years after Bleyer's death, I found his students in leadership positions everywhere.

When Bleyer's former students talk about him, they usually speak of his contribution in welding together the study of social science and the study of journalism—and his insistence that they contribute to knowledge. In 1941, when the Association of Schools and Departments of Journalism approved a set of standards, it included a rather plaintive suggestion: that instructors be encouraged to carry on research work and contribute to the literature of journalism. Thanks to the impact of Bleyer, and others like him, that suggestion was already behind the times.

By the 1940s, there were name as well as curriculum changes. A few institutions began to call themselves Schools of Journalism and Schools of Communication (or Communications). Among these were such pacesetters as Minnesota and Wisconsin. A few went further: Illinois combined journalism and several other departments into the School of Communication headed by a dean. Stanford, on the other hand, established a department of communication.

In all, the names themselves were less important than the changes. For one thing, a number of schools were looking at journalism more broadly. They were also making room for other kinds of journalism. Stanford's Department of Communication, for example, absorbed radio and film. At Iowa, the Department of Speech beat the Department of Journalism with a name change: It became the Department of Communication, while down the street journalism had to keep its nameplate, Journalism and Communication. Adding the name Communication to Journalism had a deeper significance, however; communication was a social science name, rather than a vocational one. It said to the rest of the university that the study of journalism, like business and education, had joined academia and was looking at its problems and conducting its research with the same standards that other social sciences demanded.

Schools of journalism also found it convenient to establish research units. Forming research units had an advantage: It was easier for their members to get time and money for research. These units also provided laboratories for students to research communication topics. At the same time the students were themselves a source of research assistance. The existence of research units made it easier to bring in talented researchers and teachers from other departments to direct or advise on projects. Minnesota, for example, appointed Robert Jones, a psychologist, to head its research unit.

The next step was the creation of institutes for communication study. But in most cases they were not separate from journalism schools, as Lazarsfeld's Bureau of Applied Social Research was at Columbia. Most were like Hovland's research program at Yale or Lewin's at Iowa. Indeed, most were within the journalism departments or had wide open access to it.

Why an institute? For one thing, an institute dramatized the importance of research and advanced study in the academic structure of journalism. It made going back and forth between journalism and older social science disciplines somewhat easier. At Stanford, for instance, Quinn McNemar, who had been Lewis Terman's psychological statistician, not only taught graduate students but also came to many of our own meetings. So did others, including Richard LaPierre from sociology and Gabriel Almond from political science. Whether these scholars would have worked as closely with the department of journalism as they did with the institute, I do not know. In any event, the institute could appoint faculty members from other disciplines somewhat more easily than could the Department of Journalism.

Thus, at Illinois, we were able to appoint Charles Osgood, an assistant professor of psychology from the University of Connecticut. At Stanford, our first such "outside" appointment was Nathan Maccoby, head of psychology at Boston University. It is perhaps noteworthy that the men who succeeded me as directors of the Institute at Illinois and at Stanford were, respectively, Osgood and Maccoby. Perhaps the greatest contribution of the communication institutes was to provide a focus for cooperation among social science and journalism and students who cared about communication research.

The contribution of journalism schools and communication institutes to research in the universities can, of course, be measured in qualitative, rather than quantitative, terms, but let me record one or two quantitative measures. About 5,000 journalism and communication graduate students are currently enrolled in U.S. universities. About 1,500 graduate degrees are awarded each year. Thus, journalism really made a considerable contribution to advanced communication study.

We can illustrate by events in and around the Institute for Communication Research at Stanford. In the half dozen or so years after I came there, Festinger was finishing his theory of cognitive dissonance. Festinger was in psychology, but he helped teach our students and he talked over his new book with us. Almond and Sydney Verba were finishing *The Civic Culture* and talking with us and others about this immense study of developing countries in Asia.

In our own institute we were completing the surveys that went into the first U.S. book on *Television in the Lives of Our Children* in 1961. We had just published *One Day in the World's Press*, a study that compared how newspapers in 12 countries handled the news on November 12, 1956, when the Soviet Union invaded Hungary and when France, England, and Israel moved to invade Egypt. William Rivers, a former Washington correspondent, was finishing a book. Jacques Kayser, who went from editing a French newspaper to the Institute of the Press at the University of Paris was with us for 6 months, talking about the European press to our 15 or 20 graduate students. Maccoby, who had worked with Hovland during the war, was exposing these same students to the elegance of communication experiments.

I think you will agree that this was a lively time, one that saw the work of men like Park, Lasswell, Lazarsfeld, Bleyer, Lewin, and Hovland flourish. It was a time in which academic work in journalism matured within our universities.

Chapter 11

Research as an Instrument
of Power

Leo Bogart
Newspaper Advertising Bureau

In 1959, I was working for Revlon, a company headed by a gentleman named Charles Revson, whose place in history is assured by the fountain he endowed in the courtyard of Lincoln Center. I had been there just a couple of months when I was called one day by Charles' assistant and told, "Watch out on Monday. All hell is going to break loose."

I had been vaguely aware that a Congressional committee down in Washington was about to hold hearings on the rigging of television quiz shows, but I had never drawn any connection between the quiz shows and the meteoric marketing success that Revlon enjoyed just before it decided to grow up and start a professional market research department, hiring me away from McCann–Erickson to run it.

I asked, "What's going to happen?" and was told that the true story about *The $64,000 Question* was about to come out. That story has been told many times, most amusingly in Robert Foreman's 1958 novel *The Hot Half-Hour.* It describes the sponsor, thinly disguised, picking the contestants as they appeared and deciding who would live and who would die. Of course, I knew nothing of this at the time. The message was, "Find out what's going on and what attention the public will pay." Organizing this research project from scratch was something of a feat in those days, before telephone polling had become conventional and replaced the personal interviews that were then standard, before computers were in everyday use in survey research, and before we had the capacity that we have now to bring information quickly together from around the country by mobilizing a network of interviewers and supervisors. We managed it late on a Friday afternoon with the help of Don Cahalan, later a distinguished professor of sociology at the University of California at Berkeley, but then the president of the custom surveys division of Arbitron.

Our plan was to go out to a cross section of the public every night for the duration of the hearings and to track awareness and interest in what was being revealed from day-to-day knowledge of the players. The key question was whether there was any identification of the sponsors of the rigged programs and what effect this might have on consequent consumer opinion—indignation or possibly effects on purchasing behavior. All of this was duly organized, and the first set of interviews was done Monday night.

By that time all of the evening newspapers, of which New York was then blessed with quite a number, had come out with great blazing headlines about the quiz-show scandals. The news was on the radio, too. To us, at the center of the storm, it seemed as though the entire country had just that one subject on its mind. We had a complicated processing procedure set up, and at 6 o'clock the following morning I got the raw percentages on the phone and quickly wrote a brilliant, two-page, single-spaced memorandum summarizing the data. By 8 o'clock I was in my office awaiting a call from the great man.

Revson called and asked, "Did you do your survey?" and I said, "Yes, we did our survey." "Well, what did you find?" I started to recite to him from my carefully scripted report, and he cut me short after about two sentences and uttered the unforgettable words: "Just give me the net net." I said, "Well, the net net is the company won't be hurt." He said, "That's great. Thank you," and hung up.

THE "NET NET" IS POWER

The notion of knowledge as power is self-evident in the academic world, where we value the pursuit of truth for its own sake. We know that truth also helps us to control the world around us. I want to distinguish the use of knowledge as power from the use of research data—or research process or research institutions—as repositories of power, where the data really have no meaning apart from an end value.

An ad that ran in The New York Times and Wall Street Journal after a New York Arbitron ratings report appeared in October, 1986, said: "We're delighted to bring you a picture with this kind of resolution," and compared channels 2, 4, and 7 in New York for the 5, 6, and 11 o'clock local news time periods. It shows CBS the leader with numbers ranging from 8 to 6.6.

The ad is wrong on four counts. It is wrong because the graphics are a flagrant distortion of the truth, which is that base zero should be zero and not 6. It is wrong because the differences based on a sample of the kind that

Arbitron's meter sample has in New York are of dubious statistical significance. It is wrong because the validity of the meter measurement as a true count of the audience is dubious. And it is wrong because, to my mind, it has nothing to do with the nature of news or of how information is processed or how communication works.

We are all aware that there is a staggering imbalance between the measurements that are shown for daily exposure to any and all news media and the inability—constantly being documented by the polls—of people to play back some of the most elementary pieces of information in the news that they are, in fact, being exposed to daily. Somehow the opportunity for exposure is not automatically translated into a mental connection. Let me illustrate this with another example.

Deborah Lipstadt's 1986 book, *Beyond Belief*, describes the treatment by the U.S. press of what is today called the Holocaust and shows that there was in fact very substantial coverage by the news media of all the events that were going on at the various stages of the extermination process. Although these were not displayed with the degree of prominence that might in retrospect seem appropriate, the information was there for people to get.

As it happens, in 1947, when I was looking for a theme for my master's thesis, I selected as my subject the impact of what I called "the European Jewish catastrophe" on U.S. Jews. While researching the topic, I went out and talked to about 100 people in Jewish neighborhoods in Chicago. Looking back at the interviews, I am shocked by the fact that I failed to ask, "How did you find out about this? How did you learn what was going on?" At the time, I assumed there was no reason to ask. A few years ago, at a meeting of the Association for Education in Journalism, there was a paper presented on the treatment of the Holocaust by the U.S. press. The speaker asked, "Who could have known these events were taking place?" I raised my hand, but of course, no one paid attention, including the speaker, who went ahead blithely pursuing his thesis that, of course, nobody could possibly have known about what was happening. But having lived through those years, I knew perfectly well that those obscure items, one inch high in the middle pages of *The New York Times*, were being devoured, discussed, and fed into the mainstream of conversation and thought of people concerned with the subject.

Consider the obscure little half-inch item that I just noticed buried somewhere in the back of *The Times*: "Sheikh Yamani has gone to live in Switzerland." Who pays attention to that until everything hits the fan in Riyadh? Then suddenly, it becomes an important political item. My point is simply that the mere exposure of people to information—as measured in the way that we conventionally measure it—is not in itself an index of the impact of that information.

We can extend that reasoning if we contrast the reaction to the Iran/Contra affair both by the press and by the public and the reaction to the first revelations of the Watergate break-in. I recall Katharine Graham's amazement very shortly after the *Washington Post* started covering the Watergate story. Nobody else in the press had picked it up, and she could not understand why it was not seen as news. If we consider the reaction to the first broadcast of the Senate hearings on the Iran/Contra affair, the ratings were not only extremely low, but they generated an extraordinary amount of protest because they were pre-empting some awfully good soap operas. That was, of course, before Ollie North.

WHAT IS A "HARD" NUMBER?

The bulk of communication research is commercial research and is addressed to the question of measuring audiences, rather than to study of the process through which audiences reject or ingest the information presented to them. And there is what I call a kind of pathetic fallacy at work in the treatment of survey research numbers in the business world, which imbues them with the character of the numbers used by the accounting department in making up a payroll or calculating a profit or loss. The measurement of audience size, whether for news broadcasts or anything else in print or broadcasting, essentially accepts the notion that audience size can be taken as a surrogate and working substitute for effectiveness and can be translated somehow into the kinds of dollars-and-cents quantities with which business people are familiar.

I certainly would not pose as an authority on bookkeeping practices. But I have always been impressed by the fact that when one starts digging away behind the numbers that look to be so hard—of which those of us in communication research would say, "You know, those are really hard numbers!"—they turn out to be not so hard after all.

Probably the hardest numbers one can look for are returns on investment or net earnings. Back in my Revlon days at the end of every year, a lot of executives were called over to the factory to work late over the holidays, right up to midnight of New Year's Eve, placing shipments in the mail so that they would show up as sales in the year-end statement and make the numbers look good for the stock market. Since those rather naïve days, we have seen manipulation on a massive scale in many corporations. The objective of U.S. business appears to have changed from the production of goods and services to the making of massive gains on Wall Street. But quarterly earnings statements may look very good at the expense of gains or earnings over the long haul.

In the area of market research, the numbers that seem to be very, very hard and with which audience research numbers are often contrasted are the numbers on sell-through in the marketplace; that is, how many units of a given product consumers are actually buying. These can presumably be linked eventually to some kind of marketing, advertising, or promotion. As a matter of fact, the production of this kind of number—whether done through the old methods of Nielsen store audits or warehouse withdrawal reports—all involve sampling procedures. They all require estimates, a considerable element of human judgment, and often human desire.

Let me again cite a specific example. On one occasion when I was working for McCann–Erickson, Marion Harper, the legendary president of the company, called a bunch of executives into his office. He had been called by the president of Nabisco, a major client, who was deeply concerned because Ritz crackers' share of the dry cracker market in the Pacific region had plummeted. We had to do something about it. So high-powered people were mobilized, and some were sent out to the West Coast to investigate what was going on and why consumers were turning away from Ritz crackers.

When I looked at the data, they were not just penciled squiggles on a work sheet. They were in a very official-looking, beautiful, hard-number bar chart, and they bore the name of A. C. Nielsen. We never did find out what had caused the squiggle, but of course it was a squiggle. It represented an erratic variation caused by human error or the particular sample of stores. Something got screwed up in that particular report. But large numbers of grown people were wasting a lot of time agonizing about the meaning of that inexplicable variation in the trend line.

SCANNER DATA AND MEASURABLE EFFECTS

In the mid-1970s, we at the Newspaper Advertising Bureau were struck by the fact that supermarket scanner data represented a much better measurement of sales at the retail level and of consumer buying behavior than any other available method. Scanner data are the numbers that come from bar codes on everything now purchased in stores. With laser beams automatically recording purchases, both the store and the manufacturer get a very accurate record of what was bought.

We were intrigued by the possibility of using these scanners for a large sample of stores, but our sample was flawed because some stores got scanners faster than others and there was no way of controlling for that. So we went to Jerome Greene, one of the top sampling statisticians in the business, and asked him to help us make accurate national projections using the proper adjustments and weights. We showed some companies the results, and they said, "The numbers are wrong." We said, "Why are they wrong?" "Well, because they're different from the Nielsen numbers." Those were the yardstick. The large corporations were never willing to make independent assessments of market size because they had such a tremendous vested interest in the trend lines and the numbers that had been built up historically.

After we sold our scanning service, it went though several changes of ownership. Ultimately, the new management went to their major clients and asked, "How big is the total market?" And the clients said, "According to Nielsen, it's x million dollars or y million units." The management then proceeded to manipulate the data to conform with what the client accepted as the total, rather than working from the original sampling frame.

This last anecdote is more than discursive. Scanner data are important for a reason closely related to the issue I raised earlier, that commercial communication research too often mistakes audience data for the real effects. There has been a proliferation of services that try to relate buying information from scanners to information on exposure to various types of advertising. When we investigated that relationship, it was possible to relate, very closely, short-run changes in a brand's market share to its newspaper advertising. It was not possible to do that with other media that we analyzed in the same way. In my capacity as an advocate for newspapers, I took that analysis to a rather intelligent fellow at one of the large packaged goods companies, which spends no money in newspaper advertising at all but spends it all in television. And he said, "Oh, we know that newspapers work. That's not the problem. We're not interested in sales. We're interested in building image." In other words, he was not interested in the measurable effect.

If the hardest of data are full of flaws and become soft to the touch, think about image data for a while. One of my first encounters with image data was when I worked many years ago for Standard Oil of New Jersey (now the Exxon Company). I found myself heir to a service called the Link Audit, produced by a company called the Psychological Corporation—a wonderful name. It was led by Dr. Henry Link, a psychologist, naturally. For years, Henry had been going out in the spring and the fall and asking samples of the public their feelings about individual large companies: "Are you extremely favorable, somewhat favorable," and so on.

Quite apart from the fact that people loved, say, General Electric more than they loved U. S. Steel or Standard Oil, for some reason it absolutely fascinated me that they also loved all of these companies more in the fall than in the spring. In effect, their image of them had changed over the course of the summer.

I spent quite a bit of time trying to find anything in the way of seasonal variations in behavior that could possibly explain this. I never did come up with a satisfactory explanation. But these polls, spring and fall, were awaited by people in the public relations departments of these large companies with bated breath. Public relations directors were called on the carpet by their managements to explain why the companies' standing with the public had risen or fallen. To me, it seemed obvious that all of it was nonsense, that the seasonal changes were either reflections of forces beyond anybody's control or cyclical variations in the quality of field work.

I do not mean to imply that real changes trackable by these kinds of methods do not exist. If companies get into trouble, if individual industries are faced with a crisis, that will be reflected in their standing with the public. But a great deal of the variations in these trends represents nothing that is subject to control. And when the numbers are taken seriously, it implies that there has been a failure on the part of a company's communications. It is like Patrick Buchanan's remarks after the revelations on the Iran/Contra affair. The problem, he said, was a failure of the White House staff to communicate adequately and properly the very fine story that they had to tell. The idea that there might be a failure in the policy itself was never considered.

SHADOWS ON THE WALLS OF THE CAVE

Business users of communication research data have a very great intolerance for any kind of ambiguity. There is an inner necessity among people in media institutions to deal with audience numbers as though they were real instead of shadows on the walls of the cave. There is a need for an independent arbiter to refer to when the industry players represent so many different interests and forces. Somebody has to stand above the fray, which is why the late Arthur Nielsen, Sr. has just been named to the Advertising Hall of Fame. Think of that! And there is an unwillingness to support anybody in media research who represents, in effect, alternative sources of evidence, who measures things differently, for example by using a technique like deviant case analysis.

No form of mass communication has more than two competing services supplying similar information, and the figures they provide also tend to be rather similar, because they are produced by similar methodologies. This is true for the print audience measurement services. And in broadcasting, the absolute validity of the numbers produced by the ratings services has always been called into question. There are many possible approaches, and many methodological experiments have borne out the fact that there is no perfect truth. On the local station level, the rate of return of the diaries that are used as the basis for measurement represents a fraction of the original sampling universe. The whole enterprise rests on a frail reed.

Now all of a sudden, a genius in England discovered that television sets do not watch television but that people watch television. So they came up with this misnomer, the "people meter," to give a computerized diary-type record of who is in the room when a particular program is on. It arrived on the scene at a rather critical juncture. Nielsen, the big company in national broadcast ratings, had used a sample of audimeters that electronically recorded to which channel a set is tuned at which time and for how long. Nielsen also had a national diary sample that measured the characteristics of the audience. To avoid ambiguity, they melded the national results on viewer characteristics with the audimeter results, taking the audimeter results as the yardstick of truth.

This was fine during the era of one television set per household. Nielsen could estimate the number of viewers per set from one database and apply it to the other database. But over the years, what with black-and-white and color sets, changes in lifestyle, and increasing affluence, a lot of people have three or more. Program ratings were produced on one basis, and home-us-ing-television levels were produced on another. Theoretically, if everyone in the country had turned on his or her television set at the same time, the total number of ratings would have been higher than the number of homes using television.

Sophisticated buyers of advertising were, of course, aware of this dis-crepancy, but they were locked into the processes of decision making in their own organizations. They all had histories of back data. Nobody wanted to rock the boat. The people who worried about such things were considered the back-room drones. The people making the big "up-front" deals at the "21" Club or at the Polo Lounge do not get involved with trivia. They just want the net net.

So the people meter comes along at this point, and its advocates say, "Look, one data source! We give you a total viewing level and we give you the people level." There is just one little drawback: Once Nielsen started using the people meter, the numbers do not come out the same as those we are used to; they come out about 10% less. Well, now there is a difference of strategy at the research departments of the different networks on how they cope with this anomaly and on how long they can stonewall the change.

"HEY, WE WANT BETTER NUMBERS"

The complexity of all this is enormously exacerbated by the profound changes taking place in the patterns of television viewing, with cable now in over three fifths of all households and VCRs in four out of five of those. But it fits perfectly with my basic point—that numbers used for their own sake develop a life of their own. Ratings and audience measurement represent an instrument of power quite apart from the communications they were originally intended to represent. The reality—for instance, the number of people exposed to news items as opposed to how much news is actually being absorbed—defies quantification. In the way numbers are used in media institutions, research is all part of a bargaining process. Heads roll and people's careers depend on whether the numbers for which they are responsible look good or bad, even though there may be no way of holding them accountable for changes and the numbers may be meaningless as a true measure. In the current discussion of ratings, the battle lines now seem to be drawn between the agencies saying, "Hey, we want better numbers," and the networks holding fast. There are many other factors, mostly having to do with the networks' declining share of the total audience. People meters are just one small additional weight on the scale. But it is an old battle.

In the early days of radio measurement, as researchers moved away from counting postcards into the era of Hooper ratings and sophisticated sampling techniques, they came up with very big numbers compared with the audited circulation numbers that newspapers and magazines had used since the early years of this century. Cornelius Dubois, who was research director at *Life* magazine, pulled together a consortium of experts and started what was called the Continuing Study of Magazine Audiences. *Life* seemed to appear miraculously on the parched media scene in 1936, a picture book and a fast read, ideal for barber shops and beauty parlors and dentists' and doctors' offices. Nobody ever threw out a copy of *Life*, the pictures were so beautiful. One passed it from hand to hand, or if one left it in the trash heap, someone was bound to pick it up. *Life* managed to demonstrate that it had an audience that was a huge multiple of its actual circulation, an audience not only comparable to, but even better than, the vast radio audiences for Jack Benny or Fred Allen or whomever.

Dubois' study set in motion a vast machinery that is still relentlessly grinding away today and that has been revitalized by the computer. Audience data can now be melded with data about consumer behavior to produce pseudodemonstrations of something that presumably everybody with a product to sell has always known—namely, that certain kinds of people are more apt to buy certain products than other kinds of people. Most of the audience accumulated by *Life* magazine represented *pass-along*. In print, the term *pass-along* refers to copies of a periodical that are read by someone other than members of the original household in which it was bought. The concept is inseparable from the concept of "total audience." Newspapers are in a different position, because a newspaper is more fragile in time and gets obsolete very quickly. The measurement of a one-day audience for a newspaper would never show as much pass-along as the measurement of a 4- to 6-week audience for a magazine. Why is this important? One of the most compelling insights of the *American Soldier* series, in the 1949 volume produced by Carl Hovland called *Experiments on Mass Communication*, shows that although we usually think of change as something based on the percentage of people already doing or thinking something, we really should think of change as based on the potential that remains to be converted. *Life*, with a circulation in the 1950s of 5 or 6 million, could generate total audience numbers approaching 30 million readers. Its 6 million in circulation, part of an adult population of 120 million, left room for an enormous number of readers who were nonsubscribers or nonbuyers, whereas a newspaper subscribed to by 75% of the households in its market had only a very small potential for additional pass-along readership. Newspapers never latched on to the pass-along concept until they were forced to in recent years. In the magazine field, publications like the *Saturday Evening Post* and *Collier's*, which required a more thorough reading than *Life* or *Look*, generated smaller audiences relative to their actual circulations. They tried to prove their value in other ways. "Reader heat" and similar terms were brought into the battle.

In print research, the number of *readers per copy* is always an artifact. It is simply the audited circulation of a publication divided into the total audience. This derivative rather than original projection varies widely across individual publications and also for the same publication from one survey to the next. It is great for *The New York Times*, because it publishes more media advertising than anyone else and can carry the conflicting claims of *USA Today*, or *The Wall Street Journal*—each of which is the best-read newspaper in the country—or of the various women's books or other media that vie with each other using the nonsensical statistics I have been talking about.

RESEARCH AND THE STATUS QUO

Research is always used in the commercial world in a very conservative sense to reinforce the status quo. It always points to what people say, what they do, or what they want and is taken as a guideline by people who set policy, whose aim it is to maximize profit and who view the maximization of audience size as *the* way to maximize profit. This is true at media organizations, which try to maximize audiences in order to sell them to advertisers, and at agencies, which buy time or space and try to generate as large a market as possible. The illusion is that maximizing the audience maximizes the effect. If this is true, the *National Enquirer* is an infinitely more influential publication than the *Economist*.

This drive toward maximization of audience size is not unique to our commercial society. It is true in socialist countries as well, and true for publicly managed broadcasting systems as well as privately managed systems. The British Broadcasting Corp. is very ratings conscious, and always has been. But it recognizes that ratings are not all that matters. If we can establish that point here, we will be a long way ahead.

Why don't intelligent businesspeople understand and accept it? They will understand and accept it if one talks to them about it in neutral settings, but once they get back to the office and get caught up in the planning process at J. Walter Thompson or elsewhere, they have to play the customary role. They have to make believe that the numbers really make sense and deserve to be taken seriously. Of course, sometimes the numbers do make sense, especially if one is comparing one kind of bad number against another of the same kind.

The universal access to personal computers and the enormous opportunity to play off different types of numbers against each other should greatly enrich the amount of information that people have to work with in the future. Instead, what is happening is that the databases are becoming further disembodied from the reality. It is like program trading on Wall Street. Formula programs for market planning or media buying take one number from Group A and one from Group B and put them together. What comes out is gospel. If one is a Procter & Gamble agency, it is one result. If one is a Lever agency it is another. But whatever it is, it is gospel.

As a result of the proliferation of all this consumer and media data, the illusion is created on the part of people who have learned to operate a personal computer—or, God forbid, have gotten a master's degree in business administration—that they are now research experts. They endow those numbers with an independent life of their own, and take them as a substitute for the kind of real understanding that only comes from a firsthand acquaintance with primary sources. Some large advertising agencies have abolished their research departments and have started media planning and marketing ones instead. They assume, "We don't have to go out and do surveys; we've got access to wonderful sources. We've got all these numbers." So they put some young kids together as a team to crunch—that is the word—the numbers. There is nothing left of what many of us have experienced pursuing inquiries of our own—of going out and talking to people, trying to get a direct sense of what they are saying, and then taking whatever numbers might be produced from that conversation and saying, "This is what it really means." Nobody cares what it means, because research is an instrument of power and not of understanding. I think the only solution is to get across to the MBAs of 10 to 15 years from now the notion that communication is really a process and does not represent an aggregation of things. That will be a long, hard struggle.

ACKNOWLEDGMENT

This chapter, given as an extemporaneous talk in 1986, later appeared as an article in the 1988 summer issue of the *Gannett Center Journal* (now the *Media Studies Journal*).

REFERENCES

Foreman, R. (1958). *The hot half-hour*. New York: Criterion Books.
Hovland, C. I., Lumsdaine, A. A., & Sheffield, F. D. (1949). *Experiments on mass communication* (Vol. 3 in a series of studies in social psychology in World War II). Princeton, NJ: Princeton University Press.
Lipstadt, D. (1986). *Beyond belief: The American press and the coming of the Holocaust, 1933–1945*. New York: The Free Press.

Chapter 12

Addressing Public Policy

Douglass Cater (1923–1995)*

I have spent a great many years pondering the impact of communication. I would like to give a very brief personal journey, explaining how I got into the field, because I am not by nature or pedigree a scholar or a researcher. I had my one brush with research in World War II when they put me in the USSR division of OSS, the predecessor to the CIA, where I spent 2 years trying to figure out whether there were one or two tracks on a certain railroad in the Soviet Union. I took a mighty oath then never to become a specialist again. I think I have lived up to being a generalist by moving from journalism to editing to publishing to being a college president.

I arrived in Washington, DC, in early 1950, the same month that Joseph McCarthy went to Wheeling, West Virginia, and declared that he held in his hand a list of how many card-carrying communists he had found in the State Department. As a young journalist, I held the high-sounding title of Washington editor of *Reporter* magazine, which meant I was chief of the bureau, and the bureau was just me!

This allowed me to be a backseat driver in the Washington press corps at a very dramatic and interesting period in communication history. McCarthyism represented a newfangled demagoguery. The old-style demagogue was the master of the stump speech who knew how to sway the emotions of the masses by his appeals. McCarthy was not all that eloquent. He did not really give a very good speech. Yet he was a master of manipulation of the communication media, and he came on the scene just at the time television was cutting its eye teeth on systematic coverage

---

*Trustee Emeritus of the Aspen Institute; Author, *The Fourth Branch of Government* (1959).

of the processes of government. He had an instinctive genius for knowing how to deliver and time his messages so that he achieved a continuing impact.

Thus, in the course of a remarkably short time, he managed to distract Washington from the true business of government. He ushered out the Truman administration and ushered in Eisenhower. I do not give McCarthy all the credit, for as Henry Adams once said, "Washington seems to be prone to seizures every once in a while." This was a time when the politicians and the press were prepared to be seized. Even an austere man like Robert Taft had succumbed to it and was quoted as saying, "Let's give McCarthy his play and see how far he can get." That mentality was based on frustration at having "lost" China—as if we had had it to lose.

In any case, I was a wide-eyed, young journalist watching my colleagues witness this phenomenon. The first *Reporter* story I wrote from Washington was "The Straitjacket of Straight Reporting," in which I described how the norms of journalism at that time had put the press into a straitjacket so that they were capable of being manipulated by McCarthy, despite the fact that reporters personally thought him to be a demagogue, not to be believed.

That got me thinking about what I regarded as the great uncovered story in Washington, which was how the press covered Washington. I had not read, and I do not believe any of my colleagues at that time had read, Marshall McLuhan. In fact, I am not even quite clear exactly where McLuhan was in his own writings in the early 1950s. I did read Walter Lippmann and got to know him. I still admire and believe his book, *Public Opinion*, published in 1922, is a classic that can be as edifying today as when it came out. It was Lippmann who shaped my own concepts as I began to do various stories relating to the role the press plays in the United States.

Then in 1957, I was awarded an Eisenhower Fellowship, which was not a government award, but something set up in Eisenhower's honor in Philadelphia. It permitted the recipient and his or her spouse to spend 10 months wherever in the world they wanted to go, looking at whatever they wanted to see. My wife and I picked as our project travel to four countries—Great Britain, Germany, India, and the Soviet Union—looking at the relationship between government and the press in those nations. From that fellowship came *The Fourth Branch of Government* (1959), a book that is 99% about the U.S. system but is based on comparisons so that the reader knows what is unique about the U.S. system compared to other systems.

In that book, I put forth the thesis that the correspondents, not the editorial writers, were the ones who held the frontier by determining the front pages and the inside news pages. Along with television and radio broadcasts, this power constituted a quasi-official, *de facto*, "fourth branch of government." In this country, sovereignty lies with the people, so it is vitally important who communicates to the sovereign. The journalist, who has no more mandate than that somebody who hired him and sent him to Washington, plays the gatekeeper role. This role allows the journalist to determine what is and is not news. But I think this perspective offended some journalists who did not want to be called a branch of anything. They regarded themselves as independent sovereigns, and many of them still do.

Eventually I wrote a book called *Power in Washington* (1964), which was an attempt to define what was different about the power system between the postwar world of Washington and the prewar, pre-Roosevelt era. At the time I wrote that book, Eisenhower had finished his presidency and the Kennedy years were beginning. With John F. Kennedy, we had the first of the presidents whose selection was largely shaped by bypassing the party and making a direct appeal to the people through the primary process. Kennedy was not a consequential member of Congress, but he used the communication system to create the image that gave him the *imprimatur* that got him into the White House.

One would have predicted in those days, as many of us in our darker moments did, that we were fast moving into the age of the president who would be a consummate actor. We predicted Reagan long before Reagan came onto the scene, and it was surprising to me how many presidents after Kennedy were comparatively incoherent and certainly not chosen for their power of oratory or their power of looking good on the tube.

During my White House years with Johnson, I was responsible for writing speeches, which I did not particularly enjoy. It required an adaptation that I as a magazine writer did not find congenial. We had to use a lot of alliteration; it took Richard Goodwin, who grew up in the Boston suburbs and served under John F. Kennedy, to write the kind of deep Texas rhetoric that pleased the president. We called it Perdenales prose.

I made it my job to affect other people's speeches, and I think the president saw me as an idea man. So overall, I had what was to me a very satisfying 4½ years trying to work on the do-good programs of the president, such as education, Medicare, and Medicaid.

In the area of communication I was the midwife who worked closely with the Killian Commission to get the Public Broadcasting Act passed in 1967 and funded in 1968. It was one of the final acts of the Johnson presidency and helped stimulate thinking about communication and public policy.

The Public Broadcasting Act was triggered when one of the people closely connected with National Educational Television (NET) in New York invited me to lunch and said, "Congress has just passed the renewal of the Educational Television Facilities Act. It's going to bankrupt us. Stations are springing up all over the country, generously financed by the Act. We do not have the capacity to provide the programming for them."

I was asked to intercede with the president. They offered two options: (a) to have him sponsor a commission that would look into this predicament, or (b) to have the Carnegie Corporation sponsor such a commission and to have the president endorse it. So I talked it over with the president, and we both agreed that educational television should try to keep an arm's length relationship with government.

Carnegie was invited to do it. We endorsed having Dr. James Killian as chairman, and when the commission was announced, the president welcomed it. I was kept closely informed by Killian and his associates so that we were ready within a week after the report reached us to send draft legislation to Congress to create the Public Broadcasting Act.

This represents an area of my research in public policy—to examine the continuing problem of how to sustain a noncommercial system in this important area of communication. Public television and radio have had many ups and downs since coming into existence when Johnson was going out of office. For starters, they had to survive their infancy under the Nixon administration. We learned belatedly just how difficult that was. Indeed, it is a remarkable fact that the institution continues to survive, although if British television had not provided some of the programming, I sometimes think public television in this country would have gone down the tube.

There was also the Eugene Rostow commission's report on government's approach toward long-range problems related to communication technology. DeVier Pierson, associate counsel in the White House, and I worked together to set up the commission. By the time the report was finished, Johnson was getting ready to leave the White House and was not disposed to embrace anything. So, it ended up with Rostow simply releasing it to the press. The White House remained silent. I could not say what was the impact of that heavily researched report on the development of policy.

When I left the White House in 1968, a number of friends with whom I had worked urged me to consider the future of communication. With modest funding from the Ford, Markle, and Carnegie foundations, an associate and I were able to travel around the country and conduct long interviews with key people in every area of communications. I came forth with a plan for a Communications Media Council, because I felt that communications was too sensitive an area to be headed by a single executive officer.

I also proposed to have a larger council that we would call the Communications Academy with distinguished people from journalism and broadcasting, such as Frank Stanton, who showed a willingness to think about the broader problems of communication and society. All this turned out to be a pipe dream when I presented my plan to a consortium of foundations.

They were not prepared to fund it, even though I had proposed a modest budget.

I went to the West Coast, associated myself with Stanford University and the Aspen Institute. Joseph Slater, the president of the Aspen Institute and a more patient man than I, convened a group that worked on a more modest agenda. He called me in and presented the priorities derived from my report, but they were considerably shrunken. Then he called in Lloyd Morrisett of the Markle Foundation who said he was prepared to commit funding. Bill Benton, a philanthropist in this field, also said he was prepared to commit funding. We launched what was called the Aspen Institute Program on Communications and Society, which had a starting budget of approximately $200,000 a year, which eventually grew to approximately $300,000 a year. I remained at my Stanford University base, with the headquarters of the program there. The program was sponsored by the Aspen Institute and became the first of the Aspen Institute's "Thought Leading to Action" programs.

Of the starting priorities, one was the future of public broadcasting. I would like to think the examinations we undertook and the groups we convened helped nurture public broadcasting through the difficult birthing years in the hostile environment of the Nixon administration. Each year, we held a summit conference on public broadcasting at which we were able to convene key people, including Killian, McGeorge Bundy, and Fred Friendly. The Ford Foundation, stimulated by Bundy and Friendly, began to help fund our program.

We also enlisted Ralph Rogers of Texas, who became chairman of the Public Broadcasting System. A conservative Republican, Rogers served as a great champion of public broadcasting. He attended these conferences along with other people who could exert considerable clout. We gathered around the table and calculated how to stave off those in the White House who thought that it was going to be easy to manipulate public broadcasting.

Another priority for the Aspen program was the impact of television technology on the future of communication. We worked by convening conferences, assigning research projects, and then reconvening and publishing. We identified a number of the problems that have continued to mount with the arrival of the new technology.

A third area was television and social behavior. It so happened that we were founded a few months before the Surgeon General's 1977 report on television and social behavior was due to be published, examining the effect of televised violence on aggressive behavior of children. I developed a close liaison with Eli Rubinstein, head of the commission that the Surgeon General had set up.

Within a few days after the report was released, we convened a review meeting at Stanford. Under the chairmanship of O. Meredith Wilson, we gathered some important players. Over a 3-day period, we examined the full substance of the Surgeon General's report and its implications for the evolution of public policy.

Out of that and the events that followed, Stephen Strickland and I were given a grant from the Russell Sage Foundation to write a book on the whole experience. Thus, we examined the events from the day Senator John O. Pastore called on the Surgeon General right through the period when research was being conducted and finally, to the review of the report and its aftermath.

I would like to focus on what we found, because I think it illustrates the enduring questions about communication research and public policy. In those days far more than today, a single chairman, Senator Pastore from Rhode Island, had a special claim of oversight of matters in Congress relating to communication. He played the role of a Dutch Uncle. He was a well-motivated man who had a decent respect for the First Amendment without being overwhelmed by it.

Pastore had an expectation that social science could replicate what physical science had done in the area of smoking. That was why he chose the Surgeon General to carry on the television violence study. As it turned out, there were shortcomings in HEW's response. The Office of the Surgeon General simply lacked the power to give much direction to the task. Political expedience helped shape the selection of the scientific advisory committee. Bureaucratic caution led to weak decisions. This damaged the integrity of the project.

The social science on this project was frail. Prior research into the effects of television provided a very insubstantial base on which to build this investigation. There had been no study involving children over an extended period of observation. Time imposed other handicaps. It turned out that many of the prestigious social scientists were just too busy with other projects to respond to this very important call. It was difficult to recruit the researchers who would have been considered first rate.

Finally, the communication of the actual findings was confusing. I believe any future historian will be bewildered by the conflicting interpretations that appeared after the report was published. These were led off by *The New York Times*, which got the scoop about 10 days before the report was formally issued. *The Times* carried it on the front page with an erroneous headline and misinterpretation of the findings. It reported that the Surgeon General's committee had found no evidence of a causal relationship between televised violence and subsequent behavior. What the report did conclude in the guarded language of social science was that there was tentative and preliminary evidence of a direct causal relationship between televised violence and subsequent aggressive behavior on the part of some children. Whether this could constitute a sizable number of children, they were not able to say.

Social scientists felt they had been fairly strong in their conclusions, but for those who wanted black-and-white answers, it obviously was not enough. Many critics, including many of those in the press, belittled the report for being circumscribed with all sorts of *ifs*, *ands*, and *buts*. Thus, the report was made a mockery by some, although there were a few press reports, including a story in *Newsweek* magazine, that attempted to redeem it.

Government operates with questionable effectiveness when pursuing social objectives, which, as in the case of television programming, cannot and should not be reduced to legislative fiat. First, the regulatory commission must be wary of activities that come into conflict with the First Amendment. Even if the report's findings had been more decisive, it was questionable how one could use those findings to formulate a public policy that would have been both rational and legal.

The most immediate short-term results in the area of television programming stem from the demands of organized groups, including parents, Blacks, ethnic groups, and women's rights advocates. Both the licensee and the advertiser have shown a capacity to listen when aroused citizens speak. This also raises a dilemma for public policy, for the citizens most likely to speak forcibly tend to be minorities tightly united around a grievance. Such concentrated pressure-group activity may help to curtail abuses, but it may also discourage the freedom and diversity by which creative television can flourish.

In our concluding chapter, we were fairly pessimistic. Although we were writing only 2½ years after the Surgeon General's report became public, the situation, as far as we could see, remained confused and muddled. One could not discover that any public policy consensus had been arrived at by this rational approach of employing social science research to help answer major societal problems. It is time now for communication research to return to that issue and see where we stand.

There have been other studies published, but in my opinion, the broadcast industry has never faced up to the effects of television violence. Instead, it has come up with every alibi conceivable. With the new competition of cable and satellite television, one can only gloomily predict that we have seen nothing yet in terms of both violence and pornography.

Something seems to be relentlessly driving television producers toward the promiscuous use of violence as a way of holding on to a share of the market. It seems at times that violence is used as a punctuation point just in time to break for the commercial.

Working in a number of areas in the White House, I was shocked by how little disposition there was for policymakers to seek the simplest kind of research. We were in the frenetic atmosphere of the Johnson White House, where so many laws were being passed there was hardly time to keep pace. We did not, for example, take account of the fact that the rest of the world was struggling with the same problems; we did not compare the way they handled them. We still do not do that. One may find simplistic comparisons, such as the statement that we do not want to socialize medicine the way the British did. But we do not ask exactly how bad British medicine is compared to ours. We are in a primitive stage in the use of comparative research to inform public policy.

Lippmann, after having examined the phenomenon of how public opinion is shaped, declared that if one were to equate news with truth, one would get nowhere. News is an intermittent, roving spotlight that briefly illumines the events of society. But the function of truth in society Lippmann said, is "to bring to light the hidden facts, to set them into relation with each other, and make a picture of reality on which men act."

I have been preoccupied with this for a number of years. How do we create that picture of reality? That is the ideal. If we do not strive for that ideal, I think our form of government is doomed to go the way of the dinosaur—unable to adapt to the environment.

I see little sign at the moment that we are wedded to that ideal. We are so bedazzled with the technology of communications. We are prepared to sit mute, while our media pump the refuse of this vast wasteland into our home. We do not even protest, except for tight little protests such as those of Tipper Gore, who is fed up with rock and roll music that contains hidden porn. People ask why protesters are making such a fuss, or they offer the traditional response that "you can always turn off the television." Well, of course one can switch the channel. It is a little bit harder when there is a house full of children and the mother and the father are working, and somebody has to preserve that institution known as the family.

I am concerned to find stimulating and creative ways to hook up research with public policy. I do not think that research should be made a lapdog of the politician. On the other hand, I think there might be better ways of creating intermediaries between the pure researcher and the public policy-maker. These are the translators, if you will, who take the research that is not easily understandable and make the best prediction based on examining the evidence. And they must say it in language that the politician and the public can understand. Otherwise research climbs into its own navel.

Lippmann, having dismissed news as capable of serving the function of truth, called for the creation of centers of organized intelligence that would perform the truth-telling function in society. Unfortunately, then and later, he never spelled out exactly what he meant by a "center of organized intelligence."

When I wrote *The Fourth Branch of Government*, I speculated about such centers that could create a common body of information in which conservative and liberal, Black and White, Jew and gentile could have faith. One example was the Bureau of Labor Statistics. In those days, the *Congressional Quarterly* was playing a remarkably good role in providing the organized intelligence about how Congress acted in terms of specific votes on specific bills so that the informed citizen, ready to make an effort, could make sense out of the public policy process.

Lippmann said that without these centers, it was like playing tennis on a court where there are no lines and no net. There is no way to measure what is going on.

REFERENCES

Cater, D. (1959). *The fourth branch of government*. Boston: Houghton Mifflin.
Cater, D. (1964). *Power in Washington: A critical look at today's struggle to govern in the nation's capital*. New York: Random House.
Lippmann, W. (1922). *Public opinion*. New York: The Free Press.

PART III

REASSESSMENT

Chapter 13

Constructing a Historiography for North American Communication Studies

Gertrude J. Robinson
McGill University

Since the 1980s, we have been bombarded with numerous articles and books debating our field's theoretical foundations. One harbinger was the *Journal of Communication* issue titled "Ferment in the Field" (Vol. 33, No. 3, Summer 1983) in which 35 scholars from 10 countries debated the field's critical issues and research tasks. It was followed by Brenda Dervin's edited volume, *Rethinking Communication* (Dervin, Grossberg, O'Keefe, & Wartella, 1989). In addition, there seems to have been a sudden proliferation of theoretical approaches and vigorous debate and promotion of the so-called critical approach to communication studies by a group of young scholars. What does all of this intellectual ferment signify? Why is it happening at this particular point in time? And are there similar debates going on in other fields or disciplines and in other countries?

No one has as yet offered any convincing answers to these questions, although there are some conjectures why such answers may be difficult to find. In a provocative article titled "On the History and Systematics of Sociological Theory" (1967), Robert K. Merton commented that all intellectual disciplines go through a maturation process and that young disciplines can be distinguished from mature ones by their lack of theoretical cohesion. Young disciplines, he argued, are consequently marked by theoretical contest. Communication studies belong to such a discipline, one which has an even shorter pedigree than sociology. We demonstrate that such reasoning is based on a relatively narrow definition of the nature of social science, which Merton himself modified in later scholarship (Merton, 1977).

Paul Heyer, a Canadian theorist, provided a slightly different reason for the lack of consensus in our field. In his *Communications and History* (Heyer 1988), he argued that communication is more a study of *forms* than of *content* and that its issues are therefore less visible as well as less concrete. To study the social interactional role of language and speech as well as systems of writing and knowledge technologies requires interdisciplinary theorizing about communicational practices. These would have to trace the complex and multilayered interconnections between language, codes, meaning creation, and the social production and distribution of knowledge. Such theorization is at present incomplete and thus makes the field prone to theoretical ferment. Although Heyer's conceptualization of the field is certainly provocative, it fails to describe how to go about this type of intellectual enterprise. The contemporary theoretical turmoil in communication studies, I suggest, is not so much a result of disciplinary idiosyncrasies as of a lack of viewing idea structures in their relevant historical contexts.

What would a proper historiography of our field look like and how would it differ from the supposedly "historical" accounts that are presently available in texts like Susan Lowery and Melvin DeFleur's *Milestones in Mass Communication Research* (1983)? In his 1962 volume, *The Structure of Scientific Revolutions*, Thomas Kuhn demonstrated that intellectual work is a "human activity" that is situated in a particular place and a particular time. It involves many groups of people developing unique, intellectual schemas to explain selected disciplinary issues. The development of a field must therefore be viewed as a social process in which various groups of researchers compete for the ascendancy of their scholarly interpretations. Partial, ahistorical accounts, such as the ones mentioned previously, record assorted operating theories, methods, and techniques without capturing the social processes involved in doing the intellectual work. They fail to mention the false starts, the archaic doctrines, the discarded theories that help to frame the questions a field sets out to answer. In Merton's words, "The task of a historiography is to describe the complex filiations of social and institutional influences on ideas" (Merton, 1967).

Edward Tiryakian (1979) expanded on this historiographic agenda by noting that groups of scholars developing idea structures often form into "schools" or "invisible colleges." Here the "masters" carefully and systematically recruit disciples and then institutionalize themselves at certain universities and institutes. Their students and associates spread and perpetuate the groups' ideas through conferences and publications, generating more "carrying power" for their ideas than can be marshalled by an individual scholar working alone. Examples of important schools with far-reaching influences on the thinking of our field are the Chicago circle, Paul F. Lazarsfeld and Robert Merton's Bureau of Applied Social Research, and others whose idea structures I have explored in greater detail elsewhere (Robinson, 1988).

In the remainder of this chapter, I want to illustrate how historiographic accounts of our discipline provide answers to three types of questions that have remained unexplored to date. Historiography provides evidence for the genealogy of U.S. communication studies and their interconnection with the disciplinary developments of sociology and psychology. Historiographical accounts also enable us to circumscribe periods where intellectual schemas changed and predominant concerns in communication studies were redefined. In addition, historiographic inquiries provide means for tracing Canadian and European theoretical borrowing, both past and present, and their influence on U.S. communication thought.

A GENEALOGY FOR U.S. COMMUNICATION STUDIES

Ahistorical accounts continue to perpetuate the "fourfathers" myth, which places the beginning of U.S. communication research in the late 1930s and attributes the first scholarship to Paul F. Lazarsfeld, Harold Lasswell, Carl Hovland, and Kurt Lewin (Berelson, 1959). This "creation" myth overlooks the fact that there were thinkers who worked on media and society issues in other institutional settings before this time. Contrary to the Berelson account, the origin and parentage of U.S. communication studies must be sought in the work done by sociologists and social psychologists who grappled with problems of industrialization and social change at the turn of the century. The site of these first studies was in Chicago; the motivating orientation was progressivism and the pragmatic revolt against the intellectual formalism of Eastern universities.

Different historians of ideas have argued that three to five scholars participated in the genesis of communication studies, developing a novel conception of the relationships between what they called "agencies of communication" and society. Daniel J. Czitrom (1982) named three: John Dewey, the philosopher and educator (1859–1952); Robert E. Park, the journalist turned sociologist (1864–1944); and Charles H. Cooley, the social psychologist (1864–1929). To these James W. Carey (1981) added George H. Mead, another philosopher (1863–1931), and Franklin Ford. There is a great deal of controversy about Mead's role as a founding member of the Chicago group, because he worked primarily in philosophy and did not publish widely on communication issues. Yet, his role as an important source of ideas for later symbolic interactionists seems to warrant the inclusion of his name. Much more problematical is Carey's nomination of

Ford, an itinerant journalist who never went to Chicago and functioned more as a visionary than a thinker (Matthews, 1977).

From a history-of-ideas point of view, it is probably more accurate to consider William I. Thomas (1863–1930) the fifth progenitor. He joined the Sociology Department at the University of Chicago in 1895, the same year that Mead arrived (Coser, 1977). Dewey, Park, and Thomas, all of whom had been born in small U.S. country towns, followed European thinkers in indicating that modern society was different because it engendered a division of labor that had not existed before. They did not, however, accept the mass-society theory, arguing that a moral unity corresponding to the new "economic web" developed by economic progress could be achieved through the technology of communications (Quandt, 1970). Agencies of communication, the progressive scholars argued, would convert the "Great Society" created by the industrial revolution into a great community, using communication technologies to create a platform for the creation of common understandings. Such a belief in communication as the "cohesive force" in society was, of course, part of the Progressive creed.

Although substantial, the impact of the Chicago circle on Canadian practitioners and thinkers has not yet been carefully detailed. We know that John Grierson, who became the National Film Board commissioner during World War II, came to Chicago from Great Britain to study film in the mid-1920s; his "documentary" ideas were based on these experiences. Harold Innis was also influenced by the Chicago circle; his summer course in "political economy" caused him to exchange the study of law for that of economics (Heyer, 1988). Innis learned from Park that communication technologies were important to an understanding of social history and that different communication technologies facilitate different social arrangements. In his 1950 book, *Empire and Communications*, Innis combined the metaphors of "transport" with those of knowledge/power to describe the cultural effects of communication systems in terms of the monopolies of knowledge and power, which these technologies bestow on changing types of ruling elites.

PARADIGM CHANGES IN NORTH AMERICAN COMMUNICATION STUDIES

If historiographic scholarship is beginning to understand the intellectual roots of communication studies in North America, considerably less is presently known about the field's development since the 1940s. Here the influences from additional disciplines like philosophy, anthropology, linguistics, journalism, and speech communication must be taken into account (Littlejohn, 1967). Scholars in these disciplines define human communication issues much more widely than mass media thinkers did at the time, which makes the interconnections, borrowing, and transfers of ideas more difficult to understand and trace. At present, few such attempts exist. In another paper, I argued that there may be as many as five distinguishable periods in which the major questions about communicational behavior have shifted since the Chicago circle created a symbolic interactionist theory of communication (Blumer, 1969). These include the work done by Lazarsfeld and Merton's Bureau of Applied Social Research at Columbia University; two groups of Marxian scholars transplanted to New York City in the 1940s; Wilbur Schramm's redefinition of social communication issues in cybernetic terms; Herbert Blumer's 1960s reinterpretation of symbolic interactionism in Berkeley; and from the 1970s onward, the inclusion of phenomenological and literary approaches to address issues of interpretation. Some scholars reject this theoretical plurality as fragmentation, whereas others view it as an enrichment of the enlarged agenda of communication studies.

It has been pointed out that Lazarsfeld and Merton's collaboration in creating the second paradigmatic change is closely linked to the rise of market research and the spread of radio in the 1930s. In this period, privately owned newspapers and radio stations were searching for advertising sponsors and wondering about the differential impact of messages transmitted via print and radio. Investigators, in turn, were preoccupied with developing new methodologies to survey the "ethereal" radio listener and to help advertising agencies figure out how to charge for radio time. As a consequence, research agendas were redrawn and explanatory paradigms were changed (Hurwitz, 1988). David Morrison (1978, 1988) and others such as William Buxton (1993) wrote about how these socio-political changes translated into new questions for academic investigations and how Lazarsfeld's career blossomed after becoming director of the Princeton radio research project (Robinson, 1990).

Based on the cofounders' development of methods for studying audience motivation, the Columbia Bureau's institutionalization of the new paradigm is well documented. These experiments demonstrated that human communication is more strongly influenced by group membership than by media content (Barton, 1982; Katz, 1987). Much less is known, however, about the synergetic relationship between Lazarsfeld and Merton in creating their theoretical idea structure. It is also not known whether the Bureau's research agenda was negatively affected by government contracts during World War II, which some scholars claim skewed the study of media impact toward immediate rather than long-term effects (Rowland, 1983). Partial descriptions by Samuel Stouffer (1949), Alan Winkler (1978), Lazarsfeld (1969), and Merton (1979) need to be re-evaluated to trace the emergence of the Bureau's theoretical paradigm and to assess the influence of Washington, DC, on its agenda (Robinson, in press).

In spite of its unquestioned dominance throughout the 1940s, the Lazarsfeld–Merton paradigm was not the only one in the field. The famous administrative-critical debate with Theodor Adorno (1969) indicates that various versions of Marxism transplanted to New York, offered alternative ways of conceptualizing media-state relations for both the Frankfurt School (Jay, 1973) and for the refugee scholars at the New School for Social Research (Coser, 1984).

Schramm played a key role in the third instance of paradigm change, which introduced communication science as the new theoretical outlook for the 1950s and 1960s. Between 1946 and 1956, he was involved in the founding of two of the five Midwest communication research institutes (Iowa and Illinois), which began to train a new breed of communication scholar. In Schramm's estimation, these were headed by methodologically sophisticated social scientists who were interested in mass media studies per se and were "travelling with a new disciplinary map" (Schramm, 1983). This map can be called system theory or cybernetics. It offered legitimation for the emerging enterprise of communication studies by embracing the positivistic hope for a unified science of humanity. For the burgeoning, revamped post-World War II communication departments in U.S. universities, system theory offered a glamorous interdisciplinary justification for the field's academic centrality and uniqueness. Of course, Schramm was the initiator/translator of this new paradigm, which was based on C. E. Shannon's and D. Weaver's famous paper, "The mathematical theory of communication," published under Schramm's auspices at the University of Illinois in 1949.

Even this period, however, was not monolithic; rather it contained communication researchers utilizing other intellectual frameworks. Most important among these minor strains was the re-emergence of symbolic interactionism under Herbert Blumer, (1969), a student of Mead who had settled at Berkeley in the 1960s. He attracted such scholars as Erving Goffman, Dell Hymes, and others who established an invisible college with ethnomethodologists like Birdwhistell and others (Winkin, 1988). The 1960s also witnessed a revival of Marxist theory in the wake of Black and student rebellions associated with racial issues and the Vietnam War. C. Wright Mills and Herbert Marcuse began to offer new ways of analyzing the impact of ideology on social organization. In addition, pragmatism and the cultural theories of Canadian scholars Harold Innis (1950) and Marshall McLuhan (1964) began to challenge the macro-sociological and positivistic interpretations of human behavior implied in Schramm's systems model.

Historiographic studies suggest that paradigmatic plurality in communication studies become even more pronounced in the 1970s. This plurality is not the outcome of a lack of theoretical rigor or of theoretical convergence, as Karl Rosengren (1983) claimed, but rather of a more general breakdown of consensus in social theorizing (Giddens, 1983). The theoretical ferment in communication studies is thus revealed to be part of a larger theoretical challenge to the positivistic interpretations of human behavior and the critique of science, which commenced with Kuhn (1962) and Paul Feyerabend (1978). In our field, it is also a reaction to what Stuart Hall (1980) called the mislabeling of communication studies as mass media studies. This mislabeling, he claimed, had three detrimental effects. It limited communication studies to topics concerned with the "functioning" of the mass media. In addition, the preoccupation with the "mass audience" as a social category neglected the "interpretive" contributions of viewers and listeners in the communicative situation. Furthermore, media studies are neither the only, nor the major, preoccupation of scholarship in what is now recognized as a much wider "interdiscipline" of human communication studies.

Alternative paradigms from a variety of disciplines were introduced into our field to provide answers to five theoretical issues, which traditional social and system theories were unable to conceptualize. Among these was the mistaken self-identification of the goals of social science with those of the natural sciences. Kuhn and Feyerabend demonstrated that scientific descriptions are as culture based as other kinds of descriptions and therefore do not provide a privileged means for getting at the "truth" about reality. New communicational approaches were also needed to deal with the restrictive language philosophy on which many mass communication analyses were based. Ethnomethodologists and language theorists such as John Searle (1969) demonstrated that language is not only a medium of *description*, but it is also a form of action and a *social practice* in which humans participate. Natural language philosophers consequently challenged the sociological assumption that the common sense beliefs of actors were irrelevant to the analysis of communicational situations. In fact, as symbolic interactionists such as Goffman (1974) and constructivists such as Peter Berger and Thomas Luckmann (1966) indicated, common sense understandings provide the framework for social role behavior and thus for social communication practices.

A fourth source for the emergence of alternative paradigms in communication studies was the lack of a proper theory of the social actor whose behavior is both interpretive and reflexive. Here phenomenologists such as Alfred Schutz (1971) showed that communication acts involve behavior expectations in addition to common language practices and a common code. Audience analyses have benefited from these insights and are now able to explain the use of different types of narrative forms in different types of public and private speech situations, such as television news shows and conversations.

A final issue addressed by alternative approaches is the "naturalistic" bias of orthodox theory, which assumes that the *logical* framework of the natural and social sciences is one and the same. As a result of this preconception, communication as a social science was theoretically oriented toward the search for deductively related laws and systems of explanation that subsume observations under these laws. Such an interpretation of "explanation," according to Charles Taylor (1987), is inadequate for describing social conduct, because humans are "interpreting" and "learning" animals. Various versions of hermeneutic theories and forms of Marxist "critical" and "cultural" studies as well as film, literary, and feminist scholarship have all addressed these five important theoretical issues in the 1980s and thus provided improved theoretical bases for understanding communication as a reciprocal and a social process (Robinson, 1994).

EUROPEAN CONNECTIONS: PAST AND PRESENT

Historiography, or the placing of idea structures in their historical time and place, I have demonstrated, offers answers to a number of puzzles about our intellectual past. It provides a framework for finding which groups of people developed which kinds of ideas to redescribe the communicational issues of their day. The institutionalization and distribution of these ideas to other groups of scholars provide evidence for paradigm ascendancy. Through historiographic studies, we can also discover when paradigms are challenged by others and whether they result in paradigm shift. Such shifts redirect scholarly interest and give rise to the search for new methodological approaches in our field.

Our thumbnail sketches of different schools and periods indicate that paradigm changes do not follow neatly upon each other but often overlap and intertwine. In contrast to traditional accounts, I have suggested that at least six theoretical periods, rather than three or four, must be distinguished in excavating the field of North American communication studies. Within each of these periods, there are both major and minor theoretical outlooks that complement or vie with each other. Often this vying is as much for and about institutional ascendancy in university departments and academic publications as it is about theoretical issues, although all of these motivations become intertwined.

Historiography also suggests that the mere coexistence of many theoretical approaches to scholarship in the interdiscipline of communication studies does not warrant the conclusion that the field is fragmented. A variety of theories of society and of human communication are compatible with each other and few theorists, including those presenting their ideas in *Rethinking Communications* (Dervin et al., 1989), took the trouble to explicitly tease out their own philosophical assumptions. There is also no evidence on which to conclude that communication studies are theoretically more barren than other social sciences, as John Peters (1985) claimed. Taylor and others demonstrated that this assessment is based on a mistaken positivistic notion of explanation which is unable to theorize the reflexive and inter-subjective learning process which informs the human capacity to use language. A science of communication, according to Taylor, can therefore "not be based on brute data: its most primitive data are always readings of meanings" (1987, p. 75).

Historiography furthermore helps make sense out of the transcontinental borrowing and intellectual transfers that have gone on between Europe and North America since before the turn of the century. It is well known that the Chicago sociologists were inspired by August Comte and that Mead and Park studied in Germany, where they encountered Friedrich Simmel's social-action theory. Morrison (1988) furthermore traced Lazarsfeld's indebtedness to the Buehlers of Vienna and to de Mann. Added to this, there were the Marxist imports from Germany (both Frankfurt and otherwise) in the 1940s, which provided the foundations for many of the critical approaches of today. The 1960s saw the incorporation of Canadian thought through the work of Innis and McLuhan, who influenced such contemporary scholars as Joshua Meyrowitz (1985). The 1970s witnessed the import of French influences through the transfer of film theory, structuralism, and semiotics, which became the basis for the postmodernist wave, which is encompassing sections of our interdiscipline today. At the same time, British "cultural studies" were being received in Canadian and U.S. academies to explore the interpretive dimensions of class, ethnicity, and gender (Hall, 1980).

This very incomplete sketch of transcontinental intellectual borrowings indicates that they have occurred *selectively* either through the teaching of a single scholar or through the transfers of whole institutes. It also shows that they occur in every historical period, although they have not yet been completely documented. It is clear, however, that historiographical scholarship will have to pay careful attention to these transfers of ideas and their impact on North American communication studies. It is far too simplistic to assert that the U.S. communication outlook dominated German and British scholarship after World War II, as Jay G. Blumler (1981) suggested. And it is equally misleading to believe that all novel ideas in the field have come from Europe in the past two decades, as Everett Rogers (1982) seemed to infer. Historiographical inquiries show that scholarship is exchanged across geographical borders, but that this exchange often involves a reinterpretation of key terms and paradigms to fit into the importing country's scholarly traditions (Coser, 1984). To understand where the ideas fueling North American communication studies came from, we must therefore

continue our archaeological quest into the origin and transfer of these idea
structures both within North America and abroad.

REFERENCES

Adorno, T. (1969). Scientific experience of a European scholar in America. In D. Fleming & B.
   Bailyn (Eds.), *The intellectual migration: Europe and America, 1930–1960* (pp. 338–370). Cam-
   bridge, MA: Belknap, Harvard University Press.
Barton, A. H. (1982). Paul Felix Lazarsfeld and the invention of the University Institute for
   Applied Social Research. In H. Barton & J. Nehnevajsa (Eds.), *Organizing for social research*
   (pp. 17–83). Cambridge, MA: Schenckman.
Berelson, B. (1959). The state of communication research. *Public Opinion Quarterly, 23*(1), 1–5.
Berger, P., & Luckmann, T. (1966). *The social construction of reality.* Garden City, NY: Doubleday.
Blumer, H. (1969). *Symbolic interactionism: Perspective and method.* Englewood Cliffs, NJ: Pren-
   tice Hall.
Blumler, J. G. (1981). Mass communication research in Europe: some origins and prospects. In
   G. C. Wilhoit & H. DeBock (Eds.), *Mass communication review yearbook, 2* (pp. 37–49). Beverly
   Hills, CA: Sage.
Buxton, W. J. (1993). The political economy of communication research: Rockefeller sponsor-
   ship, commercial broadcasting and the Princeton radio project. In R. Babe (Ed.), *Information
   and communication in economics* (pp. 147–175). Boston: Kluwer Academic.
Carey, J. W. (1981). Culture, geography, communication: The work of Harold Innis in an
   American context. In L. Salter, W. H. Melody, & P. Heyer (Eds.), *Culture, communication, and
   dependency* (pp. 73–91). New York: Ablex.
Coser, L. A. (1977). *Masters of sociological thought.* New York: Harcourt Brace Jovanovich.
Coser, L. A. (1984). *Refugee scholars in America.* New Haven, CT: Yale University Press.
Czitrom, D. J. (1982). *Media and the American mind: From Morse to McLuhan.* Chapel Hill:
   University of North Carolina Press.
Dervin, B., Grossberg, L., O'Keefe, B. J., & Wartella, E. (Eds.). (1989). *Rethinking communication*
   (Vols. 1–2). New York: Ablex.
Feyerabend, P. (1978). *Science in a free society.* London: New Library Books.
Giddens, A. (1983). *Central problems in social theory* (2nd ed.). Berkeley: University of California
   Press.
Goffman, E. (1974). *Frame analysis: An essay on the organization of experience.* New York: Harper
   & Row.
Hall, S. (1980). Cultural studies and the centre: Some problematics and problems. In S. Hall,
   D. Hobson, A. Lowe, & P. Willis (Eds.), *Culture, media, language* (pp. 15–47). London:
   Hutchison.
Heyer, P. (1988). *Communications and history: Theories of media, knowledge and civilization.*
   Toronto: Oxford University Press.
Hurwitz, D. (1988). Market research and the study of the U.S. audience. *Communication, 10*(1),
   223–241.
Innis, H. (1950). *Empire and communications* (2nd ed.). Toronto: University of Toronto Press.
Jay, M. (1973). *The dialectical imagination.* Boston: Little Brown.
Katz, E. (1987). Communications research since Lazarsfeld. *Public Opinion Quarterly, 51*(4),
   25–45.
Kuhn, T. S. (1962). *The structure of scientific revolutions* (2nd ed.). Chicago: University of Chicago
   Press.

Lazarsfeld, P. F. (1969). An episode in the history of social research: A memoir. In D. Fleming & B. Bailyn (Eds.), *The intellectual migration: Europe and America, 1930–1960* (pp. 270–337). Cambridge, MA: Belknap, Harvard University Press.

Littlejohn, S. W. (1967). An overview of contributions of human communication theory from other disciplines. In F. E. & X. Dance (Eds.), *Human communication* theory (pp. 243–286). New York: Holt, Rinehart & Winston.

Lowery, S., & DeFleur, M. (1983). *Milestones in mass communication research.* New York: Longman.

Matthews, F. (1977). *Quest for an American sociology: Robert E. Park and the Chicago school.* Montreal: McGill Queens Press.

McLuhan, M. (1964). *Understanding media: The extensions of man.* New York: New American Library.

Merton, R. K. (1967). On the history and systematics of sociological theory. In R. K. Merton (Ed.), *On theoretical sociology* (pp. 1–37). New York: The Free Press.

Merton, R. K. (1977). *The sociology of science: An episodic memoir.* Carbondale: Southern Illinois University Press.

Merton, R. K. (1979). Remembering Paul Lazarsfeld. In R. K. Merton & J. P. Rossi (Eds.), *Qualitative and quantitative social research* (pp. 19–22). New York: The Free Press.

Meyrowitz, J. (1985). *No sense of place: The impact of the electronic media on social behavior.* New York: Oxford University Press.

Morrison, D. E. (1978). The beginning of modern mass communication research. *European Journal of Sociology, 27,* 347–359.

Morrison, D. E. (1988). The transference of experience and the impact of ideas: Paul Lazarsfeld and mass communication research. *Communication, 10*(1), 185–209.

Peters, J. D. (1985). Institutional sources of intellectual poverty in communication research. *Communication Research, 13*(4), 527–559.

Quandt, J. B. (1970). *From small town to great community: The social thought of Progressive intellectuals.* Newark, NJ: Rutgers University Press.

Robinson, G. J. (1988). Here be dragons: Problems in charting the U.S. history of communication studies. *Communications, 10*(1), 97–119.

Robinson, G. J. (1990). Paul Felix Lazarsfeld's contributions to the development of U.S. communication studies. In W. Langenbucher (Ed.), *Paul F. Lazarsfeld* (pp. 89–112). Muenchen: Verlag Oelschlaeger Gmbh.

Robinson, G. J. (1994). The study of women and journalism: From positivist to feminist approaches. In C. Hamelink & O. Linne (Eds.), *On problems and policies in communications research* (pp. 191–203). Norwood, NJ: Ablex.

Robinson, G. J. (in press). *The Columbia Bureau during World War II: Master surveyor meets master builder.* New York: Freedom Forum Media Studies Center.

Rogers, E. (1982). The empirical and critical schools of communication research. In M. Burgoon (Ed.), *Communication yearbook* (pp. 125–144). New Brunswick, NJ: Transaction Books.

Rosengren, K. E. (1983). Communication research: One paradigm or four. *Journal of Communication, 33*(3), 185–207.

Rowland, W. (1983). *The politics of TV violence: Policy uses of communications research.* Beverly Hills, CA: Sage.

Schramm, W. (1983). The unique perspectives of communication: A restrospective view. *Journal of Communication, 33*(3), 6–17.

Schutz, A. (1971). On multiple realities. In M. Natanson (Ed.), *Collected works* (pp. 207–259). The Hague: Martinus Nijhoff.

Searle, J. (1969). *Speech acts: An essay in the philosophy of language.* Cambridge: Cambridge University Press.

Shannon, C. E., & Weaver, D. (1949). *The mathematical theory of communication*. Urbana, IL: University of Illinois Press.

Stouffer, S. A. (1949). How these volumes came to be produced. In *The American soldier: Adjustment during army life* (pp. 3–53). Princeton, NJ: Princeton University Press.

Taylor, C. (1987). Interpretation and the science of man. In P. S. Rabinow & W. Sullivan (Eds.), *Interpretative social science: A second look* (pp. 33–81). Berkeley: University of California Press.

Tiryakian, E. (1979). The significance of schools in the development of sociology. In W. Snizek (Ed.), *Contemporary issues in theory and research* (pp. 311–233). Westport, CT: Greenwood.

Winkin, Y. (1988). *Erving Goffman: Les moments et leurs hommes [Erving Goffman: His research in perspective]*. Paris: Editions du soleil.

Winkler, A. (1978). *The politics of propaganda: The office of war information, 1942–1945*. New Haven, CT: Yale University Press.

Chapter 14

The History Reconsidered

Ellen Wartella
University of Texas at Austin

Over the past decade, there has been considerable interest in writing and reconsidering the history of the field of communication study by both communication historians and other communication researchers. The goal of this chapter is to reconsider these new histories of the field and identify their commonalities.

Although each author disclaims any attempt to write a "complete history" of the field, each sheds light on the motivations and experiences of earlier researchers. Typically, the goal is to identify the institutional forces shaping the current field of study with their various industry and academic arrangements (Czitrom, 1982; Delia, 1987; Sproule, 1983). In these histories, the coming together of communication as an academic field in U.S. higher education in the 1940s is emphasized, and there is an explicit attempt to critique these origins and analyze their development. In fact, one motivation for reconsidering the history of U.S. communication research has been an interest in criticizing the so-called received history of the field to demonstrate its shortcomings and to speculate on the motivations of early researchers. Scholars probing the origins of communication research usually follow this course.

At the turn of the century and through the 1920s and 1930s, there was public concern about the effects of the newly developed mass media on audiences. The political scientist Harold Lasswell is said to have coined the term *hypodermic needle model* of media impact; this model, widely believed in this early period, held that the mass media have direct, powerful, and undifferentiated effects on audiences. However, this period before the 1940s was a time of relatively little research (with the exception of

Lasswell's propaganda studies during World War I). In the 1940s, Lasswell's ideas were challenged by large-scale survey studies conducted by Paul F. Lazarsfeld and his colleagues at the Bureau of Applied Social Research at Columbia University. Indeed, Lazarsfeld is often honored as the founder of modern empirically based communication research; he is also honored as a collaborator with various communication researchers in the growing broadcasting industry, such as Frank Stanton, who through the development of ratings research helped to promote communication research beyond the academy and in administrative settings. Lazarsfeld's research questioned the ability of media to influence directly important political decisions, such as voting in presidential elections. What little influence was found was thought to operate through opinion leaders who in turn influenced others. This idea about indirect effects of media was crystallized in the "two-step flow" theory and was applied to other areas of media content, most notably fashion, product choices, and movie attendance in Elihu Katz and Lazarsfeld's *Personal Influence* (1955). Subsequent to these ground-breaking studies, communication research became institutionalized in departments of communication, institutes of communication research, and the like, beginning in the 1950s and continuing through the 1960s; and here it was Wilbur Schramm, who upon founding research institutes at Illinois (1948) and at Stanford (1955) helped to establish communication research in the academy. This is the received history.

As J. G. Delia (1987) pointed out, it was at Columbia that the first historical construction of communication study in the United States was made: In their 1955 book, *Personal Influence*, sociologists Katz and Lazarsfeld attempted to distinguish their research from earlier studies of media's influence. Later, other research monographs (Klapper, 1960) and texts (DeFleur, 1966) repeated this history for a generation of communication scholars who were educated in the 1960s and 1970s. Moreover, it should be pointed out that the literature referenced in these studies also dominated much of the coursework for graduate study in mass communication during the same period.

Delia (1987) identified four distinct parameters of this "received history" of communication study:

> These included (1) an identification of communication research with the study of the media of mass communication, (2) a presumption that the methods of communication research were the methods of social scientific research, (3) the treatment of communication research as an exclusively American research tradition, and (4) identification of the core concern of communication research as the processes by which communication messages influence audience members. Against the backdrop of these parameters, the received view constructed the history of communication research as reflect-

ing a shift from a conception of direct, undifferentiated, and powerful effects to an understanding of effects as highly limited because of processes of psychological and social mediation within the audience. In addition, for many it also privileged a particular model of scientific practice. (p. 21)

How has this history been criticized, and why? First, as Gertrude Robinson indicates in this volume (chapter 13), this tracing of the field ignores the contributions of earlier traditions of communication scholarship, in particular, the critical/cultural tradition. Indeed, several recent historical reviews of communication scholarship have tried to recover earlier qualitative and quantitative work largely forgotten in standard historical treatments. Included here, of course, is the tradition of critical scholarship brought to the United States from Europe as well as the U.S. cultural studies tradition pioneered at the University of Chicago and elsewhere as noted by W. D. Rowland (1983); the tradition of children and media research going back to the Payne Fund Studies conducted from 1929 to 1933 examined by E. Wartella and B. Reeves (1985); and propaganda analysis emphasized by J. M. Sproule (1983).

Each of these critics of traditional interpretations offers insights but fails to adequately explain in any coherent fashion why earlier work was seemingly lost. To simply argue that much of the critique was only an effort to correct the record is to miss an important second goal of much of this important re-examination. Much of this reworking of the historical record was concurrent with a debate that has been characterized as "ferment in the field," essentially a conflict between the so-called administrative and critical traditions of communication scholarship.

Students of the sociology of knowledge report that when there are challenges to the dominant research perspectives of a field, it is common for a preoccupation with history to follow. Beginning in the mid-1970s and undeniably by the mid-1980s, mainstream U.S. communication research scholarship was in considerable ferment, as a special issue of the *Journal of Communication* published in 1983 (Gerbner, 1983) noted. Challenges to the mainstream media-effects interpretation best exemplified by Lazarsfeld and several generations of audience-effects researchers were under attack from a variety of perspectives, including British culturalists like P. Golding and G. Murdock (1978) and S. Hall (1982) who argued that American research contributed little to theory explaining the social consequences of communication. U.S. culturalists such as James W. Carey (1979) and Rowland (1983) also attacked the mainstream tradition for ignoring the ritualistic nature of communication as well as its cultural and political uses. Critical scholars like Todd Gitlin (1978) examined the influences of Lazarsfeld in a searing attack, and critical scholars in the political-economic tradition, such as D. W. Smythe and T. Van Dinh (1983), argued about the limitations of the audience-effects research approach. Most of these critics were quick to warn about the limitations of the scientific claims assumed in these studies, especially that of value-free objectivity. And in the early 1980s, the MacBride Commission report on the New World Information Order (MacBride, Abel, & International Commission for the Study of Communication Problems, 1980) brought home the far-reaching policy importance of the differences between U.S. and other philosophies of communication.

One goal of the critics was to open the academy to critical/cultural scholars so that they and their research could find positions in communication schools that had themselves been rapidly expanding since the 1970s. This had clearly happened. Even a cursory review of research papers at academic meetings in recent years or of faculty job announcements shows that younger scholars in the field are attracted to this approach and are being sought by universities.

Another motivation of critics who have taken up historical study of communication research is a desire to debunk the accepted view of media-effects theory: that is the idea of a movement from strong, powerful, direct effects to theories of more limited effects of media on audiences. For example, Steven H. Chaffee and J. L. Hochheimer (1985) re-read Lasswell's work and found no evidence of use of the phrase *hypodermic needle* to refer to media effects. This term is commonly presented in standard histories as representing the theories of scholars of the pre-1940s when a "powerful effects" model was said to be in vogue.

Of course, during this same period, propaganda analysis was in vogue and did assume powerful media effects. And well beyond communication research, historians and political scientists have written persuasively about the powerful effect of Nazi and other Axis-nation propaganda programs, especially in the 1930s. Later, in works like Fredrick Siebert's *Four Theories of the Press* (Siebert, Peterson, & Schramm, 1956), both the authoritarian and Soviet-Communist press theories were shown to assume a binding relationship between propaganda and information produced by the state and directed toward audiences. The image of "captive nations," long a mainstay of Cold War analysis, not to mention the images fostered in television documentaries of the Nazi period, suggests that this study requires much more than a perusal of Lasswell's writings to see whether he used the term *hypodermic needle theory* as modern scholars have assumed.

One of the ways that this has been done has been to revisit classical studies of the past and to try to re-read them in terms of their particular historical context (e.g., the prevailing common-sense understandings of media at the time, as well as the range of social and cultural events through which the scholar was living and working). A case can be made quite specifically for the importance of understanding the historical contexts when reviewing the various classic works in the received history of media-effects research. Media researchers have come from diverse disciplinary areas—psychology, sociology, social psychology, political science, and more recently communication research—and consequently their work reflects the contemporary view of important questions within their disciplines. Additionally, media research tends to be responsive to the wider currents of social science research issues. And media scholars, as students of an important social institution in U.S. society, have tended to be responsive to the critical issues of the day.

As early as 1931, for the Payne Fund Studies of the effects of film on children and adolescents, psychologists W. S. Dysinger and C. A. Ruckmick (1933) utilized the galvanic skin response (for the first time) to study children's emotional reactions to film content. They found strong age-related differences in the children's emotional reactions to different scenes in a group of these films, primarily the adolescents' strong reaction to romance and young children's more likely responses to violent actions. These differences, they pointed out, relate to the children's different abilities to understand the film content. They then noted that these findings are in keeping with the general principles of developmental psychology of the day. That is, the obvious developmental findings of this research are consistent with early psychological conceptions of developmental and child growth. A colleague and I (Wartella & Reeves, 1985) argued elsewhere that there is reason to believe that the researchers for the Payne Fund were conversant with the more general notions of cognitive development research then being conducted by Jean Piaget in Europe. For instance, one of the other Payne Fund researchers, George D. Stoddard (Stoddard & Wellman, 1934), reviewed the findings of the Payne Fund Studies in a textbook on development psychology that he wrote in 1934, in a chapter that appeared after his discussion of the "rediscovered" work of Piaget on cognitive development. It seems likely that the developmental flavor of much of the Payne Fund Studies can be attributed to the wider understanding of developmental psychology current at the time even when no explicit reference is made to work in the area.

Similarly, the shifting social and political climate of the United States in the past 80 or so years certainly has influenced scholars and researchers in media effects. Garth Jowett (1976), for instance, noted how the waves of immigrant children and concern about assimilating them into U.S. society sparked much of the early investigation of the impact of films on children in their teens and 20s. Similarly, Walter Lippmann's classic study, *Public Opinion* (1922), has been viewed as a reaction to the growing use of public relations during the time and the success of public relations experts had in placing items in the news, as Michael Schudson (1978) argued. In addition, one can view it as a reaction to Lippmann's own experiences preparing propaganda during World War I. His work as a propagandist for the Wilson administration demonstrated to him how easily public opinion could be molded—and this fact shook his belief in the political theory of the day, which held that the average person, when presented with facts, could make reasonable decisions (Steel, 1980). Further, it is difficult to read Hadley Cantril's *The Invasion from Mars* (Cantril, Gaudet, & Herzog, 1940) and not realize it was written in the fall of 1939. Cantril took great pains to identify the kinds of people in the audience who realized that Orson Welles' radio report was a play and not reality. He made repeated reference to the European war and the threat that the U.S. would be drawn into the war as contributing to listeners' heavy reliance on the radio as a source of credible information. Just as Cantril located this study of panic behavior within the historical context of the early days of World War II, I think we can also examine his attempt to develop a profile of audience members who can develop a critical ability to "reject" and "analyze" the radio as an attempt to develop a perspective on how to defend the nation against the Father Coughlins and Huey Longs, the Hitlers and Mussolinis of the day who were using all means of communication, including radio, to enlist followers to their cause. That Cantril had a sincere concern to find limits to the powerful effects of radio cannot be denied in this context.

Thus, to understand the view of media effects adopted historically, including in our own historical context, and the motivations of various researchers in past studies, we must recognize that media scholars live within their society and respond to the shifting concerns of that society, be they cultural, political, or disciplinary/professional. In addition to revisiting classic media-effects studies to re-read them, another finding of new historical work in the field has been to reconsider the importance of certain major figures of the field; in particular, there have been several major critiques of the role of Lazarsfeld and his establishment of an individualistic focus to U.S. mass communication effects research. A number of commentators, including Gitlin (1978), M. DeFleur and S. Ball-Rokeach (1975), and R. Brown (1970), locate the beginnings of the accepted paradigm for media-effects research with Lazarsfeld, although it is not always easy to understand what precisely this paradigm is, as Gitlin (1978) wrote:

> Effects of mass media lay on the surface; they were to be sought as short term effects on precisely measurable changes in attitude or in discrete behavior. Whether in Lazarsfeld's surveys or the laboratory experiments of Carl Hovland and associates, the purpose was to generate predictive theories of audience response, which are necessarily—intentionally or not—consonant with an administrative point of view, with which centrally located administrators who possess adequate information can make decisions that affect their entire domain with a good idea of the consequences of their choices. (p. 79)

That media-effects researchers have focused on short-term knowledge, attitude, and behavioral changes in the audiences for film, newspapers, radio, books, and television seems to be the root of what Gitlin and others called the media-effects paradigm or the "dominant paradigm." One might also label it the U.S. 20th-century social science paradigm, for the conceptions of people in terms of knowledge, attitudes, and behavior is the 20th-century social scientist's equivalent of medieval physiologists' understanding of the body humors of phlegm, blood, and bile. The conception of an effect in these individualistic units of knowledge, attitudes, and behaviors reflects media researchers' common-sense understanding of how to conceive people, and people are the audiences of mass-media effects that researchers have wanted to study.

There is evidence that theorizing about media effects defined effects in these terms as early as 1911 in dissertation research conducted at the University of Chicago. There was a number of both quantitative and qualitative, empirical investigations of media effects on audience individuals that conceive of an effect in terms of knowledge, attitude, or behavior change. For instance, a 1910 dissertation by Francis Fenton Park on "The Influence of Newspaper Presentations Upon the Growth of Crime and Other Antisocial Activity" suggests that the kind of empirical evidence necessary to demonstrate newspapers' contribution to juvenile delinquency is overt behavioral evidence linking a newspaper story of a crime with an adolescent's performance of an antisocial act. Park argued that newspaper portrayals of crime stimulate imitation as well as foster positive attitudes and values toward criminal activity among some adolescents.

Other empirical investigations into media-effects research at the University of Chicago similarly conceive of effects in terms of children's acquisition of knowledge and schemes of life from movies (Stoddard & Wellman, 1934) and the effects of motion picture content in changing children's attitudes toward minority groups (Peterson & Thurstone, 1933).

Perhaps the clearest evidence of the dominant paradigm of media-effects theorizing is a 1922 study by K. S. Lashley and J. B. Watson (the John B. Watson of behaviorist psychology) that investigated the effects of a film campaign on venereal disease in producing short-term changes in audience knowledge of the causes of venereal disease, attitudes toward venereal disease, and subsequent use of contraceptives and treatment for venereal disease. Interestingly, much like later work, this study found the film's effects on audiences to be most pronounced in changing knowledge about the disease and less effective in producing attitude or behavioral change.

The point in relating these studies is twofold. First, it is historically inaccurate to locate the origin of the dominant paradigm for media research with Lazarsfeld; the roots of that paradigm are older and derive from wider influences in U.S. social science, such as a concern with research addressing social problems. Certainly, the notion that effects on audiences can be conceptualized in terms of people's knowledge, attitudes, and behavior is part of a number of empirical investigations into media effects that predate Lazarsfeld. Examination of children and media research conducted at the University of Chicago also suggests that the University of Chicago communication research studies from the early part of this century do not so clearly stand in contrast to later media effects research as some students reading the work of John Dewey and Robert E. Park have led us to believe. Although more work needs to be done, it would appear that both cultural/critical views of communication effects existed along with empirical/individualistic investigations of media effects at Chicago as well as at Princeton and Columbia under Lazarsfeld.

Once we dispel the notion that Lazarsfeld was first to conceive of media effects in such individualistic terms, we must also dispel the simplistic notion that such media-effects research is necessarily rooted in the administrative interests of media industries, another claim by the Lazarsfeldian critics. The exact roots of the paradigm are not at all clear. Moreover, there is substantial evidence from reading the literature on the effects of media on children, from the early work on film effects in the teens and 20s through today's research on the effects of new communication technologies on child audiences, that much of the motivation for this research comes from social concerns about the adoption of these new technologies voiced by parents, educators, the clergy, and social reform groups as has been argued elsewhere. At least on its face, an argument can be made that media researchers concerned with children directed their inquiries to questions posed by an anxious public more than to questions framed by interested industries. For such public forums, it might be added, media theorizing that frames effects in the individualistic terms of how children acquire discrete knowledge and perform discrete behaviors is indeed responsive to the kinds of questions parents and teachers have about media's impact on their children.

Thus, theorizing about media effects in the United States has tended to focus on individualistic, short-term changes in knowledge, attitudes, and behaviors of audiences and continues to do so today. Why this has been the case deserves closer scrutiny.

Finally, critics of what has been the common view of the shifting history of media-effects theorizing have questioned the interpretation of theories of media impact from direct effects to limited effects. Theorizing about media effects for the past 80 or so years has tended to focus on varied perspectives about the relative power of media to affect peoples' knowledge, attitudes, and behavior. Many current reviews of the media-effects literature argue that in the 1990s, media-effects theory has returned to a concept of powerful media effects on people's knowledge about the world.

However, there are still holdouts who continue to promote a limited-effects view (Gans, 1989).

For the public at large, media effects have been and continue to be viewed as direct and powerful. For instance, as R. Davis (1965) pointed out, discussions about the introduction of film, radio, and television in popular magazines have tended to express beliefs in the power of media to affect all kinds of social outcomes. Indeed, in most cases, the conception of how media influence audiences in public discourse implicitly represents a powerful, direct media effect, whether the effect in question is behavior, our notion of childhood, our attitudes toward presidents in power, or the likelihood of our buying designer jeans. The popular literature on media effects, such as Marie Winn's *The Plug-in Drug (1978)*, or on media institutions, such as David Halberstam's *The Powers That Be* (1979), serve to illustrate this point.

Similarly, our political elites tend to believe in media power and to act on it. In this regard, discussions in Congress regarding broadcasting of Radio Marti and later TV Marti into Cuba in the 1980s are illustrative. Implicit in the political debate was a belief in the power of U.S. radio to affect Cuban citizens' conceptions of the world and influence their conceptions into an Americanized view. More recently, the work of David L. Protess and Maxwell McCombs (1991) on agenda-setting on political issues notes that politicians tend to believe that media representations heighten the public's view of the importance of an issue, and thus, the media agenda affects politicians' views of issues because the politicians believe it affects the public.

However, for communication scholars in the effects tradition there have been shifting beliefs about the power of media to affect audiences. These shifts have not occurred, as others would have it, as a shift from a hypodermic-needle model of direct effects, to a limited-effects model of Lazarsfeld to middle-range effects theory. Rather, what would seem to better describe the literature on media-effects theory historically is the following: (a) Each new technologically or socially prompted media problem generates or attracts its own set of media researchers, many of them unversed in previous media research; (b) these researchers tend to believe, much like the public at large, in relatively powerful media impact and theorize accordingly; and (c) as they or others come to empirically test these theories on media audiences within the individualistic paradigm present in media-effects research, it very quickly becomes obvious that qualifications on the grand theory need to be made, usually in the initial set of studies. Thus, the movement to limited effects of media or the notion that media messages affect only some people under some conditions is quick, discontinuous, and repetitive across issues or topical domains researchers have examined. The children and media literature appears to illustrate this. There have been topical cycles of research on children and media corresponding to the introduction and rise of films, then radio, and then television as the most popular forms of entertainment. In each era of research on either film, radio, or television effects on children, similar kinds of research studies are undertaken. In addition, similar sorts of theoretical accounts of how media affect children have been offered, and gradually during a cycle of research, these theoretical accounts tend to point out the conditional nature of a medium's effect on children, that is, that the medium affects only some children under some circumstances.

There can be a resurgence of the belief in powerful direct effects of media, however, and this tends to be the case when historically, theorists have focused on how media affect people's knowledge about the world or schemes of life, as opposed to a focus on attitude or behavioral change as an effect. Such is the cycle of development of the political communication literature, as Chaffee and J. L. Hochheimer (1985) interpreted it. Certainly, what other commentators called the rise in the belief of a powerful media again in the 1970s corresponded to the introduction of the spiral of silence hypothesis of Elisabeth Noelle-Neumann and the agenda-setting hypothesis of McCombs and others, both of which posit media effects in the political arena in terms of audience cognitions of the political climate, not of behavior directly. Interestingly, again, however, these research areas also have been marked by an ever-increasing inventory of contingent conditions on their impact. Part of the reason for this is that as researchers in the media-effects tradition, our research program tends to be one that seeks to uncover the contingent conditions for effects through the accretion of new studies utilizing new methods or new samples to test a grand theory. We have a less well-developed tradition of seeking new grand theories of media effects. That is, we tend not to look for new ways in which media affect society, but rather we are more often looking for ways of refining our empirical examination of the current disciplinary boundaries of what constitutes an effect.

Thus, it might be argued that theorizing about media-effects research has tended to focus on how media affect audience's knowledge, attitudes, and behavior and that shifts in beliefs about the power of the media to effect such change are rooted in the particular historical context of the research and researchers, as well as the tendency in our field to pursue the contingent conditions that limit media effects. How we as scholars of the field view that literature as demonstrating the "power of media" or as theoretically meaningful is a function of the particular historical context from which we view it. Bernard Berelson proclaimed that communication research was "dead" in 1959, because the "founding fathers" (as he saw them, Lasswell, Lazarsfeld, Kurt Lewin, and Carl Hovland) had left the field, implying there was nothing left to study. Needless to say, the work done since 1959 demonstrates his comment was premature. New media as well as new socially prompted questions of media's impact arose to which media-effects scholars turned their attention. Furthermore, contemporary critiques of the media-effects paradigm from the traditions of cultural studies and critical and political/economic research further challenge contemporary notions of a media effect and the unity of the literature.

To the extent, then, that the historical context changes both the individual scholar who is doing the research and the social institutions under study, we need to be more aware of the particular impact historical context has on contemporary notions of media effects and, it follows, the development of theory in the field of mass communication. To this extent, it would be useful to have a historical examination of media-effects research that examines the empirical literature in greater detail and relates it to the historical context of the research. R. Brown's comment in 1970 is relevant today: "The history of mass communication research still waits to be written." (Brown, 1970, p. 41). However, the sort of remembered history of the field as presented in this volume should help future historians write more complete renditions of the unfolding of communication research in the United States.

REFERENCES

Berelson, B. (1959). The state of communication research. *Public Opinion Quarterly, 23*(1), 1–6.

Brown, R. (1970). Approaches to the historical development of mass media studies. In J. Tunstall (Ed.), *Media sociology: A reader* (pp. 41–57). Urbana: University of Illinois Press.

Cantril, H., Gaudet, H., & Herzog, H. (1940). *The Invasion from Mars: A study in the psychology of panic*. Princeton: Princeton University Press.

Carey, J. W. (1979). Mass communication research and cultural studies: An American view. In J. Curran, M. Gurevitch, & J. Woollacott (Eds.), *Mass communication and society* (pp. 409–425). Beverly Hills, CA: Sage.

Chaffee, S. H., & Hochheimer, J. L. (1985). The beginnings of political communication research in the United States: Origins of the "limited effects" model. In E. M. Rogers, & F. Balle (Eds.), *The media revolution in America and Western Europe* (pp. 60–95). Norwood, NJ: Ablex.

Czitrom, D. J. (1982). *Media and the American mind: From Morse to McLuhan*. Chapel Hill: University of North Carolina Press.

Davis, R. (1965). *Response to innovation: A study of popular arguments about new mass media*. Published doctoral dissertation, University of Iowa.

DeFleur, M. L. (1966). *Theories of mass communication*. New York: McKay.

DeFleur, M. L., & Ball-Rokeach, S. (1975). *Theories of mass communication*. New York: McKay.

Delia, J. G. (1987). Communication research: A history. In C. Berger & S. Chaffee (Eds.), *Handbook of communication science* (pp. 20–98). Newbury Park, CA: Sage.

Dysinger, W. S., & Ruckmick, C. A. (1933). *The emotional responses of children to the motion picture situation*. New York: Macmillan.

Gans, H. J. (1989). Sociology in America: The discipline and the public. *American Sociological Review, 54*, 1–16.

Gerbner, G. (Ed.). (1983). Ferment in the field: Communications scholars address critical issues and research tasks of the discipline [Special issue]. *Journal of Communication, 37*(2).

Gitlin, T. (1978). Media sociology: The dominant paradigm. *Theory and Society, 6,* 205–253.

Golding, P., & Murdock, G. (1978). Theories of communication and theories of society. *Communication Research, 5,* 339–356.

Halbestom, D. (1979) *The powers that be.* New York: Alfred Knopf.

Hall, S. (1982). The rediscovery of ideology: Return of the repressed in media studies. In M. Gurevitch, T. Bennett, J. Curran, & J. Woollacott (Eds.), *Culture, society and the media* (pp. 56–90). London & New York: Methuen.

Jowett, G. (1976). *Film: The democratic art.* Boston: Little, Brown.

Katz, E., & Lazarsfeld, P. F. (1955). *Personal influence: The part played by people in the flow of mass communications.* Glencoe, IL: The Free Press.

Klapper, J. T. (1960). *The effects of mass communication.* Glencoe, IL: The Free Press.

Lashley, K. S., & Watson, J. B. (1922). *A psychological study of motion pictures in relation to venereal disease campaigns.* Washington: U.S. Interdepartmental Social Hygiene Board.

Lippmann, W. (1922). *Public opinion.* New York: The Free Press.

MacBride, S., Abel, E., & International Commission for the Study of Communication Problems. (1980). *Many voices, one world: Communication and society, today and tomorrow: Towards a new, more just, and more efficient world information and communication order.* Paris: UNESCO; London: Kogan Page; New York: Unipub.

Park, F. F. (1910). *The influence of newspaper presentations upon the growth of crime and other antisocial activity.* Doctoral dissertation, University of Chicago.

Peterson, R. C., & Thurstone, L. L. (1933). *Motion pictures and the social attitudes of children.* New York: Macmillan.

Protess, D. L., & McCombs, M. E. (1991). *Agenda setting—Readings on media, public opinion, and policymaking.* Hillsdale, NJ: Lawrence Erlbaum Associates.

Rowland, W. D., Jr. (1983). *The politics of TV violence.* Beverly Hills, CA: Sage.

Schudson, M. (1978). *Discovering the news: A social history of American newspapers.* New York: Basic Books.

Siebert, F. S., Peterson, T., & Schramm, W. (1956). *Four theories of the press: The authoritarian, libertarian, social responsibility, and Soviet communist concepts of what the press should be and do.* Urbana: University of Illinois Press.

Smythe, D. W., & Van Dinh, T. (1983). On critical and administrative research: A new critical analysis. *Journal of Communication, 37*(2), 117–127.

Sproule, J. M. (1983). The Institute for Propaganda Analysis: Public education in argumentation, 19371501942. In D. Zarefsky, M. O. Sillars, & J. Rhodes (Eds.), *Argument in transition* (pp. 57–85). Annandale, VA: Speech Communication Association.

Steel, R. (1980). *Walter Lippmann and the American century.* Boston: Little, Brown.

Stoddard, G. D., & Wellman, B. L. (1934). *Child Psychology.* New York: Macmillan.

Wartella, E. A., & Reeves, B. (1985). Historical trends in research on children and the media: 1900–1960. *Journal of Communication, 35*(2), 118–133.

Winn, M. (1978). *The plug-in-drug.* New York: Bantam.

Appendix: Biographic Sketches of 65 Contributors to the Field of Communication Research

Theodor W. Adorno (1903–1969) was a key figure in the Frankfurt School of critical scholars. An interest in research on authority and the family led Adorno to collaborate on *The Authoritarian Personality* with Else Frenkel-Brunswik, Daniel J. Levinson, and R. Nevitt Sanford. Other works by Adorno include *Dialectic of Enlightenment*, with Max Horkheimer; *Aesthetic Theory*; and *Against Epistemology, a Metacritique: Studies in Husserl and the Phenomenological Antinomies.*

Gordon Allport (1897–1967) taught psychology at Harvard University and developed a theory of personality that emphasized the uniqueness of the individual. His research on attitudes was especially important in studies of media effects. Among his works are *Personality: A Psychological Interpretation; The Nature of Prejudice; Resolution of Intergroup Tensions; The Individual and his Religion: A Psychological Interpretation*; and *ABC's of Scapegoating.*

Erik Barnouw (1908–   ), a radio writer, editor, director, and commentator, was appointed to the Columbia University faculty in 1946 and served as Professor of Dramatic Arts in charge of film, radio, and television. He was Editor for Mass Communication at Columbia University Press and Chief of the Motion Picture, Broadcasting, and Recorded Sound Division of the Library of Congress. He is widely known for his three-volume work, *A History of Broadcasting in the United States*, and its condensed version, *Tube of Plenty: The Evolution of American Television.* He also wrote *The Sponsor: Notes on a Modern Potentate* and was Editor in Chief of the *International Encyclopedia of Communications.*

Howard S. Becker (1928–   ) has advanced the use of autobiographical information to explain socialization and deviance and is noted for the use of photographs in cultural studies to produce ethnographies. His works include *Boys in White: Student Culture in Medical School; Outsiders: Studies in the Sociology of Deviance; The Other Side: Perspectives on Deviance; Social Problems: A Modern Approach; Sociological Work: Method and Substance; Campus Power Struggle;* and *Culture and Civility in San Francisco.* He co-wrote *Making the Grade: The Academic Side of College Life* with Blanche Geer and Everett C. Hughes.

Walter Benjamin (1892–1940) was a member of the Institute for Social Research at the University of Frankfurt who believed in the consciousness-raising capability of the media and the revolutionary potential of popular art. He committed suicide while trying to escape Nazi internment. His thought is contained in *The Correspondence of Walter Benjamin, 1910–1940* by Gershom Scholem and Theodor W. Adorno (eds.).

Bernard Berelson (1912–1979), who taught at the University of Chicago, pioneered methods in content analysis. He edited *Reader in Public Opinion and Mass Communication* with Morris Janowitz; collaborated with Paul Lazarsfeld and Hazel Gaudet on *The People's Choice: How the Voter Makes Up His Mind in a Presidential Campaign,* the study of voting in Erie County, Pennsylvania; and coauthored *Human Behavior: An Inventory of Scientific Findings* with Gary Steiner.

Peter L. Berger (1929–   ), a sociologist of the phenomenological school, emphasized the need to understand and appreciate various social realities as they exist in and of themselves. A professor at the New School for Social Research in New York, his works include *The Social Construction of Reality: A Treatise in the Sociology of Knowledge,* with Thomas Luckmann; *The Human Shape of Work: Studies in the Sociology of Occupations; Movement and Revolution* and *To Empower People: The Role of Mediating Structures,* with Richard John Neuhaus; *Facing Up to Modernity: Excursions in Society, Politics, and Religion;* and *The Capitalist Revolution: Fifty Propositions About Prosperity, Equality, and Liberty.*

Edward L. Bernays (1891–1995) was considered one of the founders of modern public relations and was an early and influential practitioner. His works include *Biography of an Idea: Memoirs of Public Relations Counsel Edward L. Bernays; Crystallizing Public Opinion; Propaganda;* and *The Engineering of Consent.*

Willard G. Bleyer (1873–1935) founded the journalism program at the University of Wisconsin, where he stressed the importance of the social sciences, blazing a trail for the later work of Wilbur Schramm. His work includes *Main Currents in the History of American Journalism* and *The Profession of Journalism.*

Herbert Blumer (1900–1987), who taught sociology at the University of Chicago and the University of California, Berkeley, was author of the Payne Fund study, *Movies and Conduct*. He became the leading proponent of symbolic interactionism, advanced by George Herbert Mead, which suggests that human communication occurs by the exchange of symbols and their meanings. Blumer's other works include *Symbolic Interactionism: Perspective and Method*.

Ernest Burgess (1886–1966), a University of Chicago sociologist, was a student of human ecology and mass communication. With his mentor, Robert E. Park, Burgess wrote a leading textbook of the time, *Introduction to the Science of Sociology*. He also wrote *Urban Sociology; The Family: from Institution to Companionship*, with Harvey J. Locke and Mary Margaret Thomes; and *Predicting Success or Failure in Marriage*, with Leonard S. Cottrell, Jr.

Chilton R. Bush (1896–1972) worked as a reporter before earning his doctorate and joining the faculty at the University of Wisconsin. He later headed the Department of Communication at Stanford University and drew Wilbur Schramm to establish the Institute for Communication Research there. Bush's books include *Newspaper Reporting of Public Affairs; Editorial Thinking and Writing;* and *News Research for Better Newspapers*.

Hadley Cantril (1906–1969), a Princeton professor of psychology, collaborated with Frank Stanton in proposing a radio research project to the Rockefeller Foundation, also serving as its associate director. His book *The Invasion from Mars: A Study in the Psychology of Panic* evaluates how a radio broadcast resulted in panic for millions of listeners. His work includes *Gauging Public Opinion; How Nations See Each Other: A Study in Public Opinion*, with William Buchanan; and *The Pattern of Human Concerns*.

Ralph Droz Casey (1890–1977) is known for his analysis of propaganda and for building the social science foundations of the School of Journalism at the University of Minnesota. His works include *Principles of Publicity*, with Glenn C. Quiett; *Interpretations of Journalism*, with Frank Luther Mott; *The Press in the Contemporary Scene*, with Malcolm M. Willey; and *Propaganda, Communication, and Public Opinion*, with Bruce Lannes Smith and Harold D. Lasswell.

Peggy Charren (1928–) in 1968 founded Action for Children's Television, also serving as its President, until it closed in 1992. Appointed to the Carnegie Commission on the Future of Public Broadcasting in 1977, she has worked with many organizations promoting excellence in children's media. Her works include *Changing Channels: A Sensible Guide to Living With Television*, with Martin W. Sandler; *The TV-Smart Book for Kids: Puzzles, Games, and Other Good Stuff;* and *Television, Children, and the Constitutional Bicentennial: A Report*, both with Carol Hulsizer.

Charles Horton Cooley (1864–1929) with George Herbert Mead founded interactionist social psychology, later known through Herbert Blumer as symbolic interactionism. His main works include *Human Nature and the Social Order; Social Organization: A Study of the Larger Mind;* and *Social Process.* He was one of four academics responsible for the success of sociology and social psychology at the University of Chicago.

John Dewey (1859–1952), who taught at the University of Chicago and Columbia University, was one of the United States' most important philosophers. He held that society exists only by communication and that communication alone could create a great community. He also was a proponent of progressive education and pragmatism. His works include *The Public and Its Problems; The Child and the Curriculum; Art as Experience; The Bertrand Russell Case,* an essay in Charles S. Peirce's Chance, Love, and Logic: Philosophical Essays; and *Characters and Events: Popular Essays in Social and Political Philosophy.*

Edwin Emery (1914–1993) followed Frank Luther Mott as the leading journalism historian in the United States. Emery's reputation developed through his writing journalism history texts and for their attracting students to the study of journalism history at University of Minnesota. His leading works include *The Press and America,* with Henry Ladd Smith; and *Introduction to Mass Communications,* with Warren K. Agee and Phillip H. Ault.

George H. Gallup (1901–1984) pioneered techniques for the measurement of public opinion. He founded the American Institute of Public Opinion in 1935 while Director of Research at the Young & Rubicam advertising agency. Gallup applied market research methods to the sampling of opinion for clients in government, business, education, and the media. His works include *The Pulse of Democracy: The Public-Opinion Poll and How It Works,* coauthored with Saul Forbes Rae; *A Guide to Public Opinion Polls;* and *The Sophisticated Poll Watcher's Guide.*

George Gerbner (1919–), Professor and former Dean at the Annenberg School for Communication at the University of Pennsylvania, is noted for his research on television violence and socialization. His cultural indicators research program has investigated institutional processes underlying the production of media content, the message systems themselves, and relationships between exposure to television messages and beliefs and behaviors, including the "scary world" syndrome of interpersonal distrust. His works include *Communications Technology and Social Policy* and *Trends in Network Television Drama and Viewer Conceptions of Social Reality.*

Todd Gitlin (1943–), a cultural critic of media performance, teaches sociology at the University of California, Berkeley. His works include *The Whole World Is Watching: Mass Media in the Making & Unmaking of the New Left; Inside Prime Time; Watching Television: A Pantheon Guide to Popular*

Culture; Uptown: Poor Whites in Chicago, with Nanci Hollander; and *The Sixties: Years of Hope, Days of Rage*.

Erving Goffman (1922–1982) pioneered a new type of research by studying conversational interaction and applying the notion of symbolic interactionism. His technique, which he applied in a variety of venues, established what has become known as conversation analysis. His works include *The Presentation of Self in Everyday Life; Asylums: Essays on the Social Situation of Mental Patients and Other Inmates; Stigma: Notes of the Management of Spoiled Identity;* and *Gender Advertisements*.

Jurgen Habermas (1929–) is considered a leading critical theorist who focused on the role of communication in shaping the public sphere. He is Director of the Institute for Social Research and Professor of Philosophy at the University of Frankfurt. His works include *Theory of Communicative Action* and *Communication and the Evolution of Society*.

Herta Herzog (1906–1969) conducted in-depth interviews with a small group of panicked listeners of the radio broadcast "War of the Worlds" and collaborated with Hadley Cantril and Hazel Gaudet in analyzing and reporting results in *The Invasion from Mars: A Study in the Psychology of Panic*.

Carl I. Hovland (1912–1961), a Yale University psychologist, started studies of individual attitude change that led to a burgeoning literature in persuasion. He directed a research program on persuasion in the Pentagon during World War II to evaluate the effects of Army training films. His experiments oriented communication research toward studying effects and inspired the study of interpersonal communication. His works include *Communication and Persuasion: Psychological Studies of Opinion Change*, with Irving Janis and Harold Kelley; and *Experiments on Mass Communication* (volume 3 of Samuel Stouffer's *Studies in Social Psychology in World War II* series), with Arthur A. Lumsdaine and Fred D. Sheffield.

Robert Maynard Hutchins (1899–1977) helped establish the Institute of Human Relations at Yale University, while he was dean of its School of Law. Hutchins became president of the University of Chicago and chaired the Commission on Freedom of the Press, also known as the Hutchins Commission.

Harold Innis (1894–1952), a political economist at the University of Toronto, studied the effects of communication technology on social organization and influenced the work of Marshall McLuhan. Innis wrote *Empire and Communications; The Bias of Communication;* and *A History of the Canadian Pacific Railway*.

Irving Janis (1918–1990), a psychologist, who collaborated with Samuel Stouffer and others on *The American Soldier: Combat and Its Aftermath*. With Carl Hovland and Harold Kelley, Janis collaborated on a famous experiment on source credibility, discovering the "sleeper effect"—that people remember messages but not necessarily that they originated with a low-credibility source. The results are recorded in *Communication and Persuasion*.

Harold H. Kelley (1921–   ) worked with Carl Hovland at Yale, directed study in group dynamics at the University of Michigan, and taught at the University of Minnesota and the University of California, Los Angeles. His works include *The Social Psychology of Groups* and *Interpersonal Relations: A Theory of Interdependence*, with John W. Thibaut; *Personal Relationships: Their Structures and Processes*; and *Close Relationships*.

Herbert C. Kelman (1927–   ), a noted attitude researcher, taught at the University of Michigan and at Harvard. His books include *International Behavior: A Social-Psychological Analysis; A Time to Speak: On Human Values and Social Research*; and *Cross-National Encounters*, with Raphael S. Ezekiel.

Joseph T. Klapper (1917–1984) worked with Paul Lazarsfeld at Columbia University in the Bureau of Applied Social Research and served for many years as head of research at CBS. His book, *The Effects of Mass Communication*, summarized the belief in 1960 that media exerted limited effects on individuals and worked mainly through other individuals.

Thomas S. Kuhn (1922–   ) was a theoretical physicist at the University of California, Berkeley, and at Princeton University. He produced a general model of the processes and the evolution of scientific thought, proposing the major conceptual construct of scientific "paradigms," the cultural and historical factors that set the agenda for working scientists. His books include *The Structure of Scientific Revolutions* and *The Copernican Revolution: Planetary Astronomy in the Development of Western Thought*.

Harold Lasswell (1902–1978), a political scientist at the University of Chicago and Yale University, pioneered the content analysis of propaganda and created a now well-known model of communication based on a five-pronged question: "Who says what to whom, through what channel, with what effects?" His works include *Propaganda Technique in the World War*; and *Propaganda and Promotional Activities: An Annotated Bibliography*; and *Propaganda, Communication, and Public Opinion: A Comprehensive Reference Guide*, both with Bruce Lannes Smith and Ralph D. Casey.

Paul F. Lazarsfeld (1901–1976) pioneered the study of the effects of mass communication and founded the Bureau of Applied Social Research at Columbia University. He was a prolific writer who applied mass communication research methods directly to current communication questions, including the impact of radio and mass communication's effects on electoral choice. His works include *Radio and the Printed Page: An Introduction to the Study of Radio and Its Role in the Communication of Ideas; The People's Choice: How the Voter Makes Up His Mind in a Presidential Campaign*, with Bernard Berelson and Hazel Gaudet; and *Personal Influence: The Part Played by People in the Flow of Mass Communications*, with Elihu Katz.

Daniel Lerner (1917–1980) identified four critical communication variables that he said summarize the process of development. He also suggested that the modern individual's high degree of flexibility and empathy is the primary essential for individual modernization. His books include *Communication Research: A Half-Century Appraisal; The Passing of Traditional Society: Modernizing the Middle East;* and *World Revolutionary Elites: Studies in Coercive Ideological Movements.*

Kurt Lewin (1890–1947) was a psychologist at the University of Berlin, the University of Iowa, and the Massachusetts Institute of Technology. Although never appointed to a tenure-track position, he pioneered social psychological research in field theory, which exerted substantial influence in group dynamics and group communication. Lewin is frequently regarded as one of the founders of communication research. His works include *Principles of Topological Psychology* and *Measurement of Psychological Forces.*

Walter Lippmann (1889–1974) was the most important syndicated political columnist of his day, an adviser to U.S. presidents, and the author of *Public Opinion*—a starting point for research in agenda setting, propaganda, and public opinion. Other major works include *The Good Society; Essays in the Public Philosophy;* and *The Essential Lippmann: A Political Philosophy for Liberal Democracy.*

Leo Lowenthal (1900–1993), a sociologist who taught at Columbia University and the University of California, Berkeley, was one of four key members of the Frankfurt School of critical scholars who emigrated to the United States. He held that the individual is denigrated in the mechanized process of working and that mass culture, which he said is the result of stereotypes and manipulated consumer goods, is deleterious to modern living. His works include *Literature, Popular Culture and Society; Literature and the Image of Man;* and the multivolume *Communication in Society.*

Alfred McClung Lee (1906–1992), a sociologist at Brooklyn College and the City University Graduate Center in New York, argued that sociological influences rather than great individuals determine the course of history and that newspapers serve the business interests of their owners instead of the interests of the public and individual freedom. His 17 works include *The Daily Newspaper in America: The Evolution of a Social Instrument; The Fine Art of Propaganda: A Study of Father Coughlin's Speeches; Principles of Sociology; Race Riot*, with Norman Daymond Humphrey; *Sociology for People: Toward a Caring Profession;* and *Sociology for Whom?*

Marshall McLuhan (1911–1980), a Canadian literary critic, taught at the University of Toronto, where he directed the Centre for Culture and Technology. He studied how communication technology changes the basic senses and suggested that the characteristics of a communication medium may be more important than its content to determining what users experience. Among his works are *The Medium Is the Message: An Inventory of Effects,* with Quentin Fiore; *Understanding Media: The Extensions of Man;* and *The Gutenberg Galaxy.*

Eleanor Maccoby (1917–   ), a professor of psychology at Stanford University, conducted early research on the effects of television on children. Her works include *Patterns of Child Rearing,* with Robert R. Sears; *Experiments in Primary Education,* with Miriam Zellner; *The Psychology of Sex Differences,* with Carol Nagy Jacklin; and *Social Development: Psychological Growth and the Parent–Child Relationship.*

George Herbert Mead (1863–1931) was a University of Chicago philosopher who developed the theory of symbolic interaction, emphasizing the importance of interpersonal communication in development of the personality. The approach is outlined in his book *Mind, Self and Society from the Standpoint of a Social Behaviorist.*

Robert King Merton (1910–   ) is University Professor Emeritus at Columbia University, where he has taught since 1941; foundation scholar at the Russell Sage Foundation; and Adjunct Professor at the Rockefeller University. He served alongside Paul Lazarsfeld as an associate director of Columbia's Bureau of Applied Social Research from 1942 to 1971. His theoretical contributions to sociology are largely brought together in his classic *Social Theory and Social Structure,* which has had more than 30 printings, whereas his book, *The Sociology of Science: An Episodic Memoir* (Part 1 of *The Sociology of Science in Europe*), records his major work in this specialty that he did much to found. His work in mass communication, largely with Lazarsfeld, includes *Mass Persuasion,* a monograph on a marathon war bond drive on CBS. The recipient of more than 25 honorary degrees, Merton has also been a MacArthur Prize Fellow.

Lloyd W. Morrisett (1929–   ) has been chairman of the board of the Children's Television Workshop since 1970. He has also served as Executive Director of the Markle Foundation, a major funder of media research since the 1970s. He taught at the University of California, Berkeley; was on the staff of the Social Science Research Council; joined the Carnegie Corporation; served as vice president of the Carnegie Foundation for the Advancement of Teaching; and has served as chairman of the Riverside Research Institute, the Research Triangle Institute, and the Rand Corporation.

Frank Luther Mott (1886–1964) may be the leading historian of U.S. journalism and the only journalism educator to be awarded the Pulitzer Prize for history. He directed the School of Journalism at the University of Iowa and was Dean of the University of Missouri School of Journalism. Among the best known of the 33 books he authored, edited, or co-wrote are *American Journalism: A History of Newspapers in the United States Through 250 Years, 1690–1940;* his five-volume *A History of American Magazines;*

Interpretations of Journalism; Jefferson and the Press; Golden Multitudes: The Story of Best Sellers in the United States; The News in America; and *Time Enough: Essays in Autobiography.*

Ralph Nafziger (1896–1973) was a central figure in journalism education and research and an expert in international communication. He directed the research division of the School of Journalism at the University of Minnesota and directed the School of Journalism at the University of Wisconsin. His books include *International News and the Press: An Annotated Bibliography* and *Introduction to Mass Communications Research,* which he co-wrote with David Manning White.

Theodore M. Newcomb (1903–1984) founded the Department of Social Psychology at the University of Michigan. His studies of changing attitudes toward public affairs among students demonstrated that the characteristics of individuals and their group membership interact to influence attitude change. His works include *Personality and Social Change: Attitude Formation in a Student Community; Social Psychology; The Acquaintance Process; Deviant Subcultures on a College Campus,* with Richard Flacks; *Social Psychology: The Study of Human Interaction,* with Ralph H. Turner and Philip E. Converse; *College Peer Groups: Problems and Prospects for Research,* with Everett K. Wilson; and *Persistence and Change: Bennington College and Its Students After Twenty-five Years.*

Arthur Charles Nielsen (1897–1980) founded A. C. Nielsen Research and Business Services, later A. C. Nielsen Company, which he built into a worldwide media-marketing research firm, now with operations in 17 countries. Nielsen's published works include *New Facts About Radio Research* and *Greater Prosperity Through Marketing Research: The First Forty Years of A. C. Nielsen Company.*

William S. Paley (1901–1990) in 1928 founded the Columbia Broadcasting System, where he served as president and as chairman of the board. Department Chief of the Psychological Warfare Division under General Eisenhower in World War II, he assumed many institutional roles, including service as a lifetime trustee of Columbia University. His books include *Free Broadcast Journalism* and *As It Happened: A Memoir.*

Robert E. Park (1864–1944), a sociologist at the University of Chicago, is sometimes considered the first academic student of mass communication and one of the most influential figures in U.S. sociology. He began the scholarly study of mass communication, race relations, human ecology, and collective behavior. Among his works are *The Immigrant Press and Its Control; The Man Farthest Down,* with Booker T. Washington; and *Introduction to the Science of Sociology,* with Ernest W. Burgess.

Ithiel de Sola Pool (1917–1984), a professor of political science at the Massachusetts Institute of Technology, with his mentor Harold Lasswell, traced the rise and fall of political forces over 60 years in five countries by content analyzing prestigious newspapers. The results are recorded in *The Prestige Papers: A Survey of Their Editorials.* Pool later used systems theory to describe social communication and outlined the potential of communication system modeling to increase the understanding of communication in social systems.

Edward Sapir (1884–1939) became the primary spokesman in the 1920s for the interdisciplinary study of language and culture. Sapir is most noted for revolutionizing the study of grammar by defining the "psychological reality" of the phoneme in terms of the intuitions of native speakers, an idea later associated with the Sapir–Whorf hypothesis, named for Sapir and Benjamin Lee Whorf. In 1921, he published *Language: An Introduction to the Study of Speech,* which became a classic introductory text for linguistics.

Claude E. Shannon (1916–   ) developed information theory, which provided the basic paradigm for communication study, marked the transition from an industrial to an information society, and led to the development of the computer and microelectronics industry. His works include *The Mathematical Theory of Communication,* with Warren Weaver, and *Automata Studies.*

Fredrick S. Siebert (1901–1982) introduced legal research methods to the study of journalism law and took part in key press-law judicial appeals in the 1930s. He also directed the University of Illinois School of Journalism. His works include *Freedom of the Press in England 1476–1776: The Rise and Decline of Government Control;* and *Four Theories of the Press,* with Theodore Peterson and Wilbur Schramm.

Georg Simmel (1858–1918) explored the *a priori* grounds for order in a society made up of individuals, fastening on the notion of "vocation," which allows sociology to bridge the gap between an inner "calling" and the external requirements of human interaction. He also explored the relationship between play and social intercourse, finding that in games people engage in the purest and most sublimated kind of human relation. His major works include *The Sociology of Georg Simmel* and *Conflict: The Web of Group Affiliations.*

Frank Stanton (1908–   ) was central to the development of CBS, Inc., as Head of Research, Vice President, General Manager, and President. He collaborated with Paul Lazarsfeld on books dealing with radio research and on a "program analyzer" to test the reactions of listeners to radio programming. Under Stanton's direction, by 1965 CBS became, according to *Forbes* magazine, "the largest advertising and communications medium in the world."

William Stephenson (1902–1989), who taught at the University of Missouri, invented the Q-Method, a research tool applied in journalism and other social sciences to study correlations between individuals, communities, and other variables. His principal works include *The Study of Behavior: Q-Technique and Its Methodology* and *The Play Theory of Mass Communication.*

George D. Stoddard (1897–1981) taught educational psychology at the University of Iowa and directed the Iowa Child Welfare Research Station, where he hired psychologist Kurt Lewin. Stoddard later became president of the University of Illinois and recruited Wilbur Schramm to found the first institute of communication research there. Stoddard's works include *Child Psychology*, with Beth L. Wellman, and *The Meaning of Intelligence*.

Samuel A. Stouffer (1900–1960), a former president of the American Sociological Association, headed the team that conducted the four-volume study titled *Studies in Social Psychology in World War II* (commonly known as *The American Soldier* series) and established the Laboratory of Social Relations at Harvard University. Stouffer pioneered large-scale quantitative research in sociology and the correlational and descriptive analysis of survey data. In addition to three volumes in *The American Soldier* series, his works include *Research Memorandum on the Family in the Depression*, with Paul Lazarsfeld; *Communism, Conformity, and Civil Liberties: A Cross-Section of the Nation Speaks Its Mind*; and *Social Research to Test Ideas: Selected Writings*.

Louis L. Thurstone (1887–1955), once an assistant to Thomas Edison, invented methods for devising interval and ratio scales for psychological variables and improved the standardization of intelligence tests. His first use of the equal-appearing interval scale appeared in one of the Payne Fund Studies. His works include *The Learning Curve Equation*; *The Nature of Intelligence*; *The Fundamentals of Statistics*; *The Measurement of Attitude*, with E. J. Chave; *The Vectors of Mind: Multiple-Factor Analysis for the Isolation of Primary Traits*; *Primary Mental Abilities*; *A Factoral Study of Perception*; *Multiple-Factor Analysis: A Development and Expansion of the Vectors of Mind*; and *The Measurement of Values*.

Alexis Henri Maurice Clerel de Tocqueville (1805–1859) in 1831 was sent by the French government to the United States to conduct a study of the penitentiary system. His account of civil and political life in the United States, *Democracy in America*, became a classic study.

Graham Wallas (1858–1932) established an early reputation as a socialist critic of intellectualism, yet later expressed concern about growing anti-intellectualism, connecting it with the rise of deterministic psychology and fascism. He devoted most of his career to a defense of liberal democracy and to the exploration of ways in which the rational free will of individuals could be applied in human affairs. His works include *What to Read: A List of Books for Social Reformers; The Life of Francis Place, 1771–1854; Human Nature in Politics; The Great Society: A Psychological Analysis; Our Social Heritage; The Art of Thought*; and *Social Judgment*.

David Manning White (1917–1993), a professor of journalism at Boston University and Virginia Commonwealth University, originated study on the "gatekeeper function" of the mass media and introduced the term *mass* *culture*. His works include *Mass Culture: The Popular Arts in America*, with Bernard Rosenberg; *The Funnies: An American Idiom*, with Robert H. Abel; and two textbooks on mass communication research.

Walter Williams (1864–1935) became dean of the United States' first school of journalism at its founding in 1908 at the University of Missouri. Williams trained and placed thousands of professional journalists in newspapers across the country and press associations around the world. He helped to found the National Editorial Association, the American Association of Schools and Departments of Journalism, and the Press Congress of the World.

Wilhelm Wundt (1832–1920) founded the first experimental laboratory for psychology in 1879. He pioneered methods for the study of sensation and perception and advocated the maintenance of a relationship between experiment and the study of comparative history and culture. His works include *Lectures on Human and Animal Psychology; Ethics: An Investigation of the Facts and Laws of the Moral Life; An Introduction to Psychology; Concerning True War; Elements of Folk Psychology: Outlines of a Psychological History of the Development of Mankind;* and *The Language of Gestures*.

About the Contributors
and Editors

Hugh Malcolm Beville (1909–1988), sometimes called "the dean of broadcast research" joined NBC in 1930 as a statistician, helped to form the network's Research Department, and became Vice President for Planning and Research in 1958. After teaching at Southampton College for 6 years, Beville served as Executive Director of the Broadcast Rating Council (now the Electronic Media Research Council). Beville helped to found the American Association of Public Opinion Research and served as President of both the Radio/Television Research Council and the Market Research Council. He is the author of *Audience Ratings: Radio, Television, Cable*.

Leo Bogart, an internationally known public opinion specialist and former advertising executive for Exxon, Revlon, and McCann–Erickson, is the author of nine books, including *Commercial Culture: The Media and the Public Interest* (1995); *Polls and the Awareness of Public Opinion: Strategy in Advertising; The Age of Television; Press and Public;* and *Preserving the Press*. He has served as President of the American and World Associations for Public Opinion Research, Society for Consumer Psychology, Radio and Television Research Council, and Market Research Council. He and George Gallup were the first persons elected to the Market Research Council Hall of Fame. From 1989 to 1990, Bogart was a senior fellow at The Freedom Forum Media Studies Center. He has taught at Columbia University, the Illinois Institute of Technology, and New York University.

James W. Carey is Professor of Journalism in the Graduate School of Journalism at Columbia University. He was Dean of the College of Communications at the University of Illinois from 1979 to 1992. Prior to that he held the George H. Gallup Chair at the University of Iowa. Carey holds a PhD from the University of Illinois and taught in Illinois' Department of Journalism from 1963 to 1976. For the last 7 of those years, he was Professor of Journalism and Director of the Institute of Communications Research.

He has also taught at the University of Georgia, Pennsylvania State University, and University College, Dublin. Among Carey's books are *Media, Myths, and Narratives: Television and the Press* and *Communication as Culture: Essays on Media and Society*. Carey has held a National Endowment for the Humanities Fellowship in Science, Technology and Human Values. In, 1985 he was a senior fellow at The Freedom Forum Media Studies Center at Columbia University.

Douglass Cater (1923–1995) was a writer, editor, emeritus college president, and former government official. He was Trustee Emeritus of the Aspen Institute, where he had been a senior fellow and Director of the Program Council. He taught at Wesleyan University, the University of California, San Francisco, and Stanford University. Cater was Special Assistant to President Johnson from 1964 to 1968, Special Assistant to the Secretary of the U.S. Army in 1951, and Counselor to the Director of the Mutual Security Agency in 1952. Among the books he either authored or coauthored are *The Fourth Branch of Government; The Irrelevant Man;* and *TV Violence and the Child: The Evolution and Fate of the Surgeon General's Report*, with Stephen Strickland.

Everette E. Dennis is Executive Director of The Freedom Forum Media Studies Center at Columbia University and Senior Vice President of The Freedom Forum. Dennis has served as Dean of the School of Journalism at the University of Oregon and Director of Graduate Studies at the University of Minnesota. A past president of the Association for Education in Journalism and Mass Communication, he has received fellowships from Harvard University, Stanford University, and the East–West Center in Hawaii. Author, coauthor, and editor of 28 books, Dennis has written and lectured widely on topics such as communication research and media and society. Among his books are *Reshaping the Media; The Economics of Libel; The Media Society;* and *Understanding Mass Communication*, a leading college text on media coauthored with Melvin DeFleur. He conceptualized and directed the seminar series that led to this book and has written extensively on the history of media research.

Hilde Himmelweit (1918–1989) was Professor Emeritus in Social Psychology at the University of London. Twice a fellow at the Center for the Advanced Study of the Behavioral Sciences, she also held visiting appointments at Stanford, the University of California, Berkeley, and Hebrew University, Jerusalem. Himmelweit was a recipient of the Nevitt Sanford Award (from the International Society of Political Psychology) and received an honorary doctorate from the Open University. Her research interests were in the study of personality, television's role in society, and the way social and political attitudes change. Among her books are *Television and the Child*, with A. N. Oppenheim and Pamela Vince; and *How Voters Decide*, with Patrick Humphreys and Marianne Jaeger.

Elihu Katz is Trustee Professor at the Annenberg School for Communication at the University of Pennsylvania. He is also Scientific Director of the Guttman Institute of Applied Social Research, in Jerusalem, and Emeritus Professor of Sociology and Communications at Hebrew University. His interest in the flow of information and influence dates to *Personal Influence*, coauthored with Paul Lazarsfeld. His most recent work, *The Export of Meaning* (coauthored with Tamar Liebes), focuses on the diffusion of U.S. popular culture abroad. Katz has served on the faculties of the University of Chicago and the Annenberg School at the University of Southern California. He holds honorary degrees from Ghent University and the University of Montreal and is winner of the McLuhan Prize (1987), the Israel Prize (1989), the Helen Dinerman Award (1992), and the Murray Edelman Award (1993).

Kurt Lang, Professor Emeritus of sociology and communication at the University of Washington, received his PhD in sociology from the University of Chicago. How the medium of communication affects our view of reality has been one of his abiding interests, first pursued in his classic study of the ceremonial reception given General MacArthur upon his return from Korea and in other studies on political television, such as *Politics and Television* and *The Battle for Public Opinion: The President, the Press and the Polls During Watergate*. More recently, he has focused on the social construction and selection of past achievement as explored in his book *Etched in Memory: The Building and Survival of Artistic Reputation*. The research he and his wife, Gladys, conducted on television earned them the Edward L. Bernays Award of the American Sociological Association.

William J. McGuire is Professor of Psychology at Yale University. He has also served on the Psychology Department faculties at the University of Illinois, Columbia University, and the University of California, San Diego. Among the topics on which he has published widely are communication and attitude change; immunization against persuasion; determinants of salience in the self-concept; the content, structure, and operation of thought systems; and positive–negative asymmetries in thinking. He has received fellowships from the Social Science Research Council, the National Institutes of Health, the Guggenheim Foundation, and the Center for Advanced Study in the Behavioral Sciences. Among his awards are the 1988 Distinguished Scientific Contribution Award from the American Psychological Association and the 1992 Distinguished Scientist Award from the Society of Experimental Social Psychology. He is author of *A Content Structure and Operations of Thought Systems: Advances in Social Cognition*, with Claire V. McGuire; and *Explorations in Political Psychology*, with Shanto Iyengar.

Theodore Peterson was Dean of the College of Communications at the University of Illinois from 1957 until 1979, when he returned to full-time teaching; he retired in 1987. Peterson is author of *Magazines in the Twentieth Century*, coauthor with Fredrick Siebert and Wilbur Schramm of *Four Theories of the Press*, and coauthor with Jay W. Jensen and William Rivers of *The Mass Media and Modern Society*. He earned his BA from the University of Minnesota, MS from Kansas State, and PhD from the University of Illinois.

Gertrude J. Robinson is Professor and former Director of the Graduate Program in Communications at McGill University in Montreal. Her current research interests include studies in international communications, women in media professions, and the intellectual history of North American communication studies. She is the past editor of the *Canadian Journal of Communication* and is on the executive board of the International Association for Mass Communication Research. From 1990 to 1991 she was a senior fellow at The Freedom Forum Media Studies Center at Columbia University and a senior fellow a year later at the Center for the Study of Gender Issues at the University of British Columbia. She has published widely in North American and European journals and has authored seven books, among them *Tito's Maverick Media; News Agencies and World News; Women, Communication and Careers;* and *Women & Power: Canadian and German Experiences*.

Wilbur Schramm (1907–1987) helped to define and establish the field of communication research and theory. He founded institutes of communication research at the University of Illinois and Stanford University and directed the East–West Center in Honolulu, Hawaii. Among his important works are *The Story of Human Communication; Communication in Modern Society; Mass Communications; The Process and Effects of Mass Communication; and Responsibility in Mass Communication*. He also coauthored *Four Theories of the Press*, with Fredrick Siebert and Theodore Peterson, and *Television in the Lives of Our Children*, with Jack Lyle and Edwin B. Parker.

David L. Sills is the Executive Associate Emeritus of the Social Science Research Council in New York. He received a PhD in sociology from Columbia University in 1956 and was associated with Columbia's Bureau of Applied Social Research form 1951 to 1962, serving as study director, acting director, and director. He is the author of *The Volunteers*, a co-author of *The Japanese Village in Transition*, and the editor of five books, including the 19-volume *International Encyclopedia of the Social Sciences* and (with Robert K. Merton) *Social Science Quotations: Who Said What, When, and Where*. He has been a fellow at both the Center for Advanced Study in the Behavioral Sciences in Stanford, California, and the Russell Sage Foundation in New York.

Ellen Wartella is Dean of the College of Communication and Walter Cronkite Regents Chair in Communication at the University of Texas at Austin. She is a fellow of the International Communication Association and author or editor of six books on communication and dozens of journal articles. She was a fellow at The Freedom Forum Media Studies Center from 1985 to 1986, a recipient of the German National Science Foundation Fellowship at the University of Munich in 1985, and a postdoctoral fellow in developmental psychology at the University of Kansas from 1980 to 1981. Her research specialty is the study of children and television issues. As well, she has been researching and writing about the history of communication audience study in the United States. She is editor of *Children Communicating* and authored *How Children Learn to Buy*, with Daniel Wackman and Scott Ward. She has been a consultant to the Federal Communications Commission, the Federal Trade Commission, and Congressional investigations of children's television.

Author Index

A

Abel, E., 87, *93*, 172, *180*
Adoni, H., 80, *82*
Adorno, T. W., 3, *18*, 109, *115*, 159, 162, *166*
Allport, G. W., 9, *18*
Altenloh, E., 4, 10, *18*
Arnheim, R., 109, *115*

B

Ball-Rokeach, S., 174, *179*
Barber, B., 37, *37*
Barton, A. H., 161, *166*
Bauer, A., 25, *37*
Bauer, R., 25, *37*
Bell, D., 24, *37*
Berelson, B., 61, 63, 65, *69*, 109, *115*, 159, *166*, 178, *179*
Berger, P. L., 163, *166*
Blumer, H., 161, 162, *166*
Blumler, J. G., 165, *166*
Boring, E. G., 40, *57*
Brehm, J. W., 51, *59*
Brock, T. C., 56, *58*, *59*
Brown, D., 77, *82*
Brown, R., 43, *57*, 174, *179*, *179*
Bryant, J., 77, *82*
Bryce, J., 11, *18*
Buecher, K., 5, 12, 13, 16, *18*
Buxton, W. J., 161, *166*

C

Cacioppo, J. T., 56, *59*
Cantril, H., 108, *115*, 174, *179*

Carey, J. W., 31, *38*, 68, *69*, 159, *166*, 171, *179*
Carveth, R. A., 77, *82*
Casey, R. D., 14, *19*, *20*, 91, *93*
Cater, D., 148, 149, *155*
Chaffee, S. H., 172, 178, *179*
Chaiken, S., 56, *58*
Charters, W. W., 15, *19*, *82*
Clark, C. D., 15, *19*
Cohen, A., 80, *82*
Coleman, J. S., 64, *69*, 110, *115*, *116*
Commission on Freedom of the Press, 87, *93*
Converse, J. M., *115*
Coser, L. A., *115*, 160, 162, 165, *166*
Crain, R. L., *69*
Czitrom, D. J., 159, *166*, 169, *179*

D

Davis, R., 179, *179*
DeFleur, M. L., 158, *167*, 170, 174, *179*
Delia, J. G., 169, 170, *179*
Dervin, B., 165, *166*
Dewey, J., 32, *38*
Dollard, J. H., 44, *57*
Doob, L. W., 44, *57*
Durkheim, E., 56, *57*
Dysinger, W. S., 173, *179*

E

Eagly, A. H., 56, *57*
Ebbinghaus, H., 40, *57*
Emery, E., 88, *93*
Entman, R., 30, *38*
Eron, L. D., 76, *82*
Escarpit, R., 3, *19*

199

F

Farr, R., 41, 56, 57, 58
Festinger, L., 51, 58
Feyerabend, P., 163, 166
Field, H., 108, 116
Fiske, M., 114, 116
Fitch, F. B., 44, 46, 58
Foulkes, D., 24, 38
Frenkel-Brunswik, E., 3, 18
Furu, T., 73, 82

G

Gans, H. J., 179, 179
Gaudet, H., 61, 63, 69, 108, 109, 115, 174, 179
Gerald, J. E., 91, 93
Gerbner, G., 171, 180
Giddens, A., 163, 166
Gitlin, T., 171, 174, 180
Goffman, E., 163, 166
Golding, P., 171, 180
Greenwald, A. G., 56, 58
Gross, N., 65, 69
Grossberg, L., 165, 166

H

Halbestom, D., 179, 180
Hall, M., 44, 46, 58
Hall, S., 163, 165, 166, 171, 180
Hamilton, H., 61n, 69
Hardt, H., 30, 38
Hatin, E., 4–5, 19
Herzog, H., 108, 115, 174, 179
Heyer, P., 158, 160, 166
Himmelweit, H. T., 73, 82
Hirst, F. W., 8, 19
Hochheimer, J. L., 172, 178, 179
Hovland, C. I., 44, 46, 47, 48, 52, 54, 55, 58, 59
Huesmann, L. R., 76, 82
Hughes, H. M., 2, 15, 19
Hull, C. L., 44, 46, 58
Hunt, E. B., 54, 58
Hunt, M., 111, 115
Hurwitz, D., 161, 166
Hyman, H. H., 107n, 115

I

Innis, H., 162, 166
International Commission for the Study of
    Communications Problems, 87,
    93, 172, 180

J

Janis, I. L., 47, 48, 54, 58
Jay, M., 162, 166
Jensen, J. W., 89, 93
Jowett, G., 173, 180

K

Karpf, F. B., 41, 58
Katz, E., 1, 2, 19, 24, 35, 38, 61, 61n, 62, 63,
    64, 69, 110, 115, 161, 166, 170, 180
Kelley, H. H., 48, 54, 58
Kendall, P. L., 108, 110n, 114, 115
Klapper, J. T., 23, 24, 29, 38, 69, 108, 108n,
    115, 170, 180
Knies, K., 19
Kobre, S., 90, 93
Kreiling, A. L., 37, 38
Kuhn, T. S., 158, 163, 166

L

Lang, G. E., 8, 9, 19
Lang, K., 2, 8, 9, 19
Langenhove, F. van, 9, 19
Lare, J., 29, 38
Lashley, K. S., 177, 180
Lasswell, H. D., 14, 19, 20, 57, 58, 91, 93
Lazarsfeld, P. F., 1, 2, 19, 35, 38, 61, 62, 63,
    65, 69, 106, 107, 108, 109, 110,
    111n, 113, 115, 116, 161, 167, 170,
    180
Lefkowitz, M. M., 76, 82
Levenstein, A., 10, 19
Levin, M. L., 61n, 69
Levinson, D. J., 3, 18
Levy, M. R., 109, 116
Lippmann, W., 8, 19, 28, 38, 90, 93, 148, 155,
    173, 180
Littlejohn, S. W., 161, 167
Loebl, E., 6, 19
Loewenthal, L., 110, 116
Lowery, S., 158, 167
Luckmann, T., 163, 166
Lumsdaine, A. A., 47, 52, 58
Lyle, J., 73, 83

M

MacBride, S., 87, 93, 172, 180
Mane, S., 80, 82
Matthews, F., 160, 167
Mayhew, L., 26, 27, 38
McCombs, M. E., 179, 180

McDougall, W., 40, *58*
McGuire, C. V., 56, *59*
McGuire, W. J., 41, 56, 57, *59*
McLuhan, M., 162, *167*
McPhee, W. N., 61, 63, 65, *69*, 109, *115*
Menzel, H., 64, *69*, 110, *115*
Merton, R. K., 17, *19*, 61, *69*, 109, 110, 113, 114, *116*, 157, 158, 161, *167*
Meyrowitz, J., 165, *167*
Miller, G. A., 43, *59*
Miller, N. E., 44, *58*
Morawski, J. G., 44, *59*
Morrison, D. E., 161, 165, *167*
Moscovici, S., 56, *58, 59*
Mott, F. L., 88, *93*
Mowrer, O. H., 44, *58*
Murdock, G., 171, *180*

N

Nafziger, R. O., 85, *93*
Noussance, H. de, 9, *19*

O

Oberschall, A., 10, 16, *19*
O'Keefe, B. J., 165, *166*
Oppenheim, A. N., 73, *82*
Osgood, C. E., 43, *59*
Ostrom, T. M., 56, *58, 59*

P

Park, F. F., 177, *180*
Parker, E. B., 73, *83*
Pasanella, A. K., 107n, *116*
Perkins, D. T., 44, 46, *58*
Peters, J. D., 165, *167*
Peterson, R. C., 177, *180*
Peterson, T., 28, *38*, 86, *93*, 172, *180*
Petty, R. E., 56, *59*
Postman, L., 9, *18*
Protess, D. L., 179, *180*

Q

Quandt, J. B., 160, *167*

R

Reeves, B., 171, 173, *180*
Riley, J. W., Jr., 72, *82*

Riley, M. W., 72, *82*
Robinson, G. J., 159, 161, 164, *167*
Rogers, E. M., 67, *69*, 107n, *116*, 165, *167*
Rosenberg, M. J., 48, *58*
Rosengren, K. E., 163, *167*
Rosenthal, D., *69*
Ross, E. A., 40, *59*
Ross, R. T., 44, 46, *58*
Rossi, P. H., *116*
Rossiter, C., 29, *38*
Rowland, W. D., Jr., 161, *167*, 171, *180*
Ruckmick, C. A., 173, *179*
Ryan, B., 65, *69*

S

Salomon, L., 6, *19*
Sanford, R. N., 3, *18*
Saussaure, F. de, 56, *59*
Schramm, W., 28, *38*, 50, *59*, 73, *83*, 86, 89, 90, *93*, 162, *167*, 172, *180*
Schudson, M., 13, *19*, 173, *180*
Schuecking, L. L., 12, *19*
Schutz, A., 163, *167*
Searle, J., 163, *167*
Sears, R. R., 44, 46, 57, *58*
Shannon, C. E., 162, *168*
Sheffield, F. D., 47, 52, *58*
Sherif, M., 48, *59*
Siebert, F. S., 28, *38*, 86, *93*, 172, *180*
Sills, D. L., 1, *19*, 61n, *69*, 107n, *116*
Singer, D. G., 75, *83*
Singer, J. L., 75, *83*
Smith, B. L., 14, *19, 20*, 91, *93*
Smith, H. L., 88, *93*
Smythe, D. W., 171, *180*
Sproule, J. M., 24, *38*, 169, 171, *180*
Stanton, F., 106, 107, 108, *116*
Steel, R., 29, *38*, 174, *180*
Stoddard, G. D., 173, 177, *180*
Stoklossa, P., 9, *20*
Stouffer, S. A., 47, *59*, 161, *168*
Suci, G. J., 43, *59*

T

Tannenbaum, P. H., 43, *59*
Tarde, G., 7, *20*
Taylor, C., 164, 165, *168*
Thimme, H., 1, *20*
Thomas, W. I., 33, *38*, 42, *59*
Thurstone, L. L., 177, *180*
Tiryakian, E., 158, *168*
Tocqueville, A. de, 6, 11, *20*

Toennies, F., 7, 12, *20*

V

Van Dinh, T., 171, *180*
Vince, P., 73, *82*

W

Walder, L. O., 76, 82
Wallace, D., 107, *116*
Wallas, G., 8, *20*
Wartella, E., *166*, 171, 173, *180*
Watson, J. B., 42, *59*, 177, *180*
Weaver, D., 162, *168*
Weber, M., 13, 14, *20*
Wellman, B. L., 173, 177, *180*
White, D. M., 85, *93*

Wicklund, R. A., 51, *59*
Wilcox, D. F., 9, *20*
Williams, T. M., 77, 81, *83*
Winkin, Y., 162, *168*
Winkler, A., 161, *168*
Winn, M., 179, *180*
Wirth, L., 2, *20*
Wittkower, M., 3, *20*
Wittkower, R., 3, *20*
Wittwer, M., 10, *20*
Wolf, K. M., 110*n*, *116*
Wright, C. R., 113, *117*
Wundt, W., 41, 56, *60*
Wuttke, H., 6, *20*

Z

Znaniecki, F., 33, *38*, 42, *59*

Subject Index

A

Abelson, Robert P., 47
Ackerman, Carl, 129
Action for Children's Television, 77
Adorno, Theodor W., 3, 109, 162, 181
Advertising
    and children, 77
    and development of ratings, 97
    effects of, 12–13, 140
    growth of, 11, 22, 96
African Americans, 37
Allen, Eric, 129
Allport, Gordon W., 9, 181
Almond, Gabriel, 132
American Research Bureau, 101, 102, 103
Anderson, Norman H., 47
Annenberg Foundation, 55
Annenberg Schools, 126
Anthropology, 66
Arbitron, 101, 102, 136
Army, U.S., Information and Education
        Branch, 45, 47
Aspen Institute, 151
Program on Communications and Society,
        151
Association of National Advertisers (ANA),
        97–98
Attitudes, studies of, 42
Audience research, 10, 119, 171
Audience(s)
    active vs. passive models, 55–56
    maximization of, 144–145
    measuring, 95–103, 138, 140, 141, 143–144
    perceived of as a community, 114
    power of, 24
    test, 114
Audimeter, 99–100
Audit services, 141–142

B

Bar codes, 139
Barnouw, Erik, 71, 181
Bavelas, Alex, 127
Beach, Frank, 45
Becker, Howard S., 181
Bell, Elaine Graham, 47
Bell Telephone Laboratories, 39, 55
Benjamin, Walter, 182
Benton, Bill, 151
Berelson, Bernard, 61, 182
Berger, Peter L., 182
Bernays, Edward L., 182
Beucher, Karl, 30
Beville, Hugh Malcolm, 193
Birdwhistell, Ray L., 162
Bleyer, Willard G., 129, 130–131, 182
Blumer, Herbert, 2, 161, 182
Boas, Franz, 125
Bobo doll study, 75
Bogart, Leo, 193
Books
    buying of, 12
    readership, studies of, 10
Booth, Charles, 10
Brehm, Jack W., 45, 47, 49
Britain, 4, 8, 78–79, 165
    broadcasting in, 71–72
    television in, 77
British Broadcasting Corporation (BBC),
        71–73, 145
Broadcasting
    commercial, 170

public, 71–72, 96, 149–151
Brock, Timothy, 47, 49
Buecher, Karl, 4, 5–6, 12, 15–17
Buehler, Charlotte and Hans, 165
Bullet theory, 11, 22
Bundy, McGeorge, 151
Bureau of Labor Statistics, 155
Burgess, Ernest, 183
Bush, Chilton R., 129, 183
Butler, Nicholas Murray, 111

C

Cable television, 142–143
Cahalan, Don, 135–136
Campbell, Enid Hobart, 47
Canada, 160, 165
Cantril, Hadley, 107, 121, 174, 183
Carey, James W., 68–69, 193
Carnegie Corporation, 149, 150
Casey, Ralph D., 91, 129, 130, 183
Cater, Douglass, 194
Cavell, Stanley, 33
CBS, 75, 98, 101, 106, 107, 118–120
Ceiling effect, 13
Center for Advanced Study in the Behav-
    ioral Sciences, 121–122
Chaffee, Steven H., 81
Channel 13, 96
Charren, Peggy, 77, 183
Chicago School, 2, 5, 15, 21–37, 124, 159–160
Child, Irving, 45
Children
    advertising and, 77
    media effects on, 176–178
    television and, 71–82, 151–153
Cinema
    content of, 173
    effect of, 47
    studies of, 4, 15
Circulation, audited, 143–144
Cohen, Arthur R., 45, 47
Cohen, Bob, 49
Columbia University, 105, 111–113, 129, 170
    Bureau of Applied Social Research, 15, 23,
        39, 61–69, 90–91, 106, 108, 110,
        112, 121, 123, 126, 131, 159,
        161, 170
    Pulitzer School, 129
    School of Communication Research, 18
Committee on the Future of Broadcasting
    (U.K.), 71
Communication, see also Mass communica-
    tion
    and community building in the U.S., 32–35
    flow of, 62, 63, 170

networks of, 65
origin of word, 124
technology change and, 5, 68–69, 87
Communication research
    applied, 120, 136, 138
    beginnings of, 39, 43, 50
    centers and institutes for, 128–133, 162, 170
    clients of, 64
    computer methods, 119, 143, 145
    convergent vs. divergent, 42, 51–53
    data from, uses and misuses of, 135–146,
        176
    descriptive vs. quantitative, 85–86, 88
    empirical, 3, 22, 41
    funding support of, 54
    history of, 1–18, 124–133, 157–166,
        169–179
    in journalism schools, 86
    pioneers of, 105–114, 124–125, 159
    and public policy recommendations,
        147–155
    researchers and teachers in, 123–133
    as social science, 66
    statistical methods, 73
    systems style, 53
    theoretical foundations of, 157–166
    in the U.S., 159–164
Community studies, 126
Computer research methods, 119, 143, 145
Comte, Auguste, 165
Congressional Quarterly, 155
Conservativism, 25
Consumer(s)
    behavior, 143
    neglect of, 122
    surveys, 126
Content analysis, 9, 109
Continuing Study of Magazine Audiences,
    143
Cook, Stuart, 46
Cooley, Charles Horton, 30–31, 35–36, 124,
    125, 159, 183
Cooperative Analysis of Broadcasting
    (CAB), 97–98
Cottrell, Leonard S., Jr., 47, 55
Coughlin, Father, 22
Crawford, Nelson Antrom, 130
Crossley, Arch, 95, 97
Cross tabulations, 119
Crowds, vs. publics, 7–8
Cunliffe, John W., 129

D

Daytime serials, 119–120

Decatur study, 61
Decision making
    influence and, 65–66
    studies of, 61, 63–64, 110
De Mann, Paul, 165
Democracy, public opinion and, 26–29,
        36–37
Dennis, Everette E., 194
Deutsch, Karl, 2, 69
Deviant case analysis, 110
Dewey, John, 30–32, 35–36, 124, 159, 160,
        176, 184
Diaries, 101–102
Diffusion research, 61–69
Dissonance theory, 49, 51
Doob, Leonard W., 45
Drewry, John, 130
Dreyfus affair, 8
Dubois, Cornelius, 143
Dun & Bradstreet, 31
Durkheim, Emile, 26

E

Early adopters, 65–66
Editorials, newspaper, 16
Educational Television Facilities Act, 149
Eisenhower administration, 148–149
Election campaigns, 61
Eliot, Charles William, 129
Eliot, T. S., 26
Elites, as communicators, 25–26
Elliott, Osborn, 85
Emery, Edwin, 88, 184
Enlightenment, 87
Ethnic communities, 33, 37
Europe
    communication research in, 1–18, 164–166,
        171
    television in, 77
Eye-witness reports, 9

F

Feisel, Hans, 98
Festinger, Leon, 43, 50–53, 127, 132
Flanagan, John, 46
Fluoridation studies, 67
Focus groups, 114
Ford, Franklin, 31, 124, 159–160
Ford Foundation, 54, 121, 151
France, 4, 7–8, 11, 165
Frankfurt Critical School, 2, 12, 26, 162, 165
Freedom of press, 26–28, 87
French Revolution, 4

Freud, Sigmund, 125
Friendly, Fred, 151
Frontier, American, 32
Furu, T., 75

G

Gallup, George H., 97, 119, 128, 184
Gannett Foundation, 55
General Electric Company, 55
Georgia, University of, 130
Gerald, J. Edward, 91
Gerbner, George, 80, 91, 184
Germany, 1–2, 4, 5, 17, 30–31, 72, 80, 165
Gitlin, Todd, 184
Godkin, Edwin L., 129
Goffman, Erving, 162, 184
Goldsen, Rose, 126
Goodwin, Richard, 149
Gore, Tipper, 154
Graham, Katherine, 138
Greeley, Horace, 129
Greene, Jerome, 139–140
Grierson, John, 160
Group dynamics, 42

H

Habermas, Jurgen, 185
Harper, Marion, 139
Harvard University, Laboratory on Social
        Relations, 126
Hauser, Philip, 2
Hegel, 31
Herzog, Herta, 2, 185
Himmelweit, Hilde T., 194
Hirst, Francis W., 8
Holocaust, news coverage of, 137
Hooper, C. E., 97–99, 101
Hovland, Carl I., 1, 32, 39, 40–41, 43, 45–50,
        124, 125, 126, 127–128, 131, 133,
        144, 159, 178, 185
Hughes, Helen M., 2
Hull, Clark L., 45, 46, 127
Hutchins, Robert Maynard, 126, 185
Hutchins Commission, 87
Hybrid corn diffusion study, 65–66
Hymes, Dell, 162
Hypodermic needle theory, 11, 22, 169, 172

I

Ideas, free exchange of, 26–28
Illinois, University of, 39, 85, 89–90, 124,
        126, 130, 131, 132, 162, 170

Image building, 140
Indoctrination, 114
Influence
    cross-class, 63
    and decision making, 65–66
    interpersonal, 63, 110
Information overload, 91
Innis, Harold, 160, 165, 185
Innovation, diffusion of, 64–67
Institutes, *see* Media research centers and in-
        stitutes
Intelligence, and effect of media, 73–74
Interviews, 61
Iowa, University of, 129, 131, 162
Iowa Child Welfare Research Station, 127,
        131
Iran/Contra affair, 138

J

James, William, 31, 125
Janis, Irving L., 45, 47, 49, 185
Jazz, in Chicago, history of, 92–93
Jensen, Jay W., 89
Johnson, Joseph French, 129
Johnson, Nicholas, 76
Johnson administration, 149, 154
Jones, Robert, 131
Journalism
    gatekeeper role of, 148–149
    norms of, 148
    researchers' background in, 4
    studies of, 5–6
Journalism Quarterly, 85, 130
Journalism schools, 86, 128–131
Journal of Communication, 157, 171

K

Kansas, University of, 130
Katz, Elihu, 1–2, 194
Kayser, Jacques, 133
Kelley, Harold H., 47, 185
Kelman, Herbert C., 47, 186
Kennedy administration, 149
Kielbowicz, Richard, 5
Killian, Dr. James, 150, 151
Killian Commission, 149–150
King, Bert, 47
Klapper, Joseph T., 23–24, 61, 108, 186
Knies, Karl, 5, 30
Kobre, Sidney, 90
Kracauser, Siegfried, 2, 4
Kris, Ernst, 2
Kuhn, Thomas S., 186

L

Lang, Gladys Engel, 2
Lang, Kurt, 195
LaPierre, Richard, 132
Lasswell, Harold D., 1, 2, 9, 15, 39, 109, 124,
        125–126, 128, 159, 169–170, 172,
        178, 186
Lazarsfeld, Paul F., 1–2, 3, 18, 22, 39, 61,
        63–64, 90, 105, 106, 107–110, 111,
        120–121, 123–124, 125, 126, 128,
        131, 159, 161, 165, 170, 171, 174,
        175–176, 178, 186
Lazarsfeld-Stanton Program Analyzer, 106,
        109–110
Le Bon, Gustave, 7
Lee, Alfred McClung, 187
Lee, Robert E., 128–129
Lerner, Daniel, 186
Lesser, Gerald, 47
Lewin, Kurt, 2, 50, 124, 125, 126–127, 128,
        131, 159, 178, 187
Liberalism, classical, 26–29, 36–37
Life, 143
Linguistics, 39
Link, Dr. Henry, 140
Link Audit, 140
Linton, Harriet, 47
Lippmann, Walter, 8, 9, 28–30, 90, 148, 154,
        173–174, 187
Lipsett, Seymour, 127
Lipstadt, Deborah, 137
Literary Digest poll, 119
Lochner, Louis P., 130
Locke, John, 26
Loebl, Emil, 4, 6
Loewenthal, Leo, 2, 187
Luchins, Abraham S., 47
Lumsdaine, Arthur A., 45, 47
Lynd, Robert, 107, 111

M

MacBride Commission, 172
Maccoby, Eleanor, 72, 187
Maccoby, Nathan, 132–133
MacDonald, Dwight, 26
MacIver, Robert M., 111
Magazines
    demise of, reasons for, 96
    foreign, 91–92
    national, role of, 34
    readership, 143–144
Maier, Norman, 127
Mandel, Wallace, 47

Marcuse, Herbert, 162
Market research, 99–100, 118, 139, 161
Market share, 140
Markle Foundation, 55, 151
Marx, Karl, 4, 26
Marxism, 36–37, 162, 165
Massachusetts Institute of Technology, 126
Mass communication
    requisites for effectiveness, 95
    research, history of, 1–18, 21–37
Mass culture, resistance to, 23
Mass media
    effects of, 67, 68, 108–109, 169
    and evolution of mass society, 25–26
    functions of, 62, 113
    as socializing agents, 71, 81–82
    studies of, 21
Mass-society theory of communication,
        24–26, 34–35, 65, 160
McCann–Erickson, 139
McCarthy, Joseph, 147–148
McCombs, M. E., 178
McDougall, William, 40
McGuire, William J., 47, 195
McLuhan, Marshall, 148, 165, 187
McNemar, Quinn, 132
McPhee, W. N., 61
Mead, George Herbert, 30–32, 159–160, 162,
        165, 188
Media
    agenda setting by, 12, 24
    effects of, direct vs. limited, 10–11, 22,
        176–178
    as fourth estate, 148–149
    new, dire predictions about, 72
    ownership of, 11, 24–25
    political role of, 6–7, 12, 16, 36–37,
        148–149, 177
    power of, 6, 15–17, 22, 23, 63
    social concerns about, 153, 176–177
Media-effects research, 30, 163, 171–172,
        174–179
Media research centers and institutes,
        128–133, 162, 170
Medical innovation, diffusion of, 64–65
Meliorism, 15
Merton, Robert K., 61, 62, 90, 105, 111–115,
        159, 161, 188
Mexico, 78
Meyrowitz, Joshua, 165
Michigan, University of, 45, 128
Miles, Catherine Cox, 45
Miles, Walter, 45
Military psychology, 46
Mill, John Stuart, 28
Miller, Neal, 45

Mills, C. Wright, 34, 63, 162
Milton, John, 28, 87
Minnesota, University of, 51, 129, 131
Missouri, University of, 129
Modernization movement, Third World, 67
Modern societies, critiques of, 24–26
Montesquieu, 12
Morrisett, Lloyd W., 151, 188
Moscovici, S., 56
Mott, Frank Luther, 88, 129, 130, 188
Mowrer, O. Hobart, 45
Munsterberg, Hugo, 125
Murphy, Lawrence, 129

N

Nafziger, Ralph O., 130, 188
Narcotizing dysfunction, 91
National Educational Television (NET), 149
National Institutes of Health, 55
National Science Foundation, 55
National Training Laboratories, 51
Nation building, newspapers and, 68
NBC, 95–96, 98–99, 101–102
Nelson, William Rockhill, 88
Networks, research departments of, 96–97,
        118–120
Newcomb, Theodore M., 189
News
    content analysis studies, 9
    determination of newsworthiness, 137–138,
        148–149
    influence of, 16–17
    relation with truth, 154
New School for Social Research, 51, 162
Newspaper Advertising Bureau, 139
Newspapers
    and 19th-century nation building, 68
    effects of, 175
    news coverage, 137–138
    readership, 143–144
News programs, television, 120
Nielsen, Arthur Charles, 99–102, 141, 189
Nielsen reports, 140, 142
Nixon administration, 150–151
Noelle-Neumann, Elisabeth, 178
Northwestern University, 129
Nuclear family, 35

O

Oberschall, A., 15–16
Olsen, Theodore, 129
Opinion leaders, 62
Oregon, University of, 129

Osgood, Charles E., 39, 43-45, 132

P

Paley, William S., 106, 189
Panel studies, 61, 119
Park, Robert E., 2, 4, 7, 14–15, 30–32, 35–37,
      124–125, 159, 160, 165, 176, 189
Pass-alongs, 143–144
Pastore, Sen. John O., 152
Payne Fund Studies, 15, 72, 171, 173
Pennsylvania, University of, 129
People meter, 142
Peterson, Theodore, 195
Pfizer Corporation, 64
Phenomenistic approach, 24
Piaget, Jean, 173
Pierson, DeVier, 150
Political parties, relation with media, 6–7,
      12, 16
Politicians
      as "samurai class" (Lippmann), 29
      use of media by, 149, 177
Politics
      media coverage of, 148
      role of media in, 8, 30, 36–37
Polling, 118, 126
Ponsonby, Arthur, 9
Pool, Ithiel de Sola, 1, 126, 189
Postman, Leo, 9
Pragmatism, 37
Press
      freedom of, 26–28, 87
      influence of, 7, 11–12
      political role of, 8, 30
      as social institution, 85–93
      studies of, 4, 6–14
      Weber's plan for study of, 13–14
Primary group, 35, 62
Princeton University, 107, 176
Office of Radio Research, 15, 107–108, 111,
      121
Progressivism, 159–160
Propaganda, 6, 9, 22, 30
      resistance to, 23
      studies of, 15, 172
Protestant Reformation, 68
Pseudo-*Gemeinschaft*, 114
Psychological Corporation, 140
Psychology, history of, 40–42
Public broadcasting, 71–72, 96, 149–151
Public Broadcasting Act of 1947, 149–150
Public Broadcasting System, 151
Public opinion
      and democracy, 26–29, 36–37
      polling of, 118, 126

      studies of, 6–7, 11–12, 128
Public Opinion Quarterly, 130
Public policy, communications and, 147–155
Public relations, 12, 22, 173–174
Publics, vs. crowds, 7–8
Pulitzer, Joseph, 129

Q

Questionnaire studies, 10
Quiz show scandals, 135–136

R

Radicalism, 25
Radio
      effects of, 107, 174, 177
      ratings, 97, 102–103, 126, 143
      studies of, 15, 107–108, 123, 161
Radio Marti, 177
Radio's All-Dimension Audience Research
      (RADAR), 102–103
Radox company, 101
Rahmel, Henry, 100
Railroads, growth of, 34
Ratings, 95–102, *see also* Radio; Television
Readership, 143–144
Reagan administration, 149
Reformism, 15, 36, 176
Reid, Whitelaw, 129
Religion, history of, 66, 67
Research, *see* Communication research
Revlon, 135
Revson, Charles, 135–136
Right-to-know doctrine, 87
Rivers, William, 132
Robinson, Gertrude J., 89, 196
Rockefeller Foundation, 47, 54, 107
Rogers, Everett M., 67
Rogers, Ralph, 151
Roper, Elmo, 118, 119, 128
Rosenberg, Milton J., 45, 47
Ross, E. A., 40
Rosten, Leo, 15
Rostow, Eugene, 150
Rovere Study, 61, 62, 63
Rowntree, Benjamin Seebohm, 10
Rubins, Bill, 102
Rubinstein, Eli, 151
Rumors, 9
Russell Sage Foundation, 54, 152

S

Sales, measuring, 139–140
Salomon, Gabriel, 80

Sampling, 139
Sapir, Edward, 39, 124, 125, 190
Sarnoff, Irving, 45
Scanner data, 139–140
Schaeffle, Albert, 4, 30
Schools (of researchers), 158–159
Schramm, Wilbur, 1, 22, 39, 43, 50, 73–75, 85,
        87, 88, 161, 162, 170, 196
Science
    history of, 157–159, 171
    sociology as, 3
Sears, David, 47
Sebeok, Thomas, 39
Seiler, James, 101–102
Sell-through, 139
Sesame Street, 78
Sex education, on television, 78–79
Shaker, Ted, 101
Shannon, Claude E., 39, 190
Sheffield, Fred D., 45, 47
Sherif, Muzafer, 47
Siebert, Fredrick S., 88–89, 130, 190
Sills, David L., 196
Simmel, Friedrich, 165
Simmel, Georg, 125, 190
Sincerity, perceived, 114
Slater, Joseph, 150–151
Small-group research, 63
Smith, Henry Ladd, 88
Smith, M. Brewster, 46
Snowball sampling, 110
Social class, and influence, 63
Social cognition, 42
Social Darwinism, 30
Social network theory, 64
Social psychology, history of, 40, 41–42
Social-representation movement, 41, 53, 56,
        80
Social science
    and communication research, 66
    methods of, 17–18, 126
    in the U.S., 15
Social Science Research Council, 54
Sociology, 3, 159
Soviet Russia, 89
Speechwriters, 149
Speier, Hans, 2
Spence, Kenneth, 45
Stanford University, 50–53, 126, 129, 131,
        132, 150, 170
Institute for Communication Research, 132
Stanton, Frank, 98, 101, 105, 106–107, 170,
        190
    interview with, 117–122
Stephenson, William, 190
Stoddard, George D., 190

Stouffer, Samuel A., 47, 126, 127, 191
Strickland, Stephen, 152
Sweden, 72
Sweeps, 102
Symbolic interactionists, 36
System theory, 53, 162

T

Tarde, Gabriel, 7–8, 17
Technical-assistance movement (Third
        World), 67
Telegraph, 5, 34
Telethons, 114
Television
    children and, 71–82, 151–153
    effects of, 71–82, 151
    program content, 68, 153
    ratings, 98–103, 142–143, 145
    technology changes in, 142–143
    time spent watching, 74, 79
    as wasteland, 154
Terman, Lewis, 132
Third World, diffusion of innovation in, 67
Thomas, William I., 160
Thought News, 31, 124
Thurstone, Louis L., 191
Tiedhard, Hubbard, 80
Tocqueville, Alexis de, 4, 6, 7, 11, 26, 191
Toennies, Ferdinand, 7, 8, 11, 12, 30
Totalitarianism, 6, 25
Toy companies, and television, 77
Tradition, vs. mass media, 32
Truman administration, 148
Tunstall, Jeremy, 2
TV Marti, 177

U

United States
    communication systems in, 34
    lack of tradition in, 32
    liberal culture of, 28
    role of communication in community build-
        ing, 32–35
    social studies in, 15
Universities, communication studies at,
        128–133, 162, 170
University of Berlin, 125
University of Chicago, 31, 128, 171, 175–176
University of Vienna, 125
Urban society, 33–35
Uses and gratifications studies, 24, 109
Utilitarianism, 26–27, 30

V

Van Gennep, Arnold, 9
VCRs, 143
Verba, Almond and Sydney, 132
Versailles Peace Conference, 28–29
Violence, on television, 75–77, 151–153

W

Wallas, Graham, 8, 191
War Department, Division of Information
      and Education, 23, 46, 55, 127
"War of the Worlds" broadcast, 22
Wartella, Ellen, 197
Washington, Booker T., 125
Washington and Lee University, 128–129
Watergate story, 138
Watterson, Henry, 129
Weber, Max, 4, 6, 13–14, 26, 30
Weiss, Walter, 47
Welles, Orson, 22
Wharton School of Business, 129
White, David Manning, 191
Why We Fight films, 47, 127
Williams, Raymond, 35
Williams, Talcott, 129
Williams, Walter, 129, 130, 192

Wilson, O. Meredith, 151
Wilson administration, 28, 174
Wire services, 34
Wirth, Louis, 2
Wisconsin, University of, 126, 129, 130–131
Word-of-mouth, 12
World War I, 9
World War II, 46
Wundt, Wilhelm, 40–41, 192

Y

Yale University
    Attitude-Change Program, 39–57, 127, 131
    Center for the Study of Communications,
        127–128
    Institute of Human Relations (IHR), 44
    Psychology department, 44–45
Yellow press, 8
Yerkes, Charles, 45
Yugoslavia, 89

Z

Zambarga, Phil, 128
Zimbardo, Phil, 47, 49